D1239729

Incarnation

The Harmony of One Love in the Totality of Reality

Martin J. Schade

University Press of America,® Inc.
Lanham • Boulder • New York • Toronto • Plymouth, UK

Copyright © 2016 by University Press of America,® Inc.
4501 Forbes Boulevard, Suite 200, Lanham, Maryland 20706
UPA Acquisitions Department (301) 459-3366

Unit A, Whitacre Mews, 26-34 Stannary Street,
London SE11 4AB, United Kingdom

Library of Congress Control Number: 2016934212
ISBN: 978-0-7618-6757-9 (pbk : alk. paper)—ISBN: 978-0-7618-6758-6 (electronic)

∞™ The paper used in this publication meets the minimum requirements of American
National Standard for Information Sciences Permanence of Paper for Printed Library
Materials, ANSI/NISO Z39.48-1992.

Dedicated to

The Society of Jesus, the Jesuits, of the New England Province

and

Charles Edward Schade, Jr. and Dorothy Elinor Martin Schade

Contents

Preface

It is not by accident that Bob Marley's "One Love/People Get Ready"[1] was named Song of the Millennium by the BBC. It is not by accident that the universal Hindu *Aum*, the Chinese *Tao* and Rastafari are all expressions of a dialectical unity found in the universe. It is not by accident that there is a *riddim of creation*, which was discovered and expressed in Jamaica. It is not by accident that Dialectical Incarnation is actually a dialectical "one love" and "one heart" of all reality. This book will explain why none of these events are accidents, but actually historical incarnations of the one harmony of love that is human, divine and the totality of reality.

This philosophy emerged when I came to Jamaica in 1982 to teach philosophy at St. Michael's Roman Catholic seminary in Kingston. While teaching Marxism, and its Dialectical Materialism, as part of a Contemporary Philosophies course, I found that I also needed to teach Hegel's Dialectical Idealism. Marx had found it necessary that Hegel's dialectic be "turned right side up again" since it was "standing on its head."[2] In explaining the dialectical method that both philosophers use, I indicated that Hegel's idealism could be the thesis while Marx's materialism is the antithesis. This necessarily, as the reader will discover, brings forth a synthesis. Upon initial, and then continued, reflection I discovered that incarnation is the synthesis of idealism/transcendence, i.e., spirit and materialism/immanence, i.e., matter. I began to do research which led me to formulate the philosophy I originally called dialectical incarnationalism. It is through the influence and fluidity of Rastafari (as will be discussed), and its adage of "No -ism, no schism" that this new philosophy is now called dialectical incarnation. Dialectical Incarnation cannot be confined to a closed "-ism" of philosophy. Incarnation is constantly, dialectically and evolutionarily creating itself in diverse particular expressions, which are culturally lived out by conscious and intentional incarnational beings, in their material "supernatural existential."[3] The first formal written articulation of Dialectical Incarnation is *'God is Love and the totality of reality': Karl Rahner: A Proposal for Dialectical Incarnationalism,* the research paper that I wrote for a STL (Licentiate in Sacred Theology) degree at Weston Jesuit School of Theology in 1997.[4] In this philosophical theological essay, I used Pierre Teilhard de Chardin's cosmological metaphysics as a foundation for Karl Rahner's systematic dialectical ontology of the divine and human, the transcendence and the immanence, of all reality. This philosophy of incarnation found various forms of expressions in two articles I later wrote—"Christ the Alpha and the Rasta"[5] and *"Riddim* of Creation."[6] I also use parts of these in this book.

I now go beyond these preliminary presentations and offer a more complete and specifically philosophical explanation of Dialectical Incarnation. The major parts of this dissertation are the historical and philosophical explanations of how there is a unity of all reality and how much of Western philosophy has separated the polar entities of spirit and matter, divine and human, transcendence and immanence, subject and object. Dialectical incarnation breaks down this dualism and offers philosophical arguments that support the understanding that all of reality is a unified whole, that the dualism of Western philosophy is an illusion, and that God and Nature comprise a single harmony of incarnate love.

I have discovered that no one has written or articulated a philosophy of incarnation and the oneness of all reality in this complete manner. In this way the book has significance not only in philosophy, but natural theology and the understanding of reality in general. There have been attempts at unifying bi-polar entities in different forms of monism, but no philosophy has surfaced as it is expressed in Dialectical Incarnation. Unfortunately, much of Western philosophy has identified incarnation as being a revealed theological phenomenon, and specifically a Christian one which is exclusively associated with the person of Jesus the Christ.

The first limitation within this philosophy is not within the philosophy itself but rather with having to argue against the predisposed, revealed theological perspective mentioned. Incarnation is present in all of reality. The anthropomorphism expressed by the majority of humanity towards the transcendence of all reality is restricting the true understanding of incarnation. As will become evident, the synthesising of spirit and matter, divine and human, transcendence and immanence, is required to explain the complete and dialectical nature of the totality of reality.

A second limitation is the fact that dialectical reasoning is difficult in itself. Hegel admits this when he says that "[dialectical reasoning] is perhaps taken for a joke [for it] is one of the hardest things thought expects to do."[7] Because it is difficult does not mean that one should hesitate in trying to expand human reasoning. Within these initial limitations the philosophy still maintains a theoretical framework of demonstrating a new dialectical method in perceiving all of reality. Seeming contradictions of opposites are in fact able to be resolved. The antagonism toward dialectical reasoning has been present since its discovery, yet philosophy must not be hindered by anthropomorphism and a strict Aristotelian logic. The hypothesis that "all of reality is one" is conceivable when dialectical reasoning is properly understood. The fact that different entities are, in fact, distinct from one another does not constitute a separation. Therefore, the ultimate objective of this philosophy is to finally break down the dualism which has insidiously established itself within the major framework of Western philosophy. In that this planet earth and its consciousness through humanity have entered into a new millennium it is of paramount importance that one remains open to the ongoing evolution of all of reality. With all said and done, I welcome all readers to the discovery and the philosophical explanation of and argumentation for the philosophy I call Dialectical Incarnation: a harmony of one love, one heart in the totality of reality.

NOTES

1. Bob Marley, "One Love/People Get Ready." New York: Universal Music Publishing Group, 1965.

2. Karl Marx, *Karl Marx: Selected Writings* (Oxford: Oxford University Press, 1987), 420.

3. The phrase "supernatural existential" is a term coined by Karl Rahner, who will be discussed at length in Chapter .

4. Martin Schade, '*God is Love and the totality of reality': Karl Rahner: A Proposal of Dialectical Incarnationalism* (Boston, MA: Weston Jesuit School of Theology, 1997).

5. Martin Schade, "Christ the *Alpha* and the Rasta: A Reflection on Christology within the Emergence of Rastafari." *Caribbean Journal of Religious Studies*, 17.1 (1996): 38-64.

6. Martin Schade, "Riddim of Creation: An Incarnational Expression of Caribbean Theology." *Caribbean Journal of Religious Studies* 19.1 (1998): 28-38.

7. G.W. Hegel, *Encyclopaedia of the Philosophical Sciences* (Oxford: Clarendon Press, 1984), 71.

Acknowledgments

The first acknowledgement must go to the Society of Jesus, the Jesuits, who gave me the vision to "find God in all things" and the intellectual and spiritual stimulation to desire such a pursuit; to Dorothy and Charles Schade, whose love is the condition of the possibility of my own individual incarnation. Acknowledgements go to Professor Ron Tacelli, SJ, of Boston College, my first mentor in studying philosophy; to Dr. James Gillon, SJ, who invited me to teach philosophy at St. Michael's Seminary in Jamaica, where the idea was first conceived; to Professor John Randall Sachs, SJ and Professor Roger Haight, SJ of Weston Jesuit School of Theology for guiding me through Pierre Teilhard de Chardin and Karl Rahner; to Professor Harvey Cox of Harvard University for guiding me through Paul Tillich and the understanding of incarnation through culture. Acknowledgements continue to go to the University of Technology in Jamaica, who gave me study leave; and to John and Barbara Schade Ferraro, who assisted financially. Finally, acknowledgement must go to the universe, which is the very condition of the possibility of this book.

Introduction

Dialectical Incarnation is a philosophy that identifies a unity found in the infinite and diverse particularities (both "spiritual" and "material") of the universe, i.e., the totality of reality. This philosophy is aimed at clarifying how seemingly opposing concepts, such as spirit and matter, transcendent and immanent, divine and human, are distinct "conditions of the possibility" but are never separate in actual reality.[1] Dialectical Incarnation breaks down dualisms by indicating that such separation is merely an illusion and that all reality can now be understood as a synthesis of bi-polar concepts. All of reality is a single dialectical entity, and this single dialectical entity is incarnation. When one says that the divine and the human, that spirit and matter, are distinct but not separate, one means that one can intellectually grasp the condition, the "concept," of each, but in actual reality one can never separate the two. That opposing entities can be "distinct but not separate" is what Aristotle had in mind when he stated that one cannot separate matter from form and form from matter.[2] Incarnation is parallel to Aristotelian substance which, as he explains, is both form and matter, distinct as conditions, as "concepts," but never separate in reality.

Incarnation is in itself dialectical. To call this philosophy Dialectical Incarnation is actually redundant. Nevertheless, as an introduction to and explanation of this philosophy I will continue to use the term because it serves as an indication that it is different from the incarnation commonly associated with Christianity. The philosophy of Dialectical Incarnation is not the theology of the incarnation of Jesus of Nazareth; rather, it is a philosophy of the dialectical "one stuff" of the totality of reality.

1

THE DIALECTIC AND THE DIALECTICAL METHOD

It is important to understand what is meant by dialectic and how a dialectical method operates, since there are a variety of meanings of both the term and the methodology. The word dialectic comes from the Greek word *dialektos,* meaning discourse or debate.[3] Any form of dialectic begins by drawing rigorous distinctions. The origin of a formal understanding of dialectic may be appropriately attributed to Zeno of Elea, Socrates and Plato. But the manner in which dialectic is understood and used in this philosophy is the way it was defined by Johann Fichte and then employed by Georg Friedrich Hegel and Karl Marx.[4] According to this understanding, dialectic is a process involving the triad of thesis, antithesis and synthesis. When the synthesis is made, it becomes a new thesis, to which there is then a new antithesis, and so on. The dialectical procedure brings to light contradictions and other types of opposition not sensed before. An example of a dialectical movement is the following: thesis: humanity is one; antithesis: humanity is many; synthesis: humanity is a unity-in-diversity.

HEGEL'S DIALECTIC

Hegel's (1770–1831 C.E.) Dialectical Idealism is important because the basic themes of his dialectic are held together by the development of the Idea, Mind or Spirit into unity. The truly real is the Absolute, and this Absolute, in philosophical and theological terms, is called God. The Idea serves as the thesis of his dialectical understanding of the Absolute. According to Hegel, the Absolute is not separate from the world of nature; all things are related and one thing relates to another, until all things lead, through the dialectical process, to the knowledge of the Absolute.[5] Hegel rejects materialism, which holds that there are particles of hard matter separated and finite but which, when arranged in different formations, exhaustively constitute a thing's nature.[6] The Absolute, which is the unity of all things, is a dynamic process, with parts that differ and yet are unified into one complex system. The Absolute is not separated from the world but is the world. Nature is the physical disclosure of the Absolute. Thought connects the Absolute, Nature and the human mind.[7] Nature thus remains one with the Absolute as an expression or disclosure of Spirit that becomes "material" in the dialectical process. Yet, Hegel's "matter" is never totally material, and so his dialectic is lop-sided. Indeed, as will be shown, most, if not all, Western philosophy is, in varying degrees, lop-sided, leaning either toward mind and spirit or body and matter. Dialectical Incarnation finally unites, synthesizes and balances a reality that is fully divine and fully human, fully spirit and fully matter, fully transcendent and fully immanent, fully Self and fully Other.

The dialectical method involves the notion that movement, or process, or progress, is the result of the conflict of opposites.[8] The term itself can be misleading because, neither in Hegel nor in Marx is dialectical thinking a set of procedures for inquiry, nor a set of rules for generating or justifying results, as it is in the Socratic Method. The Socratic Method is a form of inquiry and debate between individuals with opposing viewpoints based on asking and answering questions to stimulate rational thinking and to illuminate ideas. It is a dialectical method, very present in Plato's dialogues, involving an oppositional discussion in which the defence of one point of view is pitted against another; one participant may lead another to contradict himself in some way, strengthening the inquirer's own point ("Socratic method").

As used in this philosophy, the dialectic can be best understood as a general conception of the intelligible (and the incarnational) structure the world has to offer, and consequently a programme for the theoretical structure which best captures the world as the totality of reality.[9] The dialectic, says Hegel,

> is the principle of all the movement and of all the activity we find in reality. . . . Everything that surrounds us can be treated as an instance of dialectic. We know how all that is finite, instead of being stable and ultimate, is rather changeable and transitory: this is no other than the dialectic of the finite whereby it, being implicitly other than itself, is driven beyond what it immediately is, and turns into its opposite.[10]

According to Hegel, everything in the world involves opposed and contradictory aspects. He maintains that contradiction is the motive force of the world and that it is absurd to say that contradictions are unthinkable.[11] As we shall discover throughout the philosophy, the Dialectic is manifest and is expressed in all aspects of the world, from the smallest sub-atomic elements to the motions of the heavenly bodies, from political revolutions, to the paradoxical shifts and switches of emotional mood and expression.[12]

What is important in the dialectical method, as used in this philosophy, emerges from Hegel's "genuine dialectic." As such, the dialectic's "various stages should arise out of each other in a *necessary* manner. It is not *we* who must determine its course; it must determine itself."[13] In developing a dialectical system, much of what is discovered, Hegel admits, is derived from instances offered by experience. Findlay explains:

> these [experiences] may illustrate notions previously arrived at dialectically, or may prompt us to form such notions. All such empirical borrowings must, however, be transformed in a dialectical treatment, and must acquire a necessary connection that they did not seem to possess. [Moreover] his [Hegel's]

unilateral dialectical chain will twist round in a circle, that it will, after many windings, return to its point of origin. And . . . provide us with a *proof.*[14]

Immanuel Kant's (1724–1804 C.E.) influence on Hegel, in particular his attempt to synthesise Continental Rationalism and British Empiricism, with the category of *synthetic a priori* judgment, is crucial. Kant states,

> [t]here can be no doubt that all our knowledge begins with experience [and that a] "light dove, cleaving the air in her free flight, and feeling its resistance, might imagine that its flight would be still easier in empty space" [and] thoughts without experience are empty, experience without thoughts are blind.[15]

The *synthetic a priori* is important for the dialectical method because it is a synthesis of the thesis of *a priori reasoning* and the anti-thesis of *a posteriori reasoning.* Hegel claims that the dialectical method is intrinsic to the *structure of the world* and is also found in the external "experience" of the world. For Hegel, the Kantian antinomies are the most explicit modern expressions of dialectic. Our notions of time, space, and causal dependence can be developed in contradictory ways, contradictions that are "essential and necessary," and that spring from neither a causal error nor a conceptual mistake.[16] But Kant insists that the antinomies are within one's understanding, and not in the "things in themselves." Hegel criticises Kant for "confining his antinomies to a limited set of cosmological ideas: he should . . . .have recognised their presence in objects of *all* types, and in *all* notions and ideas."[17]

Hegel's dialectic, in comparison, attributes a dialectical structure to the world that expresses itself in external experience of the world. This change is important for the philosophy of dialectical incarnation, which also offers a historical development in the history of Western philosophy. As indicated, in Hegel's understanding, a thesis would be an idea, like continental rationalism, and the antithesis would be British empiricism, or a historical movement, such as the Napoleon "imperialism" and the French Revolution. The philosophy contains within itself incompleteness that gives rise to opposition, or an antithesis, a conflicting idea or movement. As a result of the conflict or the "dialectical strife" a third point of view arises, a synthesis, which overcomes the conflict by reconciling, at a higher level, the truth contained in both the thesis and antithesis. This synthesis then becomes a new thesis that generates another antithesis, giving rise to a new synthesis, and the process is continually generated. According to Hegel, Absolute Spirit itself, which is the sum total of reality, develops in this dialectical fashion toward an ultimate end or goal, which is once again, the Absolute, now synthesized through Nature and history.

Hegel's system, from a metaphysical perspective, begins with Being as the thesis, Nothing as the antithesis, and Becoming as their synthesis. According to our understanding of the dialectic, one must realize that Being and Nothing are One. This is a new vision, the new consciousness that is needed to grasp the philosophy of Dialectical Incarnation. Hegel himself was aware of the difficulty of seeing in this dialectical way, for he says that "the proposition that Being and Nothing are the same is so paradoxical to the imagination or understanding, that it is perhaps taken for a joke [for it] is one of the hardest things thought expects to do."[18] *Becoming,* then, is the unity of *Being* and *Nothing* (Hegel, *Philosophy of Hegel* 203–217).

Hegel's Being goes through its dialectical process toward Idea, yet the dialectical process continues, and it is from the Idea that Nature is derived. Nature is understood as the dialectical Idea "outside" of itself. Nature is not separate from Idea, it is simply the Idea in its external form. For Hegel, ultimate reality is a single organic and dynamic whole, whereby there is the inner (Idea) and the outer (Nature) aspects of the one reality. The dynamic interaction of thesis and antithesis proceeds to the synthesis which Hegel calls *Geist,* namely, Absolute Spirit. Thus, Hegel's system is called dialectical idealism.

For Hegel, reality is the Absolute, which unfolds dialectically in a process of self-development. The history of philosophy is the development of the Absolute's self-consciousness in the mind of humans. As the Absolute develops, it manifests itself both in Nature and in human history. Nature is Absolute Thought or Being objectifying itself in "material" form. Hegel's system is a species of idealism because Nature is objectified Thought, finite minds and human history are the process of the Absolute manifesting itself in that form that is most similar to itself, namely, spirit or consciousness (Findlay 34–35, 82–83).

The goal of the dialectical process can be best understood at the level of reason. As finite reason progresses in understanding, the Absolute progresses toward full self-knowledge. Indeed, the Absolute comes to know itself through the human mind's increased understanding of reality. Hegel analysed this human progression of understanding in terms of three levels: art, religion, and philosophy.[19] Art grasps the Absolute in material forms, interpreting the rational through the sensible forms of beauty that we experience in feeling. Art goes beyond itself to religion, which understands the Absolute by means of images and symbols that we experience with thought. In Christianity, the truth by which the Absolute manifests itself in the finite is symbolically reflected in the incarnation. Christianity is, thus, the absolute religion because in it "God has actually communicated the knowledge of himself to men" (Yerkes 118). In Christianity "it is revealed what Spirit, what God is" (Hegel, *History* 1:84). Philosophy, however, is conceptually supreme, because it grasps the Absolute rationally. It leaves behind the iconic forms of religion and rises to the level of pure thought. Once this has been achieved, the Absolute arrives at full self-consciousness, and the cosmic drama reaches its end and goal. It is at this point that Hegel identifies the Absolute with God. Hegel argues,

> God is God only insofar as he knows himself. His self-knowledge is further his self-consciousness in human beings and human knowledge of God, which proceeds toward the self-knowledge of human beings in God. [20]

A central element of Dialectical Incarnation is that the human person is the centre of the universe, the "centre of the circumference," [21] which is God and the totality of reality. In indicating similarities between Hegel's understanding of God and humanity, dialectical incarnation states that God needs humans to be God as much as humans need God to be human.

Hegel's doctrine of Spirit, and its relationship with the world of Nature and the centrality of the human person, would certainly have received influence from the glorious mysticism of medieval and renaissance Germany. In the systems of both Meister Eckhart and Angelus Silesius there is the approximation of the finite to the infinite Spirit, which show similarities with Hegel's notion of the dialectical method. Hegel quotes Meister Eckhart, stating that

> The eye with which God sees me, is the eye with which I see Him, my eye and His eye are one. In the meting out of justice I am weighed in God and He in me. If God were not, I should not be, and if I were not, He too would not be. [22]

The question now arises. If the Absolute reaches its end or goal, how does the Absolute remain dynamic? It remains dynamic because philosophy does not offer to humans the knowledge of that Absolute at any particular moment; because such knowledge is, itself, the product of the dialectical process. Philosophy is historical whereby God knows Godself through humanity. [23] Though the Absolute has been attained as a goal, the goal itself is a "becoming" synthesis, an ongoing developmental process which goes on, because humanity will continually be searching the infinity of God. The end of the Absolute is an end or goal, in the sense of a final stage, but not as an end which becomes static and finished. [24]

When understanding Hegel's dialectic, which is totality expressed in his philosophy, one recognises that it is the nature of everything to be a "unity of opposites." [25] Accordingly, Hegel believes he can confirm his vision of reality *a priori* in thought "by showing that in every pair of opposites the existence of each member logically or conceptually requires the existence of the other." [26] All opposites, Hegel says, "are essentially conditioned through each other, and *are* only in relation to each other." [27] The contrasting or opposite elements in the totality of reality are reciprocally dependent and therefore cannot exist without one another. In any pair of opposites, both manifest the same essence, the same organic form or principle which animates the whole. As such, opposites are *identical*, each is in its essence what its opposite is.[28] It is this dialectical reasoning which puzzles many thinkers. Hegel explains:

> The consideration of everything that is shows that *in itself* everything in its identity with itself is nonidentical with itself and self-contradictory; that in its difference, in its contradiction, it is identical with itself, and that in itself it is this movement of transition of each of these determinations into the other.[29]

Dialectical Incarnation, and its own dialectical method, accepts much of Hegel's dialectic. The fundamental point of difference is with the understanding of the Absolute as Spirit. Dialectical Incarnation supports Hegel's' *structure* of reality but not the Hegelian *idealistic metaphysics* of reality. Hegel does not hold firm to his "unity of opposites" in a complete manner, because spirit is not equal, in its essence, to its opposite, matter. It is this same difference which leads us to Marx's critique of Hegel and to Dialectical Incarnation's critique of Marx.

MARX'S DIALECTIC

Karl Marx (1818–1883 C.E.) acknowledges Hegel's system of logic as being of great service in constructing his own economic theory. He even praises Hegel as "the last word of all philosophy."[30] Marx's primary critique of Hegel is Hegel's "mysticism." Marx says:

> [the] mystification which dialectic suffers in Hegel's hands by no means prevents him from being the first to present its general form of working in a comprehensive and conscious manner. With him it [the dialectic] is standing on its head. It must be turned right side up again, if you should discover the rational kernel within the mystical shell.[31]

Marx furthers his critique when he states that:

> My dialectic method is not only different from the Hegelian, but is its direct opposite. To Hegel, the life-process of the human brain, i.e., the process of thinking, which, under the name of 'the Idea,' he even transforms into an independent subject, is the demiurgos of the real world, and the real world is only the external, phenomenal form of 'the Idea.' With me, on the contrary, the ideal is nothing else than the material world reflected by the human mind, and translated into forms of thought.[32]

Marx rejects, as does Dialectical Incarnation, Hegel's metaphysical reality. Hegel was the first to champion a dialectical vision of reality and to orchestrate a theoretical programme that helps in understanding and explaining it. Marx accepts Hegel's general method, but he makes matter the absolute and "one stuff" of the universe. Marx becomes the "prophet" of matter. Like Hegel, Marx understood history as a process of development and change from less perfect to more perfect. Materialism, then, encompasses the entirety of the natural environment, inorganic and organic, as well as social, political life and human consciousness. For Marx, matter is not defined in terms of irreducible particles. Matter is diverse, the objective reality that exists in and through all things and outside of the human mind. It is not a reflection of thought. Given the primacy of the material order, mental activity is merely a reflex action in a highly complex material organ. Hence, in a reversal of Hegel, human thought and "spirit" are merely a reflection of nature. The material order is basic and the mental realm is a derivative from it.

For Marx and Engels, the human person is the centre of materialism. However, they emphasize the human as human person-in-society, because "[one] is not merely a natural being; [one]is a human natural being . . . a being for [oneself], and therefore a species-being."[33] The person is always a person in the world and this protects one from becoming de-personalized, or alienated, from one's nature. The person must also produce or create, for it is in the process of production that persons relate both to material things and to each other. The matter out of which things are produced are the factors of production. The relations of production are the ways persons relate to each other in the process of production, including their relation to the ownership of property. The important aspect is that the human person must remain united to his or her full human nature, which is the material world and one another, for otherwise the person becomes alienated.[34]

The human person is not only a species-being but also a free being. Alienated labour abuses this freedom. "[One's] labour is not voluntary, but coerced; it is forced labour . . . [a]s a result, therefore, [one] (the worker) only feels [one]self freely active in [one's] animal functions."[35] Freedom is experienced rather in real community, i.e., in species-being: "[o]nly within the community with others has each individual the means of cultivating his gifts in all directions, hence personal freedom becomes possible only within the community."[36] Marx goes on to say,

> [a human] is a species-being not only in the sense that he [or she] makes the community . . . but also . . . in the sense that he [or she] treats himself [or herself] as the present, living species, as a universal and consequently free being.[37]

In the same way that Marx continually refers to Hegel's dialectic in comparison to his own, so too, as we uncover and reveal dialectical incarnation, we will refer to Marx. It is important to remember, (i) the centrality of the human person who is one with the material world and with the species;

(ii) the person is alienated when not sharing in this union; and (iii) the human person who is free, must create, must produce and is always in dialectical evolution.

These brief descriptions of Hegel's and Marx's dialectic serve only to set the parameters in which Dialectical Incarnation emerges. Although this philosophy serves as a general synthesis of these two opposing positions, dialectical incarnation does not incorporate both philosophies in their entirety. It is the dialectical method present in both and the bi-polar positions of idealism and materialism that bring forth the synthesis.

Both Hegel's and Marx's dialectic could be examined in detail in its similarity and or differences with Dialectical Incarnation. Examples would be how Hegel's idealism cannot let go of the physical and material aspect of reality when he refers to the sensuous dimension of the "Spirit" in art and nature. Likewise, Marx's materialism cannot let go of the spiritualistic aspect of matter when comparing his materialism to that of "vulgar" materialism and its lack of the humanistic element, or what would be called the "incarnational" aspect of matter. It is the dialectical method of both that this book uses so as to explain the philosophy of Dialectical Incarnation. As the philosophy develops one will be able make innumerable critiques in relation to specific philosophies, several of which will be discussed in the following pages.

LOVE AND A PHILOSOPHY OF INCARNATION

Dialectical Incarnation can be described as a philosophy of love. What, then, is love? Love is the dialectical energy and relationship between the subject, the lover, and the object, the beloved. Traditionally, there are three expressions of love, *eros, philia and agape*.[38] This relational energy found between a subject and object is necessarily incarnate, because it needs to be particular, and therefore, material. Love, by definition, requires a beloved. A beloved is a particular entity, and the possibilities of expressions in being the beloved are infinite. Love has the condition of the possibility of the divine, the human, and the totality of reality, because love is present in and through everything and everyone. Within the paradigm of Dialectical Incarnation, divine love has a dialectical Other, which is the human Self and all of reality. This Other is material because matter enables individuality or particularity. Love necessitates a particular beloved. The centre of the circumference is the human incarnate Self. The Self, as a beloved, is able to recognize and discover the nature of God's Self, as one discovers one's own Self.[39] The Self is the crucial link between the divine and the human. The Self is the nexus of spirit and matter, mind and body. The philosophy of incarnation thus synthesizes dualisms that separate spirit and matter; it is an expression of the oneness of all. The philosophy of Dialectical Incarnation is the dialectical "one love, one heart," as Bob Marley sang, of the totality of reality.

Besides being a philosophy of love, the philosophy of incarnation can be a universal philosophy of religion, because it allows for all expressions of religion and the infinite. It can be anthropology, because the human being is the centre of it all. It is metaphysics because it deals with the being of all reality. It is epistemology, because the Self is the subject of awareness of the infinite horizon of God and the totality of reality. It is also a natural theology. The difference between natural theology and a philosophy of God is that philosophy is a rational explanation of God. Natural theology is the "study of God" in a natural, rational manner. Theistic philosophy, then, is natural theology. God is understood through nature, which is reason.

Philosophy and natural theology, however, are distinct from revealed theology, according to which knowledge and understanding of God is through some form of revelation rather than through rational discovery. All the scriptures of the world religions are based on some manner of revealed theology. All the dogmas, doctrines, and traditions of particular religions are usually based on a revelatory experience. The doctrine of the Trinity in Christianity is a revealed truth. The Incarnation, referring specifically and exclusively to Jesus the Christ, is a revealed truth. Dialectical Incarnation is a rational understanding and expression of a similar philosophy of the Trinity. The philosophy of Dialectical Incarnation struggles with the same concerns as those faced by the early Church fathers, who battled over the philosophical and metaphysical synthesis of seeming opposing "entities" found in the Trinitarian and Christological Controversies.

Since the philosophy of Dialectical Incarnation is explained through a historical perspective, it is crucial to clarify that dialectical incarnation is not an apologetics for Christianity or Christian theology. As an incarnational philosophy, Dialectical Incarnation displays similarities with the understanding of incarnation in Christianity. References are made to such similarities, e.g., the theology of the Trinity and the structure of Dialectical Incarnation. However, unlike Hegel, Dialectical Incarnation does not say that Christianity is the "Absolute religion." To clarify the difference, the philosophy of Dialectical Incarnation is strictly rationally based, and not revealed, while Christianity is revealed and not rationally based. All of reality is incarnate, and is not exclusively found in Jesus of Nazareth.

THE PHILOSOPHY OF DIALECTICAL INCARNATION

The dialectical of incarnation is the triadic, methodological understanding that all of reality is comprised of the process of thesis, antithesis, and synthesis. All of reality is comprised of the conditions of the possibility of being idea, spirit and transcendence. All of reality is comprised of the conditions of the possibility of being body, matter and immanence. All of reality is incarnation. All of reality is the condition of the possibility to be both idea and body united *completely*. All of reality is the condition of the possibility of being both spirit and matter united *totally*. All of reality is both transcendent and immanent united *equally*. The human person is the centre of this dialectical process, because it is the human person who can recognise it, "see" it, feel it, and self-reflect upon it.[40] The human person, with a human heart and mind, are united as one incarnation, one incarnate Self, the "centre of the circumference," the centre of the universe and all of reality. One's *telos* is arrived at by discovering and co-creating one's Self, which is the material-super-natural existential of the totality of reality, moving towards perfection.

Dialectical Incarnation is Hegel's idealism united with Marx's materialism and synthesised equally in incarnation. Dialectical Incarnation is neither a monism nor a dualism but can be dialectically understood as both. Dialectical Incarnation involves both mentally "knowing" and bodily "feeling" one and/or the other. One can reason on the spiritual side equally as on the material side, the transcendent side as well as the immanent side. Dialectical Incarnation is a new metaphysics in understanding all of being. It can offer a new epistemology in how humans know reality as the condition of the possibility of incarnation and where "to be is to be known, and to be known is to be." Dialectical Incarnation is a new anthropology, by identifying the human person as an incarnational being, a material-supernatural existential. It is a new philosophy of the human person because humans can critically reflect upon themselves as incarnational beings and wonder how it is that they can "know" and "feel" themselves as the centre of the totality of reality. It is a new theology because it is a new anthropology, which is now an anthropological theology. All knowledge and study of God is in, and through, the human person. The human person is the crucial link between God and Nature. Dialectical Incarnation is a new cosmology because creation is evolution and all is sacred. It is a new ethics because the agent in ethics understands himself or herself in a new incarnational perspective and within a new incarnational context of doing ethics. Dialectical Incarnation is a new psychology of the Self, because mental processes are no longer mere "mental" processes, and observing those mental processes are no longer being passively observed. Dialectical Incarnation is a new philosophy of religion, because it recognises the harmony found in the infinite expressions of the divine experienced by the culturally conditioned incarnational human beings in the world. It is a new sociology, because the individual in society is an incarnational being of culture within the common good. Dialectical Incarnation requires the coming out of Plato's cave and seeing "The Good" in its fullness; something Plato himself could not have done, as an idealist.

In the philosophy of Dialectical Incarnation, incarnation is the "one stuff" of the universe. Incarnation is incarnate love and therefore dialectical in its own being. Love requires a lover and a beloved. The lover, as subject, as individual, must be material, i.e., incarnational, so as to be particular. The beloved as an object must be material, and therefore incarnational, so as to be particular and individual. Love is human, divine and the totality of reality.

Dialectical Incarnation understands that reality has a triadic nature and each particular incarnation, from the smallest sub-atomic particle and/or wave, to the entirety of the cosmos, is a synthesis of incarnation. With each particular synthesis (these are the infinite particular incarnations of the world), the particular synthesis becomes a new thesis. For example, I as Self, is a particular incarnation, both "idea-like" and "matter-like." I am now a subject, and a thesis. The antithesis is that which is object, i.e., the external world. Descartes had to separate these conditions of the world. Dialectical Incarnation re-unites them. I as subject, as a new thesis, is united with the novel, objective, socio-cultural, physical environment of my incarnational existence. This union brings forth a synthesis. I, as subject and object totally united as one, am synthesising and recreating. As a new thesis, the incarnational Self serves as the subject while the antithesis is the object, i.e., the totally external environment, or "situation" in which the Self finds its being. The synthesis is the new creation, with itself as a new other "Self" in a new objective world, constantly creating and evolving. Dialectical Incarnation is a process philosophy in its completeness.

A NEED FOR A SYNTHESIS AND OUTLINE OF THE BOOK

This synthesis then becomes a thesis in itself, and thus the dialectical process continues. The objective of Dialectical Incarnation is to identify and define the synthesis as incarnate love in its infinite expressions. The constant synthesis of Dialectical Incarnation is primarily through the human person, who is the resolution of the mind/body problem in its very Self. The synthesis of incarnate love is an ongoing dynamic and will continually be expressed and discovered in its own evolutionary manner. Like Hegel's end and Marx's end, this synthesis is a process that manifests itself in each particular expression. The goal is to recognise that one cannot separate the transcendent from the immanent, spirit from matter, the one from the many, but to allow the ongoing synthesis to actualise itself in its perfection.

Another reason for a synthesis is the simple fact that matter and spirit have, for too long, been separated. Can one "see" dialectically and paradoxically so as to no longer separate the two?[41] In theory we refer to the distinction between matter and spirit, but in reality we need not separate the two. The union and distinction between matter and spirit is similar to Aristotle's matter and form, which together are substance. Matter never exists without form or form without matter in nature. Instead of saying that one is the "reflection," the "expression," the "disclosure" of the other, the manner in which Hegel and Marx do, can one simply understand that matter and spirit are the "conditions of the possibility" for incarnation and recognize that they are not separate?[42] All of reality is incarnate; all of reality is ongoing incarnation.[43]

One can conceptually identify the distinction of matter from spirit as one can identify form from matter, but the two are never, in reality, separate. In dialectical incarnation, matter or spirit are equal and one is not favoured, one from the other. All of reality is the condition of the possibility to be both spirit and matter completely, totally and equally.

Given this understanding of dialectic and the dialectical method, Dialectical Incarnation synthesizes the poles of matter and spirit, divine and human, God and the world. We will move through the thought of early Western philosophy's understanding of God and the One. This will bring us to a discussion of how rationalism tries to synthesize matter and spirit, unity in diversity. The proper vision of Dialectical Incarnation will be buttressed by invoking Pierre Teilhard de Chardin. Teilhard's understanding of creation, incarnation and redemption as one single act of God's love allows us to recognize the fullness of the incarnation in the world. Following this description of Teilhard's cosmology, we will move toward the anthropological, transcendental philosophy and theology of Karl Rahner. Rahner's dialectical and incarnational understanding of God, through the incarnation of the world, grounds Dialectical Incarnation. By examining Rahner's philosophical and theological methods, and especially his notion of symbol, we are able to grasp the foundations of his philosophy and theology of incarnation. The metaphysical concept of the "hypostatic union" will serve as the "real symbol" of uniting God and the "totality of reality." In that one does not simply study philosophy or theology but actually lives it, an anthropological ethics will then be presented, emerging from Nicholas of Cusa, Baruch Spinoza and G.W. Leibniz, leading to the existential ethics of Karl Rahner and Joseph Fuchs. Within the understanding that "God is love and the totality of reality," reference will be made to the "absolute legitimate pantheism" of Teilhard de Chardin and the "truth of pantheism" of Rahner so as to present a new understanding of a dialectical pantheism.

But what contribution does Dialectical Incarnation make to philosophy, toward education or toward the academic endeavour itself? The contribution is for humanity to have greater vision and fuller being as Teilhard de Chardin passionately proclaims. The contribution is to demonstrate how the history of philosophy is dialectically expressing itself through various philosophers all seeking a summation of reality.

Although Dialectical Incarnation has its conception in early Western and Eastern philosophy, it continues to manifest itself in different contemporary philosophies. A significant example is process philosophy. Yet the incompleteness of process thought is that it is a philosophy of mere experience, emerging from the roots of British empiricism; it is not a holistic philosophy of incarnation, of matter *and* spirit, mind *and* body, human experience *and* concrete historical events.

The journey of unpacking Dialectical Incarnation through history moves first to Western thought and the dialectical movements which have emerged from it. Chapter One presents the ancient, medieval and modern philosophical bases for dialectical incarnation. Chapter Two then offers the cosmological understanding of incarnation through the insights of Pierre Teilhard de Chardin who argues that the divine is "in all that is most hidden, most solid, and most ultimate in the world."[44] After Teilhard prepares the way, Karl Rahner presents a metaphysical explanation of how the divine and the human, spirit and matter can be "distinct but not separate."

Chapter Three verifies that Dialectical Incarnation is a "legitimate pantheism" and offers as evidence expressions found in Eastern philosophies, viz. the Hindu *Aum* of Hinduism and Chinese *Tao*. The oneness of the divine and the human within all of reality is also expressed in the "I-n-I" of Rastafari and the influence of its African roots.

Chapter Four presents current philosophies which either provide alternatives to or challenge the philosophy of Dialectical Incarnation. There are similarities between Dialectical Incarnation and process philosophy, yet Dialectical Incarnation goes beyond process philosophy's limited perspective. Analytic philosophy and Logical Positivism present challenges but, unfortunately, remain lop-sided and, thus, cannot grasp Dialectical Incarnation in its completeness and simply rejects anything metaphysical, theological and ethical. The recent emergence of the New Physics remarkably supports this new philosophy by explaining that all reality is comprised of both "idea-like" and "matter-like" entities.

Since Dialectical Incarnation is a harmony of one love, one heart in the totality of reality, the human person must recognise his or her own place in maintaining that harmony. Philosophy begins with anthropology since it is the human person who seeks to know reality. An explanation of the Self is crucial for the philosophy, because in Dialectical Incarnation the Self is centre of the universe. Chapter Five offers an understanding of the Self, which leads to an ethics of Dialectical Incarnation taking a natural law, personalistic foundation. It presents an existential and virtue ethics which is grounded in an understanding of the common good. Following the ethics of Dialectical Incarnation, this philosophy offers a material-supernatural existential instantiation found in the culture and music of "the riddim of creation." The philosophy ends with a conclusion indicating the completeness of dialectical incarnation and the necessary challenge for humanity to think and "see" in a new manner.

NOTES

1. The phrase "condition of the possibility" is the term Immanuel Kant uses to clarify the use of categories in human knowledge in *Critique of Pure Reason* (London: Macmillan, 1968, 6). It was a great insight when he developed his dialectical philosophy.

2. Aristotle claimed that matter and form combine substance as one entity. Dialectical incarnation is one dialectical entity, but not the substance of Aristotle. See "Metaphysics" in *The Basic Works of Aristotle* (New York: Random House, 1941), Book VII, chapters 3, 30; Book VIII, chapters 2, 15.

3. William L. Reese, *Dictionary of Philosophy and Religion* (Amherst: Humanity Books, 1996), 174.

4. Ibid.

5. These aspects of Hegel's dialectic are clearly presented in his *Science of Logic* (London: Allen & Unwin, 1969), *Philosophy of Nature* (Oxford: Clarendon Press, 1970), and *Philosophy of History* (New York: Dover Publications, 1956), but are explained in more detail in J.H. Findlay's *Hegel: A Re-examination* (New York: Collier Books, 1962), 16–17, especially in the Introduction.

6. Hegel's rejection of materialism will be addressed in the next chapter when I examine Baruch Spinoza and G.W. Leibniz.

7. See Findlay, *Hegel: A Re-examination*, 16, 17, 26, 33; and Samuel Enoch Stumpf, *Socrates to Sartre: A History of Philosophy* (New York: McGraw-Hill Book Company, 1966), 325–344.

8. Dialectical incarnation will be referring to process philosophy which started with Heraclitus and became popular through Alfred North Whitehead in his *Process and Reality*. I will examine similarities with process philosophy as well as how the philosophy of dialectical incarnation is different.

9. Allen Wood, *Karl Marx*. 2nd ed. (New York and London: Routledge, Taylor & Francis Group, 2004), 198.

10. See *Hegel's Logic* (Oxford: Oxford University Press, 1975), 148–50; and Findlay, *Hegel: A Re-examination*, 62.

11. So as to indicate how some philosophers do think that it is absurd to reason in this dialectical, contradictory manner, I refer to the attitude of Karl Popper who repeatedly attacks the dialectic. In 1937 he wrote and delivered a paper titled "What Is Dialectic?" in which he attacked the dialectical method for its willingness "to put up with contradictions." Popper concluded the essay with these words: "The whole development of dialectic should be a warning against the dangers inherent in philosophical system-building. It should remind us that philosophy should not be made a basis for any sort of scientific system and that philosophers should be much more modest in their claims. One task which they can fulfill quite usefully is the study of the critical methods of science." See *Conjectures and Refutations: The Growth of Scientific Knowledge* (New York: Basic Books, 1962), 316.

12. Findlay, *Hegel: A Re-examination*, 62.

13. Ibid.

14. Ibid., 67–68.

15. The latter is paraphrased from "concepts" to thoughts, "percepts" to experience. See *Critique of Pure Reason* (Cambridge: Cambridge University Press, 1998), B1, B8, B75.

16. Findlay, *Hegel: A Re-examination*, 62.

17. Ibid.

18. G.W. Hegel, *Encyclopaedia of the Philosophical Sciences, The Logic* (Oxford: Clarendon Press, 1984), 71.

19. These are explained in several of Hegel's works, such as "Lectures on Aesthetics" (*(http://plato.stanford.edu/entries/hegel-aesthetics/)*), "Philosophy of Religion" (in *Hegel: A Re-examination)* and *Philosophy of History* (New York: Dover Publication, 1956). See Findlay, *Hegel: A Re-examination*, 339.

20. See G.W. Hegel, *The Philosophy of Mind* (Oxford: Oxford University Press, 1971), 292. This is very similar to Aristotle's position that God is "thought thinking itself." (See "Metaphysics" in *The Basic Works*, Book XII, chapters 7, 9).

21. This is a quote from Nicholas of Cusa that will be discussed on several occasions. See Jasper Hopkins, *Nicholas of Cusa On Learned Ignorance: A translation and an appraisal of De Docta Ignorantia* (Minneapolis: The Arthur J. Banning Press, 1985).

22. "Logic of Hegel" in *Hegel: A Re-examination,* 6.

23. Findlay, *Hegel: A Re-examination,* 347.

24. Ibid., 211–12.

25. Allen Wood, *Karl Marx* (New York and London: Routledge, Taylor & Francis Group, 2004), 208.

26. Ibid., 209.

27. *Hegel's Logic* (Oxford: Oxford University Press, 1975), 173.

28. Wood, *Karl Marx*, 211.

29. Hegel, *Science of Logic,* 412.

30. Wood, *Karl Marx*, 215.

31. Karl Marx, *Karl Marx: Selected Writings* (Oxford: Oxford University Press, 1987), 420.

32. Ibid.

33. Karl Marx and Frederick Engels, *Karl Marx, Frederick Engels: Collected Works* (New York: International Publishers, 1975), 327.

34. This philosophy is not a comparison of Marx and other philosophies, especially Christian ones. However, one will see similarities with regard to the human person in the world, and in nature. We will see that evil, for Rahner, involves the person not being in accord with his or her own human nature.

35. Marx and Engels, *Collected Works,* 274–75.

36. Ibid., 78.

37. Ibid., 275.

38. These aspects of love will be elaborated in Chapter Five.

39. The self within dialectical incarnation will be discussed in Chapter Five.

40. "It" is the philosophy of dialectical incarnation, the dialectic of the world.

41. As we will discover in Chapter Two, Pierre Teilhard de Chardin speaks about the verb, "to see," and the importance "seeing" has in having "fuller being" and "closer union." See *Phenomenon of Man* (New York: Harper & Row, 1975), 31, 33.

42. Just as the categories are the "conditions of the possibility" in knowing things in the external world, so too "matter" and "spirit" are "conditions of the possibility" of incarnation.

43. The "mind/body" or matter/ spirit problem will be discussed throughout the thesis, especially in discussing the self as a mind and body.

44. Pierre Teilhard de Chardin, *The Divine Milieu* (New York: Harper & Row, 1968), 46.

Chapter One

Ancient, Medieval, and Modern Philosophical Background to Dialectical Incarnation

ANCIENT DEVELOPMENT: PRE-SOCRATICS AND HYLOZOISM

The quest began with the understanding of the Greek word *Hyle,* meaning "primordial stuff." *Hyle* serves as the first principle out of which the objective universe was formed.[1] Hylozoism leads to pantheism, with its different forms, and finally to Dialectical Incarnation. Through the dichotomies of inorganic and organic, inanimate and animate, matter and spirit, immanent and transcendent, many of our Western philosophies have succumbed to dualism. Hylozoism breaks down a major element of this dualistic understanding. It states that all material things possess life. The inanimate/animate, inorganic/organic separation is mistaken.

This dualistic separation has been a major factor in the way modern humanity views existence. Some ancient philosophies understood that there is only One Life in all of creation, and that the universe (and all that it contains) is the outward expression of that One Life. In the Western framework one calls this universal entity God. It is not God *and* creation, but God *as* creation that is at the root of this thought. If there is only One Life manifesting as, and through, the cosmos, then nothing can escape the livingness of that One Life, not even "inorganic" matter.

The Ionian cosmologists were seeking this one, primordial stuff. Thales (640–546 BCE) called it water. Anaximander (610–547 BCE) struggled with the strict "materiality" of his predecessor and called it "the indefinite," or the "boundless." Anaximenes (588–524 BCE) synthesises these two seeming opposing poles into what he claims as the "primordial stuff" of "air." Pythagoras (570–500 BCE) brings an understanding of "form" to the materiality of the Ionians. He held that the substance of all things was number, and that the Universe came forth out of chaos, through measure and harmony acquiring form. Pythagoras, indeed, was the first to call the universe the "cosmos," meaning "the harmonious order of things."[2] The "one stuff" of the universe is music and mathematics, offering a harmony for the totality of reality. From this deeper understanding of the cosmos, Heraclitus (c. 540–475 BCE) recognises that there is a form of life in all material objects. In the attempt to find unity in diversity, Heraclitus assumed that there must be some one thing which changes. That one thing is *fire*. This was not a simple substitute for Thales' *water* or Anaximenes' *air*. Fire is simultaneously a deficiency and a surplus; fire is a process of transformation. In holding firm to the understanding of fire as the basic reality, he identified not only the something which changes but the principle of change itself. For Heraclitus to say that everything is in flux meant that the "world-order is . . . an ever-living fire, kindling in measures and going out in measures."[3] Changeability pervades the whole world; "one cannot step twice into the same river."[4] Heraclitus thought that he had explained the rudiments of the unity between the one basic stuff and the many diverse things in the world.[5] While the earlier speculative, metaphysical philosophers were seeking the one stuff, Heraclitus was trying to maintain the reality of diversity and change. The fundamental "stuff" of the cosmos is not something material but is rather a natural process. This process is the strife of Dialectical Incarnation. Therefore, Heraclitus is the first major figure of Dialectical Incarnation.

In *On Nature*, Heraclitus explained the world as a manifold of opposed forces joined in mutual rivalry, interlocked in constant strife and conflict. He proclaims that "All things happen by strife and necessity."[6] Reality is not a constellation of things at all, but rather of processes. The river is not an object, but an ever-changing flow; the sun is not a thing, but a flaming fire.[7] Heraclitus goes on to say that the "harmonious structure of the world depends upon opposite tension, like that of the bow and the lyre" and that "[i]t is opposition that brings things together."[8]

In Parmenides' (c. 515–c.450 BCE) metaphysics, the significant aspect of his doctrine on the nature of the world is his assertion that "It is." "It" i.e., Reality, Being, whatever nature it may seem to be, is, exists, and cannot not be. But what is the nature of this "It," this Being, according to Parmenides?

The material reality of Being is suggested by Parmenides' assertion that "[w]hat *is,* is a finite, spherical, motionless *plenum,* and there is nothing beyond it."[9] Being, that which *is,* is One and is finite, and finitude requires materiality. For Parmenides, the infinite meant indeterminate and indefinite, while "Being, as the Real, cannot be indefinite or indeterminate, cannot change, cannot be conceived as expanding into empty space; it must be definite, determinate, complete."[10] Parmenides struggles with the dialectical nature of Being. For him, "It" is "temporally infinite, as having neither beginning nor end, but it is spatially finite."[11] As J. Burnet notes, "Parmenides is not, as some have said, the 'father of idealism'; on the contrary, all materialism depends on his view of reality."[12]

Parmenides' difficulty in explaining "the One" is that he does not grasp the dialectical nature of reality and does not understand that the "conflict of opposites is not a calamity but the permanent condition of all things."[13] Parmenides could not grasp Heraclitus' perspective in which "what is in opposition is in concert, and from what differs comes the most beautiful harmony."[14]

Plotinus and "the One"

In discovering the evolution of hylozoism and the understanding of a "one substance," one must turn next to Plotinus' (205–270 CE) notion of emanation and "the One." Plotinus is not a metaphysical philosopher in the strict sense of the term. He is, however, frequently called a "mystical thinker," but even this description fails to express the depth of his thought. Plotinus could certainly be considered the founder of Neo–Platonism, so when one examines his understanding of Being and Life in his cosmology, one recognizes that idealism emerges.[15]

Plotinus believes that the material world, with its multiplicity of things, cannot be the true reality because it is always changing. That which is true "being" does not change so it must be something different from the material world. This true reality is God. Nothing specific can describe this being except that God, or the One, absolutely transcends or lies beyond everything in the world. For this reason:

> God is not material, is not finite, is not divisible, has no specific form either as material, soul, or mind, each of which undergoes change, cannot be confined to any idea or ideas of the intellect and for this reason cannot be expressed in any human language, and is accessible to none of the senses but can be reached only in a mystical ecstasy that is independent of any rational or sense experience.[16]

Plotinus' "concept" of the One is not, properly speaking, a concept, since it is never explicitly defined by Plotinus; yet it is nevertheless the foundation of his philosophy. No words can do justice to the One, for even the name, "the One," is inadequate, for naming already implies discursive knowledge that divides or separates its objects, in order to make them intelligible. Plotinus says that the One cannot be known through the process of discursive reasoning.[17] Knowledge of the One is achieved through the experience of its "power" and its nature, which provides a "foundation" and location for all existents.[18]

It should be obvious that Plotinus' understanding of the One, as transcending the material world, is inconsistent with both hylozoism and Dialectical Incarnation. But his struggle with the Oneness of reality, in view of a material, diverse world attracts our attention.

If God is One, God cannot create, for creation is an act, an activity which implies change. In his attempt to maintain a consistent view of the unity of God, Plotinus explained the origin of things, by saying that they come from God, not through a free act of creation but through necessity. Things *emanate*, they flow from God, from the One, the way light emanates from the sun, the way water flows from a spring that has no source.[19] Yet, the question immediately arises as to why the One, being so perfect and self—sufficient, should have any need or even any "ability" to emanate or generate anything other than itself. In answering this challenge Plotinus appeals, not to reason, but to the non–discursive, intuitive faculty of the soul. This is why he is referred to as a "mystical thinker." Although all is One, the One relates to the diversity of the world, especially the world of matter, through the soul.

The emanation of the One begins with the mind or *Nous*, which, while like the One, is not absolute and can have an attribute or character. Nous is thought and, therefore, signifies the underlying rationality of the world. This rationality does not have any spatial or temporal boundaries, but it does imply multiplicity, because thinking contains the idea of particular things.

Light emanates from the sun in ever-diminishing intensity; just so, gradations of being emanate from the One. And just as light diminishes with distance, so too each succeeding emanation is a decline in the degrees of perfection.[20]

The One, the *Nous,* the World Soul are all co-eternal; below the World Soul lies the realm of nature, of particular things, reflecting in a changing way, in time, the eternal ideas. The human soul is an emanation of World Soul and "looks up" to it. Yet, the soul is also connected to, but is not identical with, the body. While in the body, the soul provides the power of rationality, sensibility, and vitality.[21]

At the farthest remove from the One is matter. Plotinus compared matter to the dimmest, the farthest reach, of light, the most extreme limit of light. Darkness is the very opposite of light, as matter is the opposite of spirit and is therefore the opposite of the One. Insofar as matter exists in conjunction with the soul, to this extent matter is not complete darkness. In the same way that light tends to emanate finally to the point of utter darkness, so too matter stands at the boundary line of nothingness, where it tends to disappear into non-being.

Besides the fact that Plotinus sees all of reality as emanating from the One, the salient element of his philosophy is his struggle in responding to the dualism of matter and spirit while maintaining the reality of one. In trying to synthesize seeming opposing elements, i.e., matter and spirit, materiality and vitality, it is clear one cannot resort to Plotinus' understanding of reality. In consonance with the philosophy of hylozoism, the world of matter is not void of life. Plotinus' contribution to the philosophy is his struggle with the dichotomy and his seeking to resolve the conflict present in the dualism of Western philosophy. It is by comparison that one can better understand what succeeding philosophers and metaphysicians have tried to do in explaining how "All is One." Within this direction it is important that we move to Thomas Aquinas and his notion of a "hierarchy of being" and its relationship to matter.

MEDIEVAL PERIOD AND SUBSEQUENT PERIODS

Thomas Aquinas and the Hierarchy of Being

Aquinas (1225–1274 CE) acknowledges Aristotle's insistence that matter is never without form and form is never present without matter. One can speak of "matter" and "form" theoretically, indicating a conceptual distinction, but they are never separated in reality. One can speak of "inorganic" and "organic," theoretically and distinctly as concepts, but one cannot separate these concepts in reality. "Distinct but not separate" is the heart of hylozoism and Dialectical Incarnation.

Seeming opposing positions, such as transcendent and imminent, unity and diversity, divine and human, etc., can be identified and defined, but in reality they are not separate. In the way that Aristotle explains that matter and form are never separate in reality, so too, transcendence and immanence, divine and human, matter and spirit, are not separate in reality.

In trying to resolve these seeming opposing concepts, Aquinas uses the terminology of "analogy" when describing his understanding of the *Esse* (Being) of God, and the *esse* (being) of all other reality. The Being applied to God is not univocal, as it is different, when applied to the being of reality. Nor is the Being applied to God equivocal to all other beings. Rather, the Being applied to God is analogical to the being of humanity and all other creatures, angels and animals alike.[22] By using an analogical comparison, Aquinas is trying to explain the statement "distinct but not separate," as a relationship between the divine and the human, and all creation. As a concept, God is not human; that is, God is divine, and distinct from human, and from creation. Yet Aquinas wants also to explain that although distinct, God is not equivocally different and separate from creation and humanity. There is an analogical relationship between these two distinct concepts.

Like Plotinus, Aquinas is seeking a unity of all creation. The problem, from the perspective of Dialectical Incarnation, is the failure to think dialectically in a complete manner. Aquinas, as "the Doctor" of Roman Catholic philosophy and theology, needed to reconcile his philosophy with Catholic doctrine.[23] The doctrine of creation, in which God freely creates *ex nihilo,* rules out Plotinus' theory of emanation. Likewise, pantheism, which emerges from the philosophy of hylozoism, must also be rejected, because, for Aquinas, God must be separate from God's creation.[24] Let us turn to examine Thomas Aquinas' metaphysics, with the understanding of its vitality of all materiality.

According to Aquinas, God is Pure Being and Pure Act and all other being participates (Plato's influence on Aquinas) in that Being.[25] For Aquinas, to participate is to share in and be part of Pure Being. It is the analogy of participating, whereby humans and all creation, although different from God, share in, and are part of the Pure Being of God.

Aristotle's influence upon Aquinas is easily recognised. Aristotle understands the world as

> made up of active substances, each one of them giving and receiving some form of actuality, such as material qualities, motion under all its forms, and finally substantial being at the term of every process of being.[26]

The "universal dynamism of substances" attributed to Aristotle is the "universal dynamism of being" attributed to Aquinas and is similar, if not identical, to the "universal dynamism" of nature found in hylozoism.[27] If one can see the life force, or "universal dynamism" of all matter, the established dualism, which separates matter and spirit, animate from inanimate, will no longer be able to stand on solid ground and the truth of Dialectical Incarnation can be validated.

Nicholas of Cusa

Nicholas of Cusa (1401–1464 CE) is sometimes referred to as the first "modern" philosopher, because of the forward-looking elements found in his thought.[28] He was born in Kues, Germany. He became a canon lawyer and a cardinal in the Roman Catholic Church. *Of Learned Ignorance* and *De Visione Dei (On the Vision of God)* are his two best-known works. One can appreciate the academic contribution of *Ignorance* when understanding that there was an atmosphere of intellectual tension in the early fifteenth century when Nicholas was studying and writing. He was in the midst of the prolonged debate between Ockham's nominalism and Thomas Aquinas' realism.[29] So too, the emergence of the Renaissance was weakening the underpinnings of Scholastic philosophy, while at the same time humanism was opening new ways of understanding both the past and the present. Historically, it seemed evident that theoretical foundations were shifting, consequently there surfaced an encouragement of new conceptual syntheses. Nicholas's *De Doctra Ignorantia* certainly must be understood as one such synthesis, whereby the dualism of the past was reconciled into the dialectical oneness of God, whereby "in God all is God."[30]

Nicholas is a philosopher of paradoxical and dialectical reasoning. He begins by taking ignorance or lack of certain knowledge as thematic, as a starting point of his philosophy and by doing so differentiates himself from his medieval predecessors. It was hardly questioned that things outside thought are epistemologically prior and stand as thought's norm and measure. Nicholas turns to the human mind and its inadequacies, particularly when it comes to having knowledge of God. The human capacity to know even created things is inadequate in our desire to know. Nicholas explains in his first chapter of Ignorance that "[i]t so far surpasses human reason, however, to know the precision of the combinations in material things and how exactly the known has to be adapted to the unknown."[31]

Within Nicholas' epistemology and metaphysics, which are simply two sides of the same coin, God is a trinity of eternal unity, i.e., an eternal oneness of unity, an eternal unity of equality and an eternal unity of connection. Expressed in another way, God is a trinity of Oneness, Equality-of-Oneness, and the Union thereof. In that God is a trinity in unity, so too is the universe, and all diverse elements of it, a trinity of *possibility, actuality*, and the *union* between the two which is movement or motion. "Potency and act are connected by means of this movement, for movement itself, which is intermediary, springs from moveable matter and a formal mover."[32]

Aquinas states that God is pure act, neither possibility nor potentiality. In contrast Nicholas states that God and the physical world, the cosmos, are one. Pure potentiality, which is found in the physical world, especially in the human person, who is aware of the objective other, is also found in God. In brief, God is pure Act for scholastic philosophy; for Nicholas, God is pure potentiality.

According to Nicholas, God is all things through the mediation of the universe. In Book Three of *Ignorance*, there is more direct explanation of God in the world through a Christian theology. As such, there is a fine line between philosophy and revealed theology. Nevertheless, it is established that God and the world are inseparable terms, and that God is the unity of the possibility of things. God is

> the *maximum absolutum* to which the world is related as *maximum contractum*, itself as maximum because the fullest realization of active possibility compatible with the negative and passive possibility inherent in a world of finite things.[33] There is no separate world soul,[34] and motion proceeds from the dynamism of the spirit of God.[35] [36]

Nicholas understands God as the formal cause of the universe, but also seeks to establish God as the efficient and final cause.[37] Aristotle makes clear distinctions among his four causes. The material cause is that "out of which" something is made, e.g. the marble of a sculptured statue. The efficient cause is "that by which" something is made. The example would be the sculptor himself or herself. The formal cause is "that which it is." It is a statue of something or someone specific. The marble piece's form is a sculpture of Moses. The final cause is "that for which the thing is made." In the case of the sculpture, the final cause would be to be appreciated as a piece of art.

When Nicholas understands God as the formal cause of the universe, he is saying that God is the form of the universe; God is that which the universe is. As the efficient cause, God is the creator, and as the final cause, God is that for which the universe is made. The universe is dependent upon God, yet remains the essential, dialectical antithesis to God as the restricted or limited aspect of the infinite. The universe is relative to the absolute. How is this dialectical dynamic of thesis and antithesis overcome? It is through Incarnation. Incarnation is what it is through the condition of the possibility of being both God *qua* God and the universe *qua* universe. Incarnation is possible through being the formal cause *qua* formal cause and final cause *qua* final cause of the totality of reality. Incarnation is intrinsically dialectical and cannot be intellectually grasped in any other manner.

Although Nicholas is quite innovative in his philosophy, he still succumbs to the limits of doctrinal theology. His primary problem is explaining how the world can be said to be distinct from God, while at the same time insisting God is "the unity or complication of all reality and that the world is only the explication in limited forms of that same reality, so that the world seems to differ from God only by not-being or nothing."[38] The intrigue of dialectical reasoning is that the two poles remain distinct but are not separate.

Nicholas could be considered a pantheist, in its classical description. While Nicholas describes God and the cosmos as "One," he maintains a dialectical distinction whereby the two are never separate. As such he is a significant player in setting the stage for Dialectical Incarnation. As God ontologically precedes and unites contradictories, so the universe ontologically precedes and unites contraries, and the humanity of Christ, the Incarnation, ontologically precedes and enfolds all created things. God as the *maximum,* which is at once the *minimum,* is incomprehensible; and in God centre is the circumference.[39] Just as God is the centre and the circumference of the universe, so too the Incarnation is the centre and the circumference of the intellectual natures. In understanding the fullness of Incarnation expressed in Nicholas' philosophy, the human Self then becomes the centre of the circumference, where the human Self and God unite dialectically as distinct but never separate. Jasper Hopkins explains this in a more understandable way. He says:

God is in all things through the mediation of the universe, just as [God] is in all believers through the mediation of Christ. In all things God is, absolutely, that which they are, just as in all things the universe is, contractedly, that which each is, and just as Christ [Incarnation] is the universal contracted being of each creature [Self]. Just as God ontologically precedes and unites contradictories, so the universe ontologically precedes and unites contraries, and the humanity of Christ ontologically precedes and enfolds all creatable things. In God center is circumference, just as God is the center and the circumference of the universe and just as Christ [Incarnation] is the center and the circumference of the intellectual natures.[40]

The metaphor of the Self as the centre of the circumference indicates that the Self is the link between the human and the divine. The human is the divine as the centre is the circumference. As a dialectical method one entity, or identity, is at the same time the entity's opposite. This is how Nicholas can identify God as both the *maximum* as well as the *minimum.*

The fulcrum of Nicholas' philosophical system, and therefore his epistemology, is the understanding of *docta ignorantia*. What is this doctrine? He explains that it is recognition of the limitedness that has been achieved, that has been learned. It is "enlightened ignorance," an unknowing has been learned so that the one who has learned of his/her unknowing is now among the instructed rather than remaining one of the unlearned. Nicholas refers to Socrates who admits that "he knew nothing save his own ignorance."[41] The importance of *learned ignorance* is that it is "instructed"; it is not merely a lack of knowledge. Like Socrates himself, the person of *learned ignorance* is wise precisely because he or she knows that he or she does not know. As Nicholas puts it:

Nothing could be more beneficial for even the most zealous searcher for knowledge than his [or her] being in fact most learned in that very ignorance which is peculiarly his own.[42]

Learned ignorance thus distinguishes the learned from the unlearned or uninstructed, while at the same time this *ignorance* elevates the learned to the level of the "wise."

Learned ignorance has a twofold awareness. First, God, as the absolute maximum, is "completely beyond our understanding."[43] Secondly, as been stated, "[i]t so far surpasses human reason, however, to know the precision in material things."[44] Therefore, Nicholas indicates that we must acquire a *learned ign orance* both in our knowledge of God, the infinite *qua* infinite, and material things, the finite *qua* finite. When he refers to knowing something with "precision" it does not mean that we do not know anything. Nicholas does not equate knowledge with precise knowledge or understanding for the "Absolute Maximum is known but not understood."[45] When he speaks of the objects of the world, he admits that we know them but we do not know them in their "quiddity," or as they are in themselves. Thus, *learned ignorance* begins with the twofold awareness of not *precisely* knowing God and not *precisely* knowing the material world.

A very important element of Nicholas of Cusa's philosophy, for our purpose, is his claim that God is the *coincidentia oppositorum;* in God "contradictories are reconciled."[46] God is the synthesis of opposites in a unique and absolutely infinite being. In having referred to the challenge Nicholas faces when explaining his philosophy at the same time of dealing with his revealed theology, he utilizes this concept under the umbrella of the "Providence" of God.[47] He explains that "[i]t is clear, from what has been said, that God encompasses all things, even contradictories; it follows then that nothing escapes [God's] Providence."[48]

Nicholas' *coincidentia oppositorum* is especially important with regard to finite things.[49] He explains that finite things are multiple and distinct, possessing their different natures and qualities, while God transcends all the distinctions and oppositions which are found in created things. These distinctions coincide in God, because God unites them in Godself. The distinction of essence and existence cannot be in God, as they are in other creatures. In God, essence and existence coincide and are one. He goes on to explain that in created things we can distinguish greatness from smallness, where there are different degrees of particular attributes. However, in God all distinctions coincide, for God is the greatest being, the *maximum*. But, we must also say that God is the least of being, the *minimum*, for God cannot possess degrees of anything. In God *maximum* and *minimum* coincide.[50]

Although one may speak of God in this paradoxical, dialectical manner, a complete understanding of what this actually means remains elusive. Through learned ignorance, one is aware that that one comes to know a finite thing by bringing it into relation to or comparing it with an already known entity. One knows created things by means of comparison, similarity, dissimilarity and distinction. But God, being infinite, is like no finite thing. In reality the distinct predicates which we apply to finite things coincide in God in a manner which "surpasses human reason."

For Nicholas God is dialectical in nature. Hence, God is the *coincidentia oppositorum*, the synthesis of opposites in a unique and absolutely infinite being. Finite things are multiple and distinct, possessing their different natures and qualities while God transcends all the distinctions and oppositions which are found in creatures.[51] God is all things through the mediation of the universe. God and the world are inseparable terms, and God is the unity of the possibility of particular things.

Giordano Bruno: Monistic Immanentism

During the Renaissance, Giordano Bruno (1548–1600 CE) revived the doctrine of hylozoism and held a form of Christian pantheism. He had a superb love of nature and understood God and nature as one. Accordingly, the universe is infinite and is full of a plurality of heliocentric systems composed of matter and soul. Both matter and soul are, rather than principles, two aspects of a *single substance* in which all opposites and all differences are reconciled. The soul of the universe is intelligent; it is God, conceived of as "Natura naturans." The material world, the cosmos, the universe is the "Natura naturata," an effect of God.[52] Birth of life in any form, according to Bruno, is the individualization, the materiality, the finite of the infinite, nonmateriality. As a result, death is the return of the finite to the infinite.

For Bruno, the universe is infinite, full of a plurality. The fundamental principles of the universe are two: matter, the passive principle, and soul, the active principle. Matter and soul represent two aspects of a single substance, two powers of a single principle, in which they are reconciled and united, and in which their differences are annulled, according to the principle of the coincidence of opposites of Nicholas of Cusa.[53]

"All things are one," says Bruno.[54] The soul of the universe is conceived of as intelligent, the "ordinator" of the world itself, the interior force of everything. Such a force is not transcendent, but immanent; it adheres in things. It is God, conceived of as "Natura naturans," producing all and ordaining all to its end; it is infinite. The world, the work of "Natura naturans," is "Natura naturata," which, as the effect of an infinite cause, is also infinite. Individual souls (and not only the human soul, but the soul of every individual essence, since for Bruno everything is animate) are the passing shades of the eternal becoming of the world. Bruno calls them monads.[55] As stated, birth is the individuation of the infinite in the finite and death is the return of the finite to the infinite.

Bruno was charged with atheism, because in his theory the universe was God, and God was the universe. For Bruno, divinity revealed itself through individual things, and all things are infused with divinity. His statement is "All is in all things."[56] To identify God and Nature was not a negation but an explanation. God is the source, cause, medium, and end of all things, and therefore all things are participatory in the ongoing Godhead. In this way every individual thing has something of the whole within itself, and everything interpenetrated with everything else: "Each thing is within every other."[57]

There are different opinions as to the type of pantheism to which Bruno adheres. One could say he is a panpsychic rather than a materialist pantheist in that he recognises matter and spirit as distinct, although both are aspects or elements of one underlying substance. This is similar to Aristotle's distinction of matter and form but neither is separate. One can never find form separate from matter. But, as also stated, everything is infused with divinity. God animates each thing and harmonises everything into a single universal whole.

Bruno makes another distinction between God and the world, when he speaks of God as distinct from God's manifestation and, at the same time, God is considered as God's manifestations. Dialectical Incarnation constantly maintains that God is "distinct but not separate" from creation, the world and the universe. Bruno, however, remains a believer in a God as transcendent.[58] Philosophy deals with Nature and that God, in Godself, is a subject which can only be properly treated in theology. As such, Bruno cannot be a strict pantheist because he indicates a type of separation. Philosophy which deals with God is natural theology, although different from revealed theology.

When dealing with the continued struggle of a seeming dualistic world of transcendent and immanent, God and nature, spirit and matter, etc., Bruno tried to find a synthesis. However, it seems he was never able to resolve the conflict in his philosophy. Perhaps he had not yet grasped the fullness of dialectical reasoning, although Hegel himself acclaimed Bruno a prophet.[59] Bruno adds much to the evolution of hylozoism and Dialectical Incarnation through his *monistic immanentism*, yet the journey continues as we move toward Baruch Spinoza with his "pantheism" and understanding of God and nature.

THE MODERN PERIOD

Baruch Spinoza

The philosophy of Baruch Spinoza (1632–1677 CE) unites the divine with the human, transcendence with immanence. Spinoza states that the "Mind's intellectual Love of God is the very Love of God by which God loves [God's] self."[60] He goes on to elaborate this in the following Demonstration and Corollary. He says:

> [the]Love the Mind has is part of the infinite love by which God loves Himself, q.e.d . . . God's love of man and the Mind's intellectual Love of God are one and the same.[61]

Spinoza's metaphysics is based on rigorously defining terms and carefully working through the logical consequences of them. His reaction against Descartes, and earlier Scholastic philosophy, is the anthropomorphism of God and the attempt to create metaphysics pliable to orthodox religion. Spinoza disdains the falsity of religion, yet he argues at length for God's existence and concludes that the knowledge and love of God are human's greatest good.

For Spinoza, ethics is an ontology of the human person, and morality is lived by a human person's being-in-itself. The moral existence of humanity is explained by the human condition. An ethics does not offer an external theory of morality, but rather an intrinsic, radical and essential constitution of the human condition.[62] Ethical reality is the work of humans' *striving (conatus)* and acting through the power of reason and virtue. For Spinoza, the goal of ethics is to demonstrate the necessary fulfilment of human nature in the world.

Spinoza's philosophy presents the truth of God, nature and the human person. He uses metaphysics, physics, anthropology, and psychology; yet, Spinoza's overriding intention is to offer a work of ethical reasoning. Human happiness and well-being do not lie in the human bondage to passions, nor to the transitory goods for which humans strive, neither to the unreflective superstitious attachment to religion. Rather, well being comes through the power of reason itself.

The central purpose of Spinoza's work is to present a proper understanding of reality as that in which "[e]xcept God, no substance can be or be conceived."[63] Substance is that which is conceived *through* itself and which is *in* itself. God *or* Nature, in its existential character, is where Spinoza begins. Spinoza's philosophy is a humanistic existentialism, concerned with the concrete and existent, and is not an abstract metaphysical definition of the idea of God. A humanistic existentialism examines and stresses the existence of the human person and humanity's perfection rather than seeking to know the essence of what a human is in an abstract way. As such, Spinoza identifies God or Nature in the concrete existential realm where the human person strives, *conatus*, for his or her perfection.

Descartes' definition of substance is that which "we can understand nothing other than a thing which exists in such a way as to depend on no other thing for its existence."[64] Spinoza's definition of substance is similar when he writes "[b]y substance I understand what is in itself and is conceived through itself."[65] It would seem that in both definitions there could only be one substance for only God "depends on no other thing." Yet, Descartes was not willing to reduce substance to only one for he maintains that substance really means two different things, either God or those finite things (mind and body). For Spinoza there is only one substance and that is God *or* Nature.[66]

God is infinite substance and Spinoza argues that no attribute which expresses the essence of substance can be denied of God.[67] Every being has its being in God. Nothing can come into being or exist without God. God is the one and only thing which is. "Whatever is, is in God, and nothing can be conceived without God."[68] The argument placed against Spinoza is that of extension. Corporeality cannot apply to God, because this would lead to contradictions about infinitude and finitude, divisibility and perfection. Spinoza responds by distinguishing between "quantity" understood through the imagination versus "quantity" understood through the intellect.[69]

When quantity is understood through imagination, one finds quantity to be finite, divisible and made up of parts. But if one considers quantity intellectually and conceives it insofar as it is substance, then quantity will be found to be infinite, one and indivisible. Spinoza explains how "matter" is everywhere the same. There are no distinct parts in it, except insofar as one conceives matter as modified in various ways. The parts of matter are distinct only "modally."[70] He offers the example of water.

> We conceive water to be divisible and to have separate parts insofar as it is water, but not insofar as it is material substance. In this latter respect it is not capable of separation or division . . . water, qua water, comes into existence and goes out of existence; but qua substance it does not come into existence nor go out of existence [*corrumpitur*].[71]

Spinoza proceeds to claim that from "the necessity of the divine nature there must follow infinitely many things in infinitely many modes."[72] The criticism is that God, as the one substance, must express itself in modes and Spinoza never stated directly that substance must have modes. This leads to his explanation of *Natura Naturans* and *Natura Naturata*.[73]

There are two sides of God *or* Nature similar to that which was offered by Bruno. One is comprised of the active, productive aspect of the universe. Natura Naturans is God and God's attributes, from which all else follows. The other aspect is nature and the universe. *Natura Naturata* is that which is produced and sustained by the active aspect. Nature is an indivisible, uncaused, substantial whole. It is the only substantial whole and outside of Nature, there is nothing. Everything that exists is a part of Nature and is brought into being by Nature, with a deterministic necessity.

For Spinoza "God acts from the laws of [God's] nature alone, and is compelled by no one."[74] Spinoza discusses the impropriety in attributing "will" and "intellect" to God.

> For the intellect and will which would constitute God's essence would have to differ entirely from our intellect and will, and could not agree with them in anything except the name.[75]

According to Spinoza, the will and the intellect are modes of thought. The will is the same as the intellect. In God, intellect is actual and not potential, because in God intellect is fully actualized. This means that things must necessarily occur in the manner in which they occur, because the intellect or will of God is fully actualized.

In explaining his *Ethics*, Spinoza tries to rid humanity of certain pervasive misunderstandings. He claims that men think themselves as free, because they are conscious of their volitions and their appetite, and do not think, even in their dreams, of the causes by which they are disposed to wanting and willing . . . men act always on account of an end, viz. on account of their advantage, which they want. Hence they seek to know only the final causes of what has been done, and when they have heard them, they are satisfied because they have no reason to doubt further.[76]

From this position, Spinoza proceeds to explain "that all final causes are nothing but human fictions."[77] He explains that the "doctrine" of final causes "takes away God's perfection. For if God acts for the sake of an end, [God] necessarily wants something which [God] lacks."[78] Final causation also leads humans to mistake the usefulness of a thing for the essence or true nature of a thing, and "take the imagination for the intellect."[79] The fact is, for Spinoza, final causation explanations are mere confusion, "since those things we can easily imagine are especially pleasing to us, [humans] prefer order to confusion."[80] Because of necessity inherent in Nature, there is no teleology in the universe. According to Spinoza, Nature does not act for any ends, and things do not exist for any set purposes. God *or* Nature does not do things for the sake of anything else. The order of things just follows from God's essence with an inviolable determinism. When there is reference to God's purposes, intentions, goals, preferences or aims it is mere anthropomorphism, says Spinoza.

This particular aspect of Spinoza's philosophy is unacceptable. If God is the first and efficient cause, God, in the perspective of the philosophy, is also the final cause. Spinoza is clearly reacting to the ways in which humanity anthropomorphises God and "thinks" that God will change if we pray and do devotions and celebrate rituals. Spinoza wants humanity to find humanity's full purpose and destination yet he rejects God as a Final Cause. This philosophy holds strongly that all of *Natura Naturata* has as its final cause an end, i.e., to be one with *Natura Naturatans*. The goal, the end of all of creation is to synthesize what one understands as transcendence, which is God, and immanence, which is Nature. God, and therefore Nature, in Dialectical Incarnation, is the *Alpha* and the *Omega*. Spinoza makes his final cause an instrumental cause, rather than an intrinsic cause. Because of previous attention made in the past to doing good so as to attain reward, that is salvation, he had to reject, so he thought, final causality. But, if Spinoza simply understood it as an intrinsic movement, rather than an instrumental goal, final causality can fit sufficiently in his philosophy.

Having expounded the nature of God, Spinoza moves to the human person and his or her complexity, beginning with the mind. All that has been established now serves as a preface for the treatment of the human person. Spinoza is not directly concerned with the nature of God merely as an object of knowledge in itself. He is more directly concerned with human happiness, with humanity's attainment of "salvation." Spinoza begins with God but he is really concerned with the treatment of the human person. As A. Robert Caponigri states in *A History of Western Philosophy*,

> [Spinoza's] devouring interest in God is born of the conviction that only by reaching God and transforming the whole of his life in the light of God can man be rendered 'beatus.' The *Ethics* is a treatise, not so much *De Deo* [*Of God*], but as *De Vita Beata* [*Of the Blessed Life*] of man.[81]

Spinoza continues to build his philosophical edifice when he offers a definition of body which argues against Descartes' multiple substances. "By body I understand a mode that in a certain and determinate way expresses God's essence insofar as [God] is considered as an extended thing."[82]

The metaphysics of God and humans is what Caponigri calls the "descending path," by which the being of the human person flows from, but not *out* of the being of God.[83] This distinction stresses the *one*ness, the monism of Spinoza's philosophy. Spinoza goes on to explain that thought is one of the attributes of God,[84] and that extension is also an attribute of God.[85] "The order and connection of ideas is the same as the order and connection of things."[86] As such, God can think an infinite number of things in an infinite number of ways. God's infinite intellect comprehends all of God's attributes.

Substance is defined by Spinoza as a mode of being which implies necessary existence. God is infinite substance, and outside of God no other substance is possible. Thus, Spinoza's philosophy is considered pantheistic, in that it claims that God is present in and as all things. He states that the "being of substance does not pertain to the essence of [the hu]man, or substance does not constitute the form of [hu]man."[87] Spinoza argues that the human mind is a part of the infinite intellect of God, and therefore all ideas are present in the intellect of God.[88]

The key elements of Spinoza's thinking come from his dialectical understanding of God and Nature as One. The human person's *conatus* makes him or her the "centre of the circumference" of God and the cosmos. He states that the "striving by which each thing strives to persevere in its being is nothing but the actual essence of the thing."[89] As such, this striving "involves no finite time, but an indefinite time."[90]

Spinoza is demonstrating that the human person's *very nature* is to strive for perfection and to be in harmony with the oneness of God. That for which the human person is striving is to be free from the passions. But since this is not absolutely possible, the person is to learn how to moderate and restrain them and thus become active autonomous beings. If one can achieve this, then one will be "free." If one is "free," one will act from one's own nature and not as a result of one's relations with things outside. From this perspective, Spinoza should really say "freedom *in* our passions" rather than "from our passions," because we are never removed from them.

Spinoza is frequently called an idealist because of his understanding and role of the Mind. He also transcends any traditional understanding of materialism. It is Spinoza's idealism that leads to hylozoism, then to pantheism and, finally, to the forming of Dialectical Incarnation. Spinoza recognized one universal indivisible substance and created a radical monism in which the single underlying of all reality was what he called "God." According to Skrbina, this substance, however, is identical with the natural cosmos and he equates God with Nature, resulting in a strong form of pantheism.[91] If he is an idealist he certainly is a materialistic one because both Hegel and Marx saw Spinoza as a precursor to their own philosophy.

Dialectical Incarnation goes beyond Spinoza's thought. First, Dialectical Incarnation rejects Spinoza's refutation of final causality in his God or Nature paradigm. Final causality is intrinsic to God and Nature. Second, as we shall see, Dialectical Incarnation celebrates and glorifies human passions, instead of trying to get rid of their negative influences. If one understands oneself as a synthesised (body and soul) incarnational, human being who is intrinsically free, one will understand one's passions and use them in one's *conatus* of life. Life is to be lived passionately, but not destructively. This is the human person's objective of life. Third, in the end, Spinoza is best described as a monist, albeit a radical one.

Dialectical Incarnation could be called a dialectical monism, but this description lacks a focus of our next key player, i.e., the pluralism of G.W. Leibniz and his greater stress on the materiality, and therefore, the particularity of the philosophy. Spinoza's one and only substance is neither physical nor mental and therefore, for him, the problem of Descartes' (the mind/body and idea/extension connection) is resolved, because mind and body do not need to interact. Dialectical Incarnation agrees that the one substance is neither mind nor body, because it is incarnation. Incarnation is similar to Leibniz's "monad" but seen in a fuller way. The reality is that the body and mind do interact as the synthesis and also as the "condition of the possibility" of an incarnational human existence. Finally, Spinoza's sees the relationship between God and humanity in the realm of the "idea" or the mind. The focus of Dialectical Incarnation is that of the heart. The mind, the soul, spirit, idea, whatever description one gives this dialectical concept, it, in the end, serves as the condition of the possibility to "feel" with the heart and to love. Spinoza is not able to complete his rejection of dualism because he lacks that which Leibniz is going to add, i.e., plurality and more materiality. Leibniz elaborates the understanding of particularity and the mystery and beauty of a system which is one while being infinite in the possibility of particularities in the world.

Gottfried Wilhelm von Leibniz

Among his various areas of interest, G.W. Leibniz (1646–1716 CE) was a physicist and studied momentum. As a mathematician, he visualised an idea which is reflected in his concept of a universe made up of infinitesimal 'Monads.' He discovered differential calculus independently of Isaac Newton and through that discovery the finding of the area of an object is done by dividing it up into an infinite number of 'slices' and then adding them together.

Leibniz is an eclectic philosopher and a self-conscious synthesiser. He says,

> This system appears to unite Plato with Democritus, Aristotle with Descartes, the Scholastics with the moderns, theology and morality with reason. Apparently it takes the best from all systems and then advances further than anyone has yet done.[92]

In stressing materiality and plurality Leibniz claims that all the plenum of the universe is filled with tiny monads, which cannot fail, have no constituent parts and have no windows through which anything could come in or go out.[93] Leibniz goes through an elaborate explanation of these monads in his *Monadology*. Every monad is different and is continuously changing in their own identity. All simple substances or Monads have in them a certain perfection and a certain self-sufficiency. Human knowledge of necessary and eternal truths distinguishes us from the animals and gives us Reason. Truths of reason are necessary and their opposite is impossible: truths of fact are contingent and their opposite is possible. When a truth is necessary, its reason can be found by analysis, resolving it into more simple ideas and truths. The final reason of things must be in a necessary substance, which we call God. God holds an infinity of ideas in God's mind and chooses the most perfect ones. Each simple substance has relations which express all the others. Consequently, a monad is a perpetual living mirror of the universe, although it represents more distinctly the body of which it is the entelechy. Each portion of matter is like a pond full of fishes, where each drop of its liquid parts is also another pond. Thus there is nothing fallow, nothing sterile, nothing dead in the universe.

Leibniz supports the earlier mentioned notion of hylozoism. All the parts of every living body are full of other living beings, each with its dominant entelechy or soul. Thus there never is absolute birth or complete death. Minds are images of the deity, capable of knowing the system of the universe and its "harmony of love." Each and every being is like a small divinity in its own sphere. The totality of reality must compose the realm of God, where no good action would be unrewarded and no bad one unpunished. Leibniz works endlessly to establish a harmony of love where there is a true unity in a plurality of diversity found in monads. This sets the stage for Dialectical Incarnation.

For Leibniz, perfection is understood as reality. God has infinite perfection and every existent being other than God (that is the entire universe) possesses a limited degree of perfection. Creation is limited and only God has unlimited perfection. Leibniz understands metaphysical perfection as being constituted by harmony which is a unity in variety, a unity in plurality. Harmony is when a variety of "bodies" are ordered in accordance with general laws or principles. He says: "[t]hus bodies are ultimately or really (as distinct from phenomenally) independent forces (Monads), which differ from one another endlessly but are yet in such harmony that they form one perfectly regular system."[94]

In contrast to Spinoza, Leibniz perceives the existence of a plurality of substances. There was but one for Spinoza; Leibniz, to the contrary, sees an infinitude of Beings from and in the One. Again, although both admitted but one real entity, Spinoza makes it impersonal and indivisible, while Leibniz, on the other hand, divides his personal deity into a number of divine and semi-divine Beings. Spinoza's is a subjective pantheism, whereas Leibniz's is an objective pantheism. Within Spinoza's monism and one substance, particularity, materiality and plurality get lost or smothered, at least to some degree. The one substance of Spinoza's idealism needs more materiality, more particularity and more diversity. Spinoza focuses on the unity of the phrase "unity in diversity," Leibniz focuses on the diversity of the unity.

Leibniz understands perfection as reality. One could assume that he derives this understanding from Plotinus' theory of emanation and Aquinas' understanding of perfection in his hierarchy of being. As such, perfection is not an all-or-nothing entity; it is scalar, that is, it comes in varying degrees. Leibniz explains that "Perfection is the harmony of things, or the state where everything is worthy of being observed, that is, the state of agreement [*consensus*] or identity in variety."[95]

Leibniz argues that, insofar as the rational soul or spirit can know eternal truths and can act according to reason, it can reflect God. The spiritual world is a moral world, which can guide the natural world. The goodness of God ensures that there is harmony between the spiritual world and the natural world, and establishes harmony between moral laws and natural laws. A perfect harmony of moral and natural law is found in the spiritual world, which Leibniz calls the City of God.

Leibniz claims that the ultimate reason of all things must be found in a necessary and universal substance, which is God. A primary substance is not material, according to Leibniz, because matter is infinitely divisible. Every monad is produced from a primary unity, which is God. Every monad is eternal and contributes to the unity of all the other monads in the universe. Leibniz does say that there is only one necessary substance, and that this is

God. A necessary substance is one whose existence is logically necessary. The existence of a necessary substance cannot be denied without causing some form of self-contradiction. Therefore, God's existence is logically necessary. God is absolutely real, infinite, and perfect. All perfection and all reality comes from God. God, as the supreme monad, is an absolute unity and "reality cannot be found except in One single source, because of the interconnection of all things with one another."[96]

Although Leibniz offers so much to the foundation of Dialectical Incarnation, one may begin to identify some points where the current philosophy will differ and go beyond. Leibniz wants to unite the material and the spiritual world, but his descriptions of his world of monads still maintain a dualism between "spiritual world" and "City of God." Spinoza could not let go of his idealism, while Leibniz could not let go of his "spiritualism." What Leibniz must do is maintain a system whereby the two are not separate. Our new vision is to see God in the most concrete, and the most particular. The City of God is the incarnate world, not some separated spiritual or moral existence.

Another interesting aspect of Leibniz's philosophy is that he envisions the fact that there are an infinite number of possible universes in the mind of God, but that God has chosen a single universe whose sufficient reason is that it is the best possible universe (i.e., having the highest possible degree of perfection). Leibniz argues that God is supremely perfect, and that therefore God has chosen the best possible plan for the universe. God's plan for the universe necessarily produces the greatest amount of happiness and goodness, because it reflects God's absolute perfection. But Leibniz's argument may be rejected by noting that the best of all possible worlds may not necessarily contain both good and evil. The best of all possible worlds may not necessarily contain both happiness and unhappiness. The universe may not necessarily be governed by harmony, but may be governed by disharmony. The universe may not necessarily reveal unity, but may reveal disunity.[97] The dialectical method is one of bi-polar theses. In the perspective of Dialectical Incarnation, the "disharmony" and the "disunity" of a harmonious and united world is the necessary strife present in such a dialectical paradigm. This is the best possible world, the ongoing synthesis of the ongoing seemingly opposing poles of a diverse and total world.

SUMMARY

The salient aspect of Hegel and Marx is that within their own system they do not allow the "other" —i.e. the seeming opposing pole of the dialectical method—to be all that it can be. Hegel's "materialism" is a disclosure of idealism and Marx's "idealism" is merely an expression of materialism. Each system refrains from enabling the "other" to exist in its fullness. Within

Dialectical Incarnation, the concepts are clearly distinct as matter and spirit, yet each concept is able to be all that it can be within the synthesis itself. Our philosophy magnifies both spirit and matter and enables each to be all that they are as spirit and as matter, conceptually. However, it needs to be emphasized that the two, although distinct conceptually, are never separate in reality. To say again, in the manner that matter and form are distinct, as concepts, but not separate for Aristotle, so too, matter and spirit are distinct as concepts but are never separate in Dialectical Incarnation.

NOTES

1. See William L. Reese, *Dictionary of Philosophy and Religion* (Amherst: Humanity Books, 1996), 323.

2. Thessaloniki Museum of Technology, "Ancient Greek Scientists," http://www.noesis.edu.gr/.

3. Heraclitus, *The Fragments: of the Work of Heraclitus of Ephesus On Nature* (Whitefish, MT: Kessinger Publishing, 2007), 217.

4. Ibid., 215.

5. Samuel Enoch Stumpf, *Socrates to Sartre: A History of Philosophy* (New York: McGraw-Hill Book Company, 1966), 13.

6. Heraclitus, *The Fragments*, 211.

7. Ibid.

8. John Burnet, *Early Greek Philosophy* (London and Edinburgh: Kessinger Publishing, 1892), 137.

9. Ibid., 194.

10. References to secondary sources are used throughout the thesis. The philosophers are numerous, as the reader discovers, and it is not easy to find the original source. See Frederick Copleston, *A History of Philosophy* (New York: Image Books, 1962), I, 1: 67–8.

11. Copleston, *A History of Philosophy*, I, 1: 68.

12. Burnet, *Early Greek Philosophy*, 195.

13. Stumpf, *Socrates to Sartre*, 15.

14. Ibid.

15. Ibid., 125–26.

16. Ibid.

17. Plotinus, *Enneads* (London: Penguin Books, 1991), VI, 9:4.

18. Ibid., VI, 9:6.

19. Stumpf, *Socrates to Sartre*, 126.

20. Copleston, *A History of Philosophy*, I, 2: 210–11.

21. Ibid., 211–12.

22. Ibid., II, 2: 74.

23. Ibid., 20.

24. Ibid., 83–84.

25. Ibid., 27, 52.

26. Etienne Gilson, *The Elements of Christian Philosophy* (New York: The New American Library, 1960), 265.

27. Ibid.

28. Copleston, *A History of Philosophy*, III, 2: 37.

29. The attempt of philosophers to discover "What is real?" continues to go on in history. The "debate" going on here is the "reality" of concepts or universals as compared to metaphysics and being.

30. Copleston, *A History of Philosophy*, III, 2: 45–46.

31. Jaspar Hopkins, *Nicholas of Cusa On Learned Ignorance: A translation and an appraisal of De Docta Ignorantia* (Minneapolis: The Arthur J. Banning Press, 1985).

32. Nicholas of Cusa, *On Learned Ignorance: A translation and an appraisal of De Docta Ignorantia* (Minneapolis: The Arthur J. Banning Press, 1985), II, 10:105.

33. Ibid., 1.

34. Ibid, 9.

35. Ibid., 10.

36. Ibid., xxiii.

37. Ibid., 9: 103.

38. Ibid, xxi.

39. Ibid, I, 21: 47.

40. Ibid., 2.

41. Ibid., I 1:8.

42. Ibid., 8–9.

43. Ibid., 4:12.

44. Ibid., 8–9.

45. This is the title of Chapter Four in *On Learned Ignorance*.

46. Nicholas of Cusa, *On Learned Ignorance,* I, 22:49.

47. "Providence" comes from the Latin *providere* ("to foresee"). The term refers to the regulative agency of God in the world. See William L. Reese, *Dictionary of Philosophy and Religion* (Amherst: Humanity Books, 1996), 615.

48. Hopkins, *On Learned Ignorance.*

49. Copleston, *A History of Philosophy,* III, 2, section 3.

50. Nicholas of Cusa, *On Learned Ignorance,* I, 4:12.

51. Copleston, *A History of Philosophy,* II, 2:41.

52. We will also see how Spinoza uses the terms "Natura naturans" and "Natura naturata." Leibniz uses the term monad.

53. Remember how for Nicholas Cusa, God is the *coincidentia oppositorum*, the synthesis of opposites in a unique and absolutely infinite being. Finite things are multiple and distinct, possessing their different natures and qualities while God transcends all the distinctions and oppositions which are found in creatures. See Copleston, *A History of Philosophy,* III, 2:41.

54. See Paul Harrison, "Scientific Pantheism: Reverence of Nature and Cosmos." http://www.pantheism.net/paul/

55. Ibid.

56. Ibid.

57. Ibid.

58. Copleston, *A History of Philosophy,* III, 2: 68–69.

59. Ibid.

60. Baruch Spinoza, *The Collected Works of Spinoza* (Princeton, NJ: Princeton University Press, 1985), 612.

61. Ibid.

62. Alfredo Lucero-Montano, "Spinoza's Ethics, Determinism and Freedom." www.PhiloSophos.com.

63. Spinoza, *The Collected Works, Ethics* I, 14: 420.

64. Rene Descartes, *Principles of Philosophy* (Whitefish, MT: Kessinger Publishing, 2005), Part I, section 51.

65. Spinoza, *The Collected Works, Ethics* I, D3, 408.

66. Ibid., 14.

67. Ibid., Dem.: 420.

68. Ibid., 15, 420.

69. Ibid., 424.

70. Ibid.

71. Ibid.

72. Ibid., I, P16: 424.

73. Ibid., P29, Dem.: 434.

74. Ibid., I, 17, 425.

75. Ibid., 427.

76. Spinoza, Part One of *Ethics* comes to an end and Spinoza offers an overall summary in the *Appendix.*

77. The final cause of which Spinoza is addressing is that of Aristotle. The goal, the purpose, the end of that which something is, is the final cause. See *The Collected Works of Spinoza* (Princeton, NJ: Princeton University Press, 1985), 442.

78. Spinoza, *The Collected Works, Ethics,* 442.

79. Ibid., 444.

80. Ibid.

81. Robert A. Caponigri, *A History of Western Philosophy: Philosophy from the Renaissance to the Romantic Age* (Notre Dame: University of Notre Dame Press, 1963), 218.

82. Spinoza, *The Collected Works, Ethics,* II P, D 1, 447. Particular things are nothing but affections of God's attributes, *or* modes by which God's attributes are expressed in a certain and determinate way. The demonstration is evident from P15 and D5; 431. Also see IP25C.

83. Caponigri. *A History of Western Philosophy*, 210–11.

84. Spinoza, *The Collected Works, Ethics,* II, 1, 448.

85. Ibid., II, 2, 449.

86. Ibid., II, 7, 451.

87. Ibid., 454.

88. Ibid., II, 11, Cor: 456.

89. Ibid., 499.

90. Ibid.

91. David Skrbina, "Participation, Organization, and Mind: Toward a Participatory Worldview." Doctoral thesis, University of Bath, 2008. With permission from the author.

92. G.W. Leibniz , New Essays on Human Understanding (Cambridge: Cambridge University Press, 1985), 71.

93. This "windowless" aspect of the monad will be a point of difference in Dialectical Incarnation.

94. See G.W. Leibniz, "Principles of Nature and Grace, Founded on Reason" in *The Monadology and Other Philosophical Writings* (London: Oxford University Press, 1948), 418, note 49.

95. Leibniz, *G.W. Leibniz: Philosophical Essays* (Indianapolis: Hackett Publishing Company, 1989), 233–34.

96. G.W. Leibniz, "Principles of Nature and Grace, Founded on Reason." In *The Monadology and Other Philosophical Writings* (London: Oxford University Press, 1948), 344 note 27.

97. This point will be examined further when looking at the theory of entropy and Teilhard's response.

Chapter Two

The Forming of Dialectical Incarnation

Cosmological, Metaphysical and
Anthropological Foundations

PIERRE TEILHARD DE CHARDIN: PREPARING THE WAY

Pierre Teilhard de Chardin (1881–1955 C.E.) was a Jesuit, Roman Catholic priest, and palaeontologist.[1] In his works he uses philosophy, science and revealed theology. The immediate manner in which Teilhard prepares the way for the emergence of Dialectical Incarnation is through his prophetic voice, challenging us to "see" and to have fuller vision and, therefore, "fuller being." He states:

> *Seeing.* We might say that the whole of life lies in that verb—if not ultimately, at least essentially. Fuller being is closer union . . . union increases only through an increase in consciousness, that is to say vision . . . *To see or to perish* is the very condition laid upon everything that makes up the universe . . . vision is fuller being.[2]

Teilhard's challenge is to "teach how to see God everywhere, to see Him in all that is most hidden, most solid, and most ultimate in the world".[3] From the onset of his mission he breaks down the barriers that divide God and the world, for he says, "that our lives, and . . . the whole world are full of God",[4] and therefore "by virtue of the Creation and, still more, of the Incarnation, *nothing* here below is *profane* for those who know how to see".[5] In breaking down the barrier between God and the world, Teilhard also razes the wall between spirit and matter. For him, matter and spirit are not two separate substances, set side by side, differing in nature; they are two aspects of "one

41

single cosmic stuff and there is between them no conflict to baffle our intelligence".[6]

For Teilhard, creation, incarnation and redemption are seen as simultaneous acts of the one act of love. Therefore, we can understand his central position with regard to the Incarnation in this way: "God-Love reaching self-fulfilment only in love . . . is nothing more nor less than a 'phylum of love' within nature".[7] According to Teilhard de Chardin, "to create, to fulfil and to purify the world is, for God, to unify it by uniting it organically with Himself".[8] So as to grasp this act of unity by God we look more directly at how Teilhard de Chardin viewed creation and evolution.

CREATION AND EVOLUTION

Creation is linked to evolution for Teilhard. He states that "evolution is not 'creative' but is the expression of creation in space and time".[9] Evolution is our only experience of creation. And since "to create is to unite" the only way in which God can unite the world to Himself is through evolution.[10]

The cosmological history of the world, i.e., evolution, may be summed up in three stages or emergent spheres: geosphere, biosphere, noosphere. Without giving a full description of these stages, it is important to indicate the fundamental changes that occur in each. The geosphere, in which the earth's crust solidified after a process of cooling down, came first in the evolutionary process. There was no trace of biological life possible because of the tremendous heat.[11] The distinctive aspect of this first sphere was the exclusive presence of inorganic matter. From this first stage evolved the biosphere. In this stage a fundamental event took place, the emergence of biological life, the transition of inorganic matter to organic matter. Life has various levels: vegetative, animal and human. The arrival of the human person, within the biosphere, brought about another, even more significant stage of evolution, viz., the emergence of mind, the noosphere. Within all the many changes and mutations in the evolutionary process, the emergence of life and the emergence of mind are the most crucial events. These two elevations constitute the two "hinges" of cosmic history and serve as the points of junction between the three spheres of evolution.[12]

According to Teilhard, evolution is not simply change in the spheres, but is genesis, which is something different. The French word *genèse* has a wider meaning than the English *genesis*. *Genèse* or genesis applies to any form of production involving successive stages oriented towards some goal.[13] As such the entire cosmos is now cosmogenesis, with its geogenesis, biogenesis, and noogenesis. Each genesis has its goal and the entire cosmos, and evolution is oriented toward its end, its *Omega*.

To understand cosmogenesis fully and to understand Teilhard's intention to demonstrate the oneness of the universe, one needs to look more deeply into the evolutionary process. According to Teilhard, all matter, organic and inorganic, has a *within* and a *without*, a psychic and a physical dimension. The "psychic" he calls "consciousness," but it is not synonymous with "thought" as used by Hegel and others. This concept of a *within* to all things is important for Teilhard's notion of evolution, because by it he tries to eliminate the dualism between matter and spirit. Instead of two separate realms of being, each is part of one and the same pattern of the universe. "Without the slightest doubt *there is something* through which material and spiritual energy hold together and are complementary. In the last analysis, *somehow or other,* there must be a single energy operating in the world".[14] Furthermore, between "the *within* and the *without* of things, the interdependence of energy is incontestable".[15]

With the necessity of establishing the *oneness* of God and the universe, Teilhard continues to seek a solution to avoid the dualism of matter and spirit and at the same time "safeguard the natural complexity of the stuff of the universe".[16] Since all energy is "psychic in nature," he states:

> in each particular element this fundamental energy is divided into two distinct components: a *tangential energy* which links the element with all others of the same order . . . as itself in the universe; and a *radial energy* which draws it towards ever greater complexity and centricity—in other words forwards.[17]

It is radial energy that was operative in the "critical points" of cosmogenesis. It can now be seen that Teilhard's understanding of the cosmogenesis involves a moving forward of all things toward greater *complexity.* "Historically, the stuff of the universe goes on becoming concentrated into ever more organized forms of matter".[18] Teilhard understands that within the "stuff of the universe," by virtue of an inner dynamic, *radial energy,* something collects and concentrates itself to an ever greater degree of intensity. This is what he called interiorization *(enroulement).* Accordingly, there emerges within the cosmogenesis organized entities held together by their own energy, whereby each of them forms a self-contained, equilibrial system. This is the general process of involution. Involution is the dialectical nature of creation/evolution which is within. It is the inner dynamic component of the universe. It is Teilhard's understanding of *radial energy.* Evolution is *within* and *without* and, as such, dialectical in itself. Teilhard understands evolution as having an *ad intra* and an *ad extra* relation. The former maintains the unity within evolution, and the other expresses that unity in an outgoing manner. Evolution is a unifying process that expands externally.

Parallel to increasing complexity in all things, there is the other distinguishing feature of cosmogenesis and evolution itself: the orientation toward an ever increasing degree of consciousness. This raises the issue of the relation of matter and spirit. All through the process of evolution, with the many and various *elevations* which emerge, there is both an increase of complexity and also consciousness, or "psychism." The connection and relation between these two realms of the universe have consistently brought about debate; Teilhard believes it is possible to "see" with greater vision and to bring closure to this discussion. He says:

> The answer comes at once. Whatever instance we may think of, we may be sure that every time a richer and better organized structure will correspond to the more developed consciousness. [19]

The relation between complexity and consciousness of organization serve, for Teilhard de Chardin, as a "tangible 'parameter' allowing us to connect both the internal and the external films of the world, not only *in their position* (point by point), but also . . . *in their motion*" (*Phenomenon* 60). He then offers his conclusion to the discussion:

> Spiritual perfection (or conscious 'centreity') and material synthesis (or complexity) are but the two aspects or connected parts of one and the same phenomenon . . . . And now we have arrived, *ipso facto*, at the solution of the problem posed for us. [20]

We thus recognise how seemingly opposing poles are united in one reality. As indicated earlier, each genesis has an end. The question now is what is the end of this law of complexity-consciousness in the cosmogenesis? The moment in the history of the world whereby the biosphere moves to the noosphere, from life to mind, is the synthesis of "matter and spirit." As such, the universe moves toward greater consciousness and higher complexity. This direction is mind, and the human person becomes the central link between matter and spirit, body and mind. "Let us ask again," says Teilhard, "why we are turning our attention to man?" [21]

The reason is because the human person,

> the centre of perspective, is at the same time the *centre of construction* of the universe. And by expediency no less than by necessity, all science must be referred back to him [or her]. If to see is really to become more, if vision is really fuller being, then we should look closely at [humanity] in order to increase our capacity to live. [22]

When humans appear in the world it is irreducibly and altogether new. [23] Humans add to the world an entirely new aspect of reflective consciousness and freedom, which in turn changes the nature of the world. In the human person the world becomes conscious of itself. [24] Teilhard's cosmology is anthropocentric, as is the philosophy and cosmology of Dialectical Incarnation. There is no such academic discipline without the human Self as the subject and agent of the universe.

The human's importance in the process of evolution and in the *oneness* of the cosmos cannot be overestimated for Teilhard, as it cannot be for Marx, or for Dialectical Incarnation. It is through the human that matter and spirit unite. It is humans that link the animal world with the cosmos; it is humans that link the cosmos with God. Hence, humans are the "summit of creation",[25] and the "crown and climax",[26] of evolution.

Yet, as the law of *complexity-consciousness* continues to operate in humans and the world, Teilhard makes the important point that the whole sense of evolution also ascends toward personalisation. "We thus reach the personalisation of the individual by the 'hominisation' of the whole group".[27]

What is personalisation? Personalisation is comparable to Marx's concept of species being according to which the "[hu]man is not merely a natural being; he [or she] is a *human* natural being . . . a being for himself [or herself], and therefore a species-being," a person *in the world*.[28] Similarly, Teilhard states:

> The peak of ourselves, the acme of our originality, is not our individuality but our person; and according to the evolutionary structure of the world, we can only find our person by uniting together . . . Totalization and personalization are two expressions of a single movement . . . Socialization means not the end but rather the beginning of the Era of the Person.[29]

By such a description we realise that human beings, by nature, are to be *one* with the world, *one* with each other, and as we shall see, also *one* with God.

At this point Teilhard's prophetic challenge, to "see" so as to have "fuller being," becomes paramount in our discovery of Dialectical Incarnation. Teilhard's understanding of creation and evolution is understood as cosmogenesis, a process in which the human is at the summit. It is now equally important to remember his understanding of the incarnation, especially its relation to creation. For Teilhard creation is not separate from the incarnation, and therefore it is not separate from redemption. He states that there is

> no creation without incarnate immersion into it, no Incarnation without redemptive compensation . . . [these] three fundamental 'mysteries' . . . are seen to be but three aspects of a single mystery . . . the reduction of multiplicity to unity.[30]

According to this view of dialectical unity, the unity within multiplicity, Teilhard's geology, biology, physics, psychology and phenomenology become his theology, the highest of all sciences. The human is the "end" of the cosmogenesis, the God-human becomes the *Omega* of his Christogenesis. Christ as Incarnation, becomes the centre of evolution.

> A universe whose structure evolves—as long as one understands the direction of such a movement—could well be, after all, the milieu most favourable for developing a great and homogeneous understanding of the Incarnation . . . What better than an ascending anthropogenesis to serve as a background and foundation for the descending illumination of a Christogenesis?[31]

The complexity of "God is love," is now "seen" in its true unity. How does God do this? God does it by becoming matter, by becoming human. It is through the God-human Incarnation that all things are to be brought into unity under the one Head, so that the whole world is made of the "pleroma," the fullness, the completion of the Incarnation.[32] The orders of creation and of redemption, of nature and of grace although distinct from one another in theory, ultimately constitute an unsurpassable *unity*.[33] It is in the incarnation of God that the two poles—God and the universe—are united as *one*, whereby "God is love and the totality of reality."

The underlying law of the cosmos, the law of complexity-consciousness, can be seen as a law of growing amorisation. Love, according to Teilhard de Chardin, is the only energy that is capable of "personalizing by totalizing."[34] Love is consequently the highest form of radial energy; love unites human beings so as to be complete and fulfilled. In order for humans to continue freely toward the unity of the cosmogenesis, their love must gradually evolve until it is capable of embracing the whole of humankind and the whole of the earth and universe. What Teilhard de Chardin called "planetization," the intensification of the noosphere's psychic temperature from the tighter contraction of human existence around the surface of the earth, must eventually become an *amortization*.[35]

An objection to this understanding of love might come from the apparent inability to love more than only a select few and that to

> love all and everyone is a contradictory and a false gesture which only leads in the end to loving no-one . . . would answer that if, as you claim, a universal love is impossible, how can we account for that irresistible instinct in our hearts which leads us towards unity whenever and in whatever direction our passions are stirred? A sense of the universe, a sense of the *all* . . . the Whole—cosmic affinity and hence cosmic sense. A universal love is not only psychologically possible; it is the only complete and final way in which we are able to love.[36]

For Teilhard de Chardin love is the "*within* of things."

> Love in all its subtleties is nothing more, and nothing less, than the more or less direct trace marked on the heart of the element by the psychical convergence of the universe upon itself.[37]

The most fundamental aspects of Teilhard's concept of love and amorization are mutuality, otherness, and totality. Love is not something that is forced. Love is free and toward the other.[38] Amorization is, above all, personal and capable; it is the reality of being "loving and lovable *at this very moment*".[39] Personal love is from the lover to the beloved. Only in a free circulation of love energy between persons is there a capability to totalize humanity and centre humanity toward the ultimate end called *Omega*. For love to exist it must be directed toward an other; for humanity that other becomes the *Omega* as the centre of love. But it is now that we must love, for with

> love, as with every other sort of energy, it is within the existing datum that the lines of force must at every instant come together. Neither an ideal centre, nor a potential centre could possibly suffice. A present and real noosphere goes with a real and present centre. To be supremely attractive, Omega must be supremely present.[40]

> . . . no doubt: that we should overcome the 'anti-personalist' complex which paralyses us, and make up our minds to accept the possibility, indeed the reality, of some *source* of love and *object* of love at the summit of the world.[41]

Besides the "otherness" of love, love must be free. Evolution, up to the point of humanity's appearance, was deterministic and fixed by the laws of nature. With the elevation of the comosgenesis in the human and the emergence of mind, there also emerged the phenomenon of freedom. Love is a free act. Humankind must love in freedom, otherwise the act is merely an instinct or predetermined process. Evolution is no longer something humans must undergo passively, rather, it is something which humankind must actively carry forward to its ultimate point. In the end, humankind's co-operation with the evolutionary process is necessary if evolution is to achieve its final crown. As such, it is the personal aspect of love, which is given toward the beloved, toward the other, that makes real love possible. Is it possible to have a sufficient love for a future goal when it is an abstraction or a "thing"? In closing, Wildiers nicely summarizes Teilhard de Chardin's attitude of love, when he states:

> Is not all real love, in the end, focused on a person, on a Someone? If we conceive of the point Omega as no more than a condition, a state, an idea, then our attachment to it will soon wither and fall away in face of the difficulties to be surmounted. If, however, we can learn to see it as a Someone, then there is a

chance that love may tide us over every obstacle and that we shall find the strength to bring evolution to its final term.[42]

ENTROPY, EVIL, SUFFERING, AND DEATH

After this optimistic, forward oriented view of evolution and humankind's free co-operation with it through love, it is paramount that we look at the dialectical strife and opposing conditions of nature and humankind, namely, the law of entropy and the problem of evil, suffering and death.

The two laws of thermodynamics can be stated in one sentence: "The total energy content of the universe is constant and the total entropy is continually increasing".[43] The first law is the law of conservation that states that energy can never be created or destroyed; it can be transformed from one form to another. The second law, the law of entropy, states that every time energy is transformed from one state to another, there is a loss of available energy. According to nature, matter moves toward some form of disorder, degradation and disintegration. If so, how can the oneness of the whole world move forward toward its *Omega*? It is here, once again, that humankind stands as the "apex of cosmogenesis".[44] Although matter is in a gradual process of degradation, humankind appears to move onward; as a species there is no indication of a loss of vital energy. Humankind's mental activity and urge to expand is always intensifying. Of all sources of energies in the world, humankind's is the most dynamic, having dominion over every other force and utilising them for humanity's own effort toward progress. In support of Teilhard's anthropocentric cosmology, humankind, by exerting its own creative energies, is able to move forward toward completing the evolutionary process.[45]

Teilhard explains:

> To make room for thought in the world, I have needed to 'interiorise' matter: to imagine an energetics of the mind; to conceive a noogenesis rising upstream against the flow of entropy; to provide evolution with a direction, a line of advance and critical points; and finally to make all things double back upon *someone* . . . The only universe capable of containing the human person is an irreversibly 'personalising' universe.[46]

Although Teilhard offers an anti-entropic solution for the process of the evolution of the physical world, he still understands that "there is no order under formation which does not at every stage imply disorder".[47] Teilhard knows well that

> we find physical lack-of-arrangement or derangement on the material level; then suffering, which cuts into the sentient flesh; then, on a still higher level, wickedness and the torture of spirit as it analyses itself and makes choices.

> Statistically, at every degree of evolution, we find evil always and everywhere, forming and reforming implacably in us and around us.[48]

Teilhard de Chardin "sees" the world, and all aspects of it, dialectically; there is always some "tension," some "opposition" present in everything; "[t]here are no summits without abysses".[49] The world is constantly "groping" as it moves forward. So too, as humankind moves onward and forward, Teilhard de Chardin recognizes the presence of dialectical strife, for

> how many failures have there been for one success, how many days of misery for one hour's joy, how many sins for a solitary saint? . . . Death the essential lever in the mechanism and upsurge of life.[50]

As humankind co-operates in the process of evolution there is recognisably the

> *evil of growth*, by which is expressed in us, in the pangs of childbirth, the mysterious law which, from the humblest chemism to the highest synthesis of the spirit, makes all progress in the direction of increased unity express itself in terms of work and effort.[51]

Teilhard's incurable optimism does not see the world as a "bed of roses," for he agonised over the evil of humankind and misuse of the beauty of God's created world. However, there was a threshold to his tolerance, one fault which he disdained: the deliberate acceptance and delight in disgust with life, scorn for the works of humankind, and the fear of the human effort. For Teilhard de Chardin the real sin was the lack of confidence in the effectiveness of humanity's vocation.[52] As such, however, there is

> nothing . . . in this ontological (or more exactly, ontogenetic) condition of participated being which lessens the dignity or limits the omnipotence of the Creator. Neither is there anything savouring of what could be called Manichaeanism. Pure unorganized multiplicity is not bad in itself; but because it is multiple, i.e., essentially subject in its arrangement to the play of chance, it is absolutely impossible for it to progress towards unity without producing evil in its wake through statistical necessity.[53]

In view of the fact that the world is in evolution, then strife, disorder and evil are inevitable aspects of the process. Whatever is in process and yet to be completed, is always imperfect and defective. Evil is structurally part of a world in evolution.

> Beside physical evil, there is moral evil or sin. Since the elevation of the *cosmogenesis,* and the emergence of reflective consciousness and freedom, there is also moral evil. The higher the consciousness and freedom, the higher

the power of sin. As the physical world is imperfect, so too humankind is imperfect. Consequently, "sin in the sphere of freedom" remains because, as stated earlier, "there is no order under formation which does not at every stage involve disorder".[54]

BEYOND TEILHARD DE CHARDIN TO KARL RAHNER[55]

Teilhard, as he himself admitted, is not a formal theologian or formal philosopher but rather a palaeontologist and scientist.[56] He nevertheless thought philosophically and theologically and was, clearly, a man of faith. For him God was "all in all." In his works, he offers a scientific, psychological and phenomenological perspective rather than a metaphysical and theological one.

It is now time to focus on Karl Rahner (1904–1984 C.E.), who says:

> . . . try to avoid those theorems with which you are familiar from your study of Teilhard de Chardin. If we arrive at some of the same conclusions as he does, then that is all to the good. Yet we do not feel ourselves either dependent on him or obligated to him. We want to confine ourselves to those things which any [philosophical] theologian could say if he brings his theological reflection to bear on the questions posed by the modern evolutionary view of the world.[57]

Teilhard tried to break the barriers of sacred and profane, spirit and matter, and at uniting the supernatural with the natural. Rahner integrates a philosophical theology with the evolutionary understanding of the created world. The history of the world is the history of salvation. One must, therefore, have a new understanding of how God has offered God's self-communication, one in which *all* of nature will be understood as supernaturalized. A dichotomy is dissolved and made into one for humanity and the "totality of reality" are now understood as transcendental and existentially united with God. The human person *is* a "graced event" from the moment of creation.[58] The human is characterised by the "supernatural existential" and is naturally created to move toward the infinite horizon of the incomprehensible God. With these categories, Rahner goes beyond Teilhard and unites God, humanity and the world so as to recognize the "fullness of being" found in "seeing" God in the totality of reality.

When one begins to comprehend the thought of Rahner, one notices quite immediately a dialectical nature in his vision of God, humanity and the world. His philosophy and theology continually represents a dynamic relationship between *seemingly* opposing poles and contradicting statements. This tensile and paradoxical way of understanding the "totality of reality" is found in such terms as unity in diversity, transcendence and immanence, sacred and profane, divine and human, *a priori* and *a posteriori*, grace and nature, transcendental and categorical, immutable and becoming, thematic and unthematic. These different elements are always understood as distinct but not separate. It is this "dynamic unity-in-difference [which] is the pattern for the systematic coherence of Rahner's thought pattern".[59]

Within and essential to this dialectical nature of God and the "totality of reality" is the *incarnation* of God in the world. Rahner states:

> that the incarnate word is the absolute symbol of God in the world . . . He is not merely the presence and revelation of what God is in himself. He is also the expressive presence of what—or rather, who—God wished to be, in free grace, to the world, in such a way that this divine attitude, once so expressed, can never be reversed, but is and remains final and unsurpassable.[60]

In view of this understanding of reality, there is no God without the world, and this world, with humanity as its "crown," is graced by the Incarnate Logos as God's very nature. God's creative love is simultaneously God's incarnate love, through grace, to all humanity in the world.

THE DIALECTICAL AND INCARNATIONAL PHILOSOPHICAL THEOLOGY OF KARL RAHNER

Philosophical and Theological Method

In explicating the foundations of Rahner's philosophy and theology, we must first look at his method. Because the incarnate word is "the absolute symbol of God," it is appropriate to direct one's attention to Rahner's philosophical theology of the incarnation. It is through these selected aspects of Rahner's philosophical theology that his vision may be called Dialectical Incarnation.

Rahner's method is *transcendental* and *anthropological*. Its starting point is the supernaturalized human person because, although theistic philosophy and theology is the study of God, one can understand God as an object of knowledge only in and through the human person. Rahner's method is an inquiry into the conditions of the possibility of divine self-communication in the incarnation, the mediation of God. One "inquires as to the conditions necessary for it to be known by the theological subject".[61] This method is called transcendental, in the tradition of Kant, because it begins with the *a priori* condition of the human person as such, as a hearer of the Word. "We shall call *transcendental* . . . the subjective, unthematic, necessary and unfailing consciousness of the knowing subject . . . the subject's openness to the unlimited expanse of all possible reality."[62] An experience is

> called *transcendental* experience because it belongs to the necessary and inalienable structures of the knowing subject itself, and because it consists precise-

ly in the transcendence beyond any particular group of possible objects or of categories. [63]

Rahner uses 'transcendental' in contrast to 'categorical.' Because the human person is a transcendental subject, he or she transcends any concrete, historical, categorical event or experience. "Transcendental experience is the experience of *transcendence*" which is beyond the categorical. [64] The human person as a transcendental subject is able to be open to the mystery and the infinite horizon of God because, for Rahner, the person is the very event of God's own self-communication. As such, the human person is a graced event who is a self-transcending subject in relation to God, the very ground of being. As creator, God is the foundation for the existence of the transcendental subject to even be. Yet, God could not self-communicate unless the human being were a receiver of that self-communication. Rahner states:

> one thing which should be mentioned here in order to clarify what transcendence means is that if man is a being of transcendence towards the holy and absolutely real mystery, and if the term and source of the transcendence in and through which man as such exists, and which constitutes his original essence a subject and as person, is this absolute and holy mystery, then strangely enough we can and must say: mystery in its incomprehensibility is what is *self-evident* in human life. [65]

According to Rahner's transcendental philosophical theology, the mystery of the incomprehensible God is the very condition by which the human person, as the subject doing philosophy and theology, is able to know the transcendent as well at the historical world. God's free self-communication, is the condition of the possibility of the human person to receive this self-communication of God. The self-transcending dimension of the human person is always mediated by the human person's historical dimension. Rahner's method is dialectical because it takes into account not only the transcendental but also the concrete, existential and historical dimensions of the human individual. With the twofold aspects of Rahner's method, that is, the transcendental and anthropological, one realises that the human person is constantly hearing the Word as one who is transcendentally aware of both the infinite horizon and the finite concrete. This method combines the historical investigation of actual experience with a transcendental reflection on the "conditions of the possibility" to know and love God, the "totality of reality." Rahner's transcendental method is also an incarnational method because all of reality, the infinite horizon and the finite concrete, enters human awareness because of the *a priori* condition of God's self-communication, which is the incarnate word freely spoken.

In this dialectical construct one sees the essential relation between God and the human, between a "theocentricity" and an "anthropocentricity" of philosophy. These are "not opposites but strictly one and the same thing, seen from two sides. Neither of the two aspects can be comprehended at all without the other".[66]

Philosophy and Theology of Symbol

An ontology of incarnation is an ontology of symbolism. This is so because

> all beings are by their nature symbolic, because they necessarily 'express' themselves in order to attain their own nature. . . . Being expresses itself, because it must realize itself through a plurality in unity.[67]

Rahner maintains that

> it is only to be expected that no theology [nor philosophy] can be complete without also being a theology [and philosophy] of the symbol . . . in fact the whole of [philosophical] theology is incomprehensible if it is not essentially a theology [or philosophy] of symbols.[68]

In this aspect of Rahner's philosophical theology lies the clearest expression of his dialectical and incarnational thought. A symbol is dialectical because it possesses its own integrity, while at the same time a symbol represents and points beyond itself to something which is *other* than itself and makes that other present. As such, a symbol is not merely a sign or an indicator, nor is it a substitute for some absent reality. Rather, a symbol is a unity in plurality; it expresses the ontology of something more than itself. This understanding of unity in difference is not a limit of a symbol, but a perfection of itself. A symbol is not just its materiality, but expresses a complexity of being. A symbol is complex because there is a plurality in its unity. It possesses itself, its own identity, by giving itself away from itself to the other. In this self-alienation, a symbol posits the *other as its own reality* and by doing so truly becomes itself, in a real sense, for the first time.[69]

The prime example of a symbol, for Rahner, is the human person. The human person is a dialectical unity of spirit and matter. It is this unity in difference, both metaphysically and experientially, which allows Rahner to explain the dialectic of symbol. Rahner illustrates this by the "Sacred Heart" of the human person, Jesus. He states that a "prior ontological unity of the whole [person] also appears in each part of the body; as the unity unfolds, it projects its proper manifestation, its symbol, into the part in question and thus possesses itself as a whole.[70] He continues to say that "a symbol is not something separate from the symbolized . . . the symbol is the reality" (IV 9: 251). Therefore, in the example of the Sacred Heart "one cannot revere the love of Christ . . . without making a special effort to think of the 'bodily heart'".[71]

So as to understand the full significance of Rahner's philosophy and theology of symbol for our proposal, we allow Rahner to explain.

> The reality of the divine self-communication creates for itself its immediacy by constituting itself present in the symbol, which does not divide as it mediates but unites immediately, because the true symbol is united with the thing symbolized, since the latter constitutes the former as its own self-realization. [72]

The importance of understanding the concept of symbol within this philosophyis more evident when Rahner says that "being is of itself symbolic". [73]

This is so, because being is matter and form. All of reality is symbolic, all of reality is dialectical. What is said of symbol is said of being. Therefore, being is not a static reality but one in constant, intrinsic self-realization and self-expression. As we come to understand God as the "totality of reality" we can recognize that divine being gives itself away in and through the other, the other then is the symbolic expression of the divine being. Incarnation is a symbol of God as it simultaneously and equally a symbol of the totality of reality. In this process of self-realization in symbolic expression, the divine being finds itself in knowledge and love and makes itself known. The "[divine] being is known in this symbol, without which it cannot be known at all". [74]

Rahner states that a symbol "is the self-realization of a being in the other, which is constitutive of its essence". [75] On this model, the Logos becoming flesh is the self-expression of God, the Logos is God's otherness, or image, which, in fact constitutes the very essence of God. [76] One remembers that "the incarnate word is the absolute symbol of God in the world . . . He is . . . what God is in himself," really and truly, not what God is as an isolated self. [77] This symbol of God in the world means that the human nature is not carried by the Logos as a mask or a uniform. Such an understanding would mean that the

> Logos would make himself audible and perceptible through a reality which was of itself alien to him, had intrinsically and essentially nothing to do with him, and could have been chosen at random from a whole series of realities". [78]

On the contrary, Rahner asserts that the human nature is an appropriate expression of the Logos. It is the Logos' "real symbol." Humanity is the very existence of God in the world. [79] Rahner calls the human being the "abbreviation" or the "cipher" of God. When God freely chose to be non-divine, the human being appears. The human being is created as a "grammar of a possible self-expression of God". [80] Accordingly, one could "define man, within the framework of his supreme and darkest mystery, as that which ensues when God's self-utterance, his Word, is given out lovingly".[81] The human person is the condition of the possibility of God's self communication.

The human person is a real symbol of God, or the transcendent, and not just some accidental sign of divine reality. The very being of God, God's self, is communicated to the non-divine.[82] In this self-communication, God makes the reality of the world God's own reality, as God's milieu. The world belongs to God, as God's own substantial determination.[83]

The being of the Logos—considered of course *as* that which is received by procession from the Father—must be thought of as exteriorization itself, so that without detriment to its immutability in itself and of itself, it becomes *itself* in truth the existence of a created reality—which must in all truth and reality be predicated of the being of the Logos, because it *is* so.[84]

The unity in difference, understood within the dialectical structure of symbol, also represents the nature of the Trinity itself. God necessarily expresses God's self inwardly. This is the condition for God to express God's self outwardly. Therefore, as stated above, the finite, created, expression of God, *ad extra* (outside itself), constitutes the oneness and the existential nature of God. The Logos, as the *ad intra* (in itself) expression of the Godhead, becomes itself in the existence of created reality, without detriment to its immutability in God, and thereby serves as the absolute symbol of God in the world. The "humanity of Christ exists by the existence of the Logos".[85] It is important to state that although God "must" express God's self within God's divine nature, *ad intra*, it is as free gift, free grace, free love that God expresses God's self, *ad extra*, through the incarnate Logos in the world. The world becomes the very reality of God and the *oneness* of God, humanity and world are finally recognized as such. This is why Rahner can say "the flesh which is man is the self- utterance of God himself" and that "God is man to all eternity".[86] The finite, real symbol of God is the human being, as the event in which God becomes a creature. God is no longer the "horizon of the world, but the innermost, loving heart of the world".[87] This heart, once again, is the "heart of the Lord [which] is a symbol of the love of Christ".[88] Because the "word symbol cannot be avoided in the theology of devotion," Rahner uses the devotion of the Sacred Heart as a finite symbol of God.[89] But this "devotion" contains much more than a mere veneration of this Sacred Heart because the "first implication latent in this devotion is that of unity",[90] a unity of body and soul, of divine love and human love, love of God and love of neighbour. Rahner uses the symbol of the "heart of the Lord" as the "amorization" of the world found in Teilhard de Chardin. The love of God, in and through the love of humans, with the real, finite symbol of love being the God-human Christ [incarnation], ultimately constitutes an unsurpassable *unity*. Therefore, for Rahner,

this devotion constitutes the ultimate and innermost centre, the ultimate reality
from which everything else draws its light, in which everything else is, in a
certain sense, united and held together. It constitutes anunity. [91]

Like Teilhard de Chardin's law of complexity-consciousness evolving to
the law of amorization, whereby love unites human beings so as to be complete and fulfilled, Rahner's understanding of the Sacred Heart identifies "an
interior centre from which the diversification of human reality is unfolded,
and in which this diversification, which also belongs to the very nature of
[the hu]man, remains united". [92]

In light of the inherent tension and strife found in the nature of the dialectical method mentioned earlier, it is important to note how Rahner refers to
this tension between the unity and complexity of humanity and the world.

The pain we experience, then, is one of tension. There is anunity that we seek,
one which, in a certain sense, we have already grasped by anticipation, and one
to which the very multiplicity all about us points us on. Yet this unity can
never be possessed by itself alone. For just as we withdraw into this unity we
must perforce turn back again and go forth into the multiplicity which belongs
to the very mode of our existence. [93]

A real symbol, as we understand Rahner, makes present that which it
symbolizes. One cannot see God but one can see materiality, one can see
incarnation. If incarnation is the symbol of the divine then God is not merely
an agent in the world but is the very ground of the whole world process and
the unity amidst the complexity and multiplicity of humans in the world.
Incarnation is God and the totality of reality. Clearly, God is active in the
world in God's real symbol, but Rahner emphasizes a radical unity of this
real symbol by demonstrating a genuine philosophy and theology of the
Sacred Heart, whereby we come to see not only that "God is love and the
totality in reality" but that Dialectical Incarnation is a harmony of One Love,
One Heart in the totality of reality.

A Philosophy and Theology of The Incarnation

What is the incarnation for Karl Rahner? It means that the "Word of God
became *man*". [94] In explaining what this means, Rahner does not look solely
at the *"became"*, but also at the *"man"*. In this anthropology, one must
understand what the human is in order to understand the mystery of the
incarnation where the "Word became *man."* Rahner understands that one
"launches into an ocean which is literally boundless" [95] when discovering the
meaning of the human. The human is by nature open to the infinite horizon of
God and is mystery. Rahner states that

one can only say what man is by expressing what he [or she] is concerned with and what is concerned with him. But that is the boundless, the nameless. Man is therefore mystery in his essence, his nature. He is not in himself the infinite fullness of the mystery which concerns him, for that fullness is inexhaustible, and the primordial form of all that is mystery to us. But he is mystery in his real being and its ultimate reason, in his nature, which is the humble, conscious state of being referred to the fullness, the form of the mystery which we ourselves are. [96]

Therefore, according to Rahner, in order to understand God who became human, it is paramount to understand the human. And, to understand the human, one must think dialectically and recognize that there is no limit to the definition of the finiteness of the human, for the human is *mystery,* the human is *indefinability.* When one has said everything about the human, one has said nothing unless humans "allow ourselves freely to be grasped by the incomprehensible". [97] The human is mystery and this mystery "brings our existence and God's existence together; and both as mystery." [98]

In understanding Rahner's philosophy and theology as Dialectical Incarnation, one discovers the existential relationship God has with humanity. The Logos becomes human; God takes humanity as God's own reality. As such, the whole emergence of the human in the world is the process of God's own self-revelation, which reaches its climax in the Incarnate Logos. Understanding this relationship requires a return to Rahner's philosophy and theology of symbol.

It follows from what has been said that the Logos, as Son of the Father, is truly, in his humanity as such, the revelatory symbol in which the Father enunciates [utters] [God]self, in this Son to the world—revelatory, because the symbol renders present what is revealed. [99]

Rahner elaborates this relationship with humanity, where human existence and God's existence are brought together in mystery, when he states:

If this is human nature, we begin to understand more clearly—always of course within the framework of the basic mystery which is God and we—what it means to say: God takes on a human nature as his own. The indefinable nature, whose limits—'definition'—are the unlimited reference to the infinite fullness of the mystery, has, when assumed by God as his reality, simply arrived at the point to which it always strives by virtue of its essence. [100]

God takes on human nature as God's own when God freely wills, in love, to become human. God, as mystery, has emptied God's self into the fullness of the mystery by becoming human. In understanding the mystery of God and our own mystery, it is important that this mystery is not the "still undiscovered unknown . . . to be fetched," nor is mystery a "second element unmastered only provisionally". [101] On the contrary, mystery is the impenetrable . . . already present . . . and the indomitable dominant horizon of *all* understanding, that which makes it possible to understand other things by the fact that it is silently there as the incomprehensible . . . It is the propriety which always and necessarily characterizes God—and through [God], *us*.[102]

As such, in Dialectical Incarnation, God knows Godself in and through the eternal incarnation as distinct from God and yet as one with God.

Philosophy, Theology and Anthropology

Much has already been said with regard to the human person; Rahner's philosophical theology is clearly anthropocentric. From his dialectical and incarnational perspective, Rahner is uniting God and the human person-in-the-world. It is only through the human person's finite, limited, categorical, and dependent nature that he or she, as subject, is aware of his or her infinite, unlimited, transcendent, and independent nature. Although the structure of the human person, as subject totally open to the transcendent as incomprehensible mystery, is an *a priori,* the experience of God is an *a posteriori* knowledge, because the human person always lives his or her free subjectivity in the world and with other people. In other words, although the human person is marked by an openness to God, and is a "supernatural existential," all knowledge of God is in nature, in concrete experiential reality. There is, in the existential life of the human person, an on-going dialectical dynamic between the two poles of reality: the transcendental and categorical, the infinite horizon and the historical reality. The proper way of living this existential reality is by "letting oneself be grasped by the mystery which is present and yet ever distant".[103] Philosophy and theology, united with anthropology must

> return to the transcendental experience of our orientation towards the absolute mystery . . . takes place in unconditional obedience to conscience and in the open and trusting . . . moments of prayer and quiet silence".[104]

In these moments, human's subjectivity is always a transcendence which listens. Human subjectivity is "in and through the infinity of transcendence that it is a transcendence which can grasp its own finiteness and must grasp it".[105]

Because God and the human person's transcendence have an "original unity," and the "two are mutually dependent on each other",[106] it is important to understand the difference between God and the world. Rahner realizes that one may radically misunderstand how God and the world are different.

> The difference between God and the world is of such a nature that God establishes and is the difference of the world from himself. And for this reason he

establishes the closest unity precisely in the differentiation. For if the difference itself comes from God, and, if we can put it this way, is itself identical with God, then the difference between God and the world is to be understood quite differently than the difference between categorical realities.[107]

The difference between God and the world is a difference that "comes from God," and is "identical with God." God is different from the world, in a way that "this difference is experienced in our original transcendental experience" which is mystery.[108] In this mystery, the peculiar and unique difference is experienced in such a way that the "totality of reality" is intelligible only within this difference. The "totality of reality" as the antithesis of Dialectical Incarnation is intelligible only within its difference from the thesis, i.e., God. It is "precisely the difference which establishes the ultimate unity between God and the world, and the difference becomes intelligible only in this unity".[109] Distinct "genuine reality" and real "dependence" are merely two sides of the one and the same reality. The difference of God and the world is a difference that is internal to God's nature rather than external to it. There is an intrinsic, formal causality rather than an extrinsic, efficient causality. That is, it is God who posits the difference between the world and Godself, and establishes the greatest unity precisely in the differentiation. God and the world are distinct, but this distinction is a consequence of the true communion God and the world share with one another. The world and God are different because of the unity present in a dialectical, creator God who is the ground of being for humans and the world. Incarnation, the synthesis of the thesis, is the symbol of God and the symbol of the totality of reality. Incarnation is also the very ground of being *qua* God as incarnation is the very ground of being *qua* the totality of reality.

When understanding the dynamic, transcendental nature of Rahner's philosophy, theology and anthropology, one more easily recognizes how "God is love and the totality of reality." The philosophical God of Rahner is the philosophical God of Giordano Bruno and Baruch Spinoza. The latter have indicated how the *Natura naturans* and the *Natura naturata* are two indistinguishable powers of a single principle, in which they are reconciled and united, and in which their differences are annulled. As such, God does not enter into the world; rather God was already there from the outset of God freely communicating God's self in the creation of the universe. Humanity makes this reality explicit and historical, and unfortunately at times, separate.

When philosophy, theology and anthropology are united, there emerges an *anthropological-philosophical theology* rather than a theological anthropology. What is the difference? Anthropological-philosophical theology starts with the human person, as indicated. The human person serves as the condition of the possibility of knowing God, i.e., natural theology or theistic philosophy. A metaphor may help. If humanity-in-the-world, i.e., all of reality, is understood as the dance, one can know and observe the Dancer, *qua* dancer, only through the dance itself. Without the Dancer there could be no dance. Likewise, the human person-in-the-world is a transcendental subject, because the divine is the very ground of being, the "foundation," for the transcendental being to even be. Because of this essential, relational nature between God and the human-in-the-world, anthropology and theology "are not opposites but strictly one and the same thing, seen from two sides".[110] As such, neither is known without the other.

The metaphor of God as Dancer and of humans-in-the-world as dance demonstrates the necessary union of the two. However, there is an aspect of the metaphor that "limps." A dance is *not* a subject, but the expression of the Dancer. The dance is an object, necessarily and essentially related with the subject and agent of the dance, but the dance cannot look upon itself, nor upon the Dancer doing the dance. The dance is not a transcendental subject. The human person is a subject and he or she can look at and reflect on himself or herself and at his or her transcendence and horizon. The human person, who is the "most objective reality of salvation is at the same time necessarily the most subjective".[111] Yes, the Dancer is the "condition for the possibility" for the dance to be, but then it stops.[112] With the necessary and essential relation between God and the human-in-the-world, and in the relation between anthropology, philosophy and theology, the human-in the-world is transcendentally aware of the infinite horizon found in his or her existence. Therefore, to study God, i.e., theology and philosophy, and to study the human, i.e., anthropology, one has to study *both* in order to know *either*.

In philosophy and natural theology, this mystery of the incomprehensible is the very means, the very condition in which the human person is able to know all that is not mysterious, i.e., the concrete, historical world. For too long, natural theology, philosophical theology or theistic philosophy has explained the *reductio in mysterium* (reduction to mystery) as negative and as that which is not comprehensible. Actually, however, it is *mystery* that makes all things understandable when one recognises that philosophy and theology are transcendental and the human is a transcendental subject. For Rahner, the *mysterium*, alone, is that which is genuinely self-evident.[113]

God is this *mysterium*. As such, the relationship of God to world is one of mystery, but not a mystery or reality distinct from the created world. God, as mystery, is the quasi-*formal* causality of the world, which is a causality not distinct from God, but which is rather God's self and the "specification of the creature" and world.[114] Therefore, there is the *unum mysterium* (one mystery), i.e., God, who is the unity and the condition for *all* knowledge of philosophy, theology and anthropology to be comprehended and loved. Rahner consistently keeps the real distinction between humanity-in-the-world and God but does not separate them and allow for a dualism. Rahner's anthropological-philosophical theology thus enables us to recognize the true unity-in-difference, whereby God is God, world is world, and the two shall never be separate because God *is* the totality of reality. As such, God needs humans to be God, and humans need God to be human. This is the reality of Dialectical Incarnation.

NOTES

1. Teilhard de Chardin is sometimes referred to as philosopher and theologian because he studied so much of both as a Jesuit and he thinks and writes as one. He is a formal paleontologist in that he did more formal graduate studies in this area. See Christopher F. Mooney, *Teilhard de Chardin and the Mystery of Christ* (New York: Harper & Row, 1966), 5.

2. Pierre Teilhard de Chardin, *The Phenomenon of Man* (New York: Harper & Row, 1975), 31, 33.

3. Pierre Teilhard de Chardin, *The Divine Milieu* (New York: Harper & Row, 1968), 46.

4. Ibid, 47.

5. Ibid, 66.

6. Ibid, 22.

7. Ibid, 5.

8. Teilhard, *The Phenomenon of Man*, 293-94.

9. See Mooney, *Teilhard de Chardin*, 173, note 60.

10. Because of this separation of transcendence and immanence, spirit and matter, creation and evolution, much of Western Christianity sees these as opposing forces. The present debate going on in the US' educational system is a perfect example. Christians want the origin of humans and the earth to be from a creationist perspective and cannot realize that evolution is creation. Evolution magnifies the glory of God in creation and it is on-going. Creation and evolution are both an on-going process. For further interest one can find the discussion in "Teaching the origin of species in schools, Evolution / ID / creationism conflicts in U.S. public schools" in http://www.religioustolerance.org/ev_school.htm.

11. I say biological life because we now understand from hylozoism that the inorganic/organic dualism and separation is an "illusion."

12. N.W. Wildiers gives a very good description of these stages in chapter 2, "An Immense Psychic Exercise" in *An Introduction to Teilhard de Chardin* (New York: Harper & Row, 1967).

13. Mooney, *Teilhard de Chardin*, 51.

14. Ibid, 63.

15. Teilhard, *The Phenomenon of Man*, 64.

16. Ibid.

17. Ibid, 64–65.

18. Ibid, 49.

19. Ibid, 60.

20. Ibid, 60–61.

21. Ibid., 31.

22. Ibid., 33.

23. Ibid., 164ff.

24. Wildiers, *An Introduction to Teilhard*, 80.

25. Mooney, *Teilhard de Chardin*, 96.

26. Wildiers, *An Introduction to Teilhard*, 62.

27. Teilhard, *The Phenomenon of Man*, 174.

28. Marx, *Collected Works*, V 3: 327.

29. The person of Teilhard de Chardin is similar to the Self as will be discussed later in the final chapter. The philosophy of the Self within Dialectical Incarnation is a philosophy called

personalism, which is in contrast to individualism. See "Understanding the Self within Dialecti-cal Incarnation" in Mooney, *Teilhard de Chardin*, 46.

30. Mooney, *Teilhard de Chardin*, 176–77.

31. Ibid, 160.

32. Wildiers, *An Introduction to Teilhard,* 128.

33. Ibid., 146–47.

34. The love which Teilhard de Chardin is speaking of here is universal, as explained below, and is best described as both *philia* love and *agape* love. This will be explained more in the final chapter on Ethics. See Mooney, *Teilhard de Chardin*, 52.

35. Mooney, *Teilhard de Chardin*, 52–53.

36. The psychology of love is a very complex element of the human person. Some people may not be able to love, but this is not an intrinsic aspect of the human person. All of humanity is created in the image of God who is love. It is the human person who creates the psychologi-cal barriers of persons to love. There is not an intrinsic inability to love. Any inability to love is a socio-psychological aspect which then inhibits humans from loving in the way Teilhard de Chardin calls us in *The Phenomenon of Man*, 266–67.

37. Teilhard, *The Phenomenon of Man*, 64.

38. A "litmus paper" in determining an emotion and experience of love can be in the acronym of CARING. Love is Concern for the other, Acceptance for the other, Responsibility in loving the other, Integrity in loving, Nurturing is loving, and Giving in love.

39. Teilhard, *The Phenomenon of Man*, 269.

40. Ibid.

41. Ibid, 267.

42. Wildiers, *An Introduction to Teilhard,* 103.

43. Jeremy Rifkin, *Entropy Into the Greenhouse World* (New York: Bantam Books, 1989), 47.

44. Wildiers, *An Introduction to Teilhard,* 82.

45. Ibid.

46. Teilhard, *The Phenomenon of Man*, 290.

47. Mooney, *Teilhard de Chardin,* 108.

48. Teilhard, *The Phenomenon of Man*, 312.

49. Ibid., 288.

50. Ibid., 312.

51. Ibid.

52. Teilhard, *The Divine Milieu*, 41.

53. Mooney, *Teilhard de Chardin*, 108.

54. Ibid.

55. Karl Rahner, like Teilhard de Chardin, is a Jesuit RC priest. He is both a metaphysical philosopher and theologian. He will use revealed terms, such as Christ, grace, Trinity, sin, etc., but he offers a genuine metaphysical understanding of his terms, his philosophy and his theolo-gy.

56. By "formal" I mean being a degreed scholar. Teilhard de Chardin studied much philoso-phy and theology as a Jesuit and reasons in both capacities.

57. Karl Rahner, "The Theology of Symbol", in *Theological Investigations* (Baltimore: Helicon Press, 1966), IV 9: 237.

58. Grace, for Rahner, is God's self-communication. The human as a "graced event" means that the human is supernaturalized.

59. Musser, Donald W., and Joseph L. Price, eds., *A New Handbook of Christian Theolo-gians.* (Nashville: Abingdon Press, 1996), 376.

60. Rahner, "The Theology of Symbol", IV 9: 237.

61. Rahner, "Theology and Anthropology", in *Theological Investigations,* IX 2: 29.

62. Karl Rahner, *Foundations of Christian Faith: An Introduction to the Idea of Christianity* (New York: Crossroad, 1992), 20.

63. Ibid.

64. Ibid.

65. Ibid., 21.

66. Rahner, "Theology and Anthropology", in *Theological Investigations,* IX 2: 28.

67. Rahner, "The Theology of Symbol", IV 9: 224, 229.

68. Ibid., 235.

69. This notion of symbol could evoke certain epistemological and metaphysical questions. The crucial aspect of a symbol from both perspectives is its dialectical nature. A symbol does not separate the two poles. A symbol goes beyond sensation and even perception when looking at the knowledge of a symbol. The two seeming opposing poles of a symbol and the dialectical method are united in the third component, the synthesis.

70. Rahner, "The Theology of Symbol", IV 9: 249.

71. Ibid., 252.

72. Ibid.

73. Ibid., 229.

74. Ibid., 231.

75. Ibid., 234.

76. *Logos* is 1: the divine wisdom manifest in the creation, government, and redemption of the world and often identified with the second person of the Trinity 2: reason that in ancient Greek philosophy is the controlling principle in the universe, Merriam Webster Online Dictionary. http://www.merriam-webster.com/dictionary/Logos

77. Rahner, "The Theology of Symbol", IV 9: 237.

78. Ibid., 237–38.

79. Mark Taylor, *GOD IS LOVE: A Study in the Theology of Karl Rahner (*Atlanta: Scholars Press, 1986), 178.

80. Rahner, *Foundations of Christian Faith*, 223.

81. Karl Rahner, "On the Theology of the Incarnation", in *Theological Investigations,* IV.4:116.

82. For the person who says "there is no God" or does not believe in the personal God of many religions, one can still believe in a form of transcendence in contrast to immanence. The significant point of symbol, as already indicated, is its synthesis of transcendence and immanence, of one and many. As such, the human person is both transcendent and immanent, both one and many.

83. Mark Lloyd Taylor, *GOD IS LOVE: A Study in the Theology of Karl Rahner* (Atlanta: Scholars Press, 1986), 179.

84. This is not a "leap of faith" in a revealed theology. It is a philosophical explanation of the dialectical nature of the human and divine. See Rahner, "The Theology of Symbol", IV 9: 238.

85. Christ is incarnation in its totality. See Rahner, "The Theology of Symbol", IV 9: 238.

86. Karl Rahner, "Christology Today", in *Theological Investigations,* XVII 7: 75, 80.

87. Taylor, *GOD IS LOVE*, 179.

88. Rahner, "The Theology of Symbol", IV 9: 221.

89. Ibid., 222.

90. The other two implications are Love and Mystery. See Rahner, "Unity –Love-Mystery", in *Theological Investigations,* VIII 12: 229.

91. "Anunity" is a Rahner creation. Rahner uses it more than once so I do not think it is a typing error. It seems to mean simply "an unity." See Rahner, "Unity-Love-Mystery", in *Theological Investigations,* VIII 12: 230.

92. Ibid.

93. Ibid., 231.

94. Rahner, "On the Theology of the Incarnation" In *Theological Investigations* IV 4: 107.

95. Ibid., 108.

96. Ibid.

97. Ibid.

98. Ibid.

99. Rahner, *"The Theology of Symbol"* IV 9: 239.

100. Rahner, "On the Theology of the Incarnation," in *Theological Investigations* IV 4: 109.

101. Ibid., 108.

102. Ibid.

103. Rahner, *Foundations of Christian Faith*, 54.

104. Ibid.

105. Ibid., 58.

106. Ibid., 68.

107. Ibid., 62–63.

108. Ibid., 63.

109. Ibid.

110. Karl Rahner, "Theology and Anthropology," in *Theological Investigations,* IX 2: 28.

111. Ibid., 36.

112. The metaphor of the Dance and the Dancer will be used again in the Chapter Four when the philosophy looks at the New Physics.

113. Karl Rahner, "Reflections on Methodology in Theology," in *Theological Investigations* XI 3, 105.

114. Ibid., 107.

Chapter Three

Pantheism and Other Expressions of Dialectical Incarnation

If "God is all things," as the philosophy for Dialectical Incarnation indicates, and there is a diversity in divine expressions, it is important to have a clear understanding of the philosophy and theology of pantheism.

GOD IS ALL THINGS: UNDERSTANDING PANTHEISM

The statement "Finding God *in* all things" emerges from the root of the incarnational spirituality and theology of St. Ignatius of Loyola, the founder of the Society of Jesus, the Jesuits. Its corollary is *Ad Majorem Dei Gloriam,* everything "for the greater glory of God," which serves as the general motto of Jesuit life and spirituality. It should not be of any real surprise, then, that the two "sons" of Ignatius, Pierre Teilhard de Chardin and Karl Rahner, would lead us to the recognition that God is Love and the totality of reality.

Pantheism comes from the Greek words *pan,* meaning *all,* and *theos,* meaning *God.* Therefore, in its most literal and simplistic definition, pantheism means "everything is God.[1] From the outset of its use, pantheism has been applied to a variety of positions, such as those offered by Baruch Spinoza, Georg Friedrich Hegel, Friedrich Schleiermacher and Josiah Royce.[2] Meister Eckhart and Nicholas of Cusa also show evidence of a form of pantheism in their philosophy and theology. In Karl Rahner's *Dictionary of Theology*, he describes the classical and common understanding of pantheism as:

> The doctrine, occurring in various forms, that God's absolute being is identical with the world; that the finite, changing reality (Contingent being) which we experience did not originate through creation by God's free omnipotence as

something distinct from himself but is a development of [God's] own being, [God's] (ontic or logical) self-expression and manifestation. It alleges that "God" is a comprehensive term for the world, either because the world is called a divine emanation, body, development, appearance or modalities of God or forms of [God's] manifestation. [3]

Pantheism, on the metaphysical level, is false, according to Rahner because

> . . . if God is grounded in finite being, instead of vice versa, then the radical difference between the finite object on the one hand and the incomprehensible source (horizon, mystery) to which the primordial, inabrogable experience of transcendence refers it on the other, disappears. Furthermore the change which finite being undergoes, and even evil itself, would be intrinsic elements of the divine nature, whereas God is perfect goodness because he possesses the whole plenitude of being. Pantheism is a doctrine which is entirely unknown to the OT and NT. [4]

Such criticisms of pantheism come from its dismissal of the dogmatic belief that God created the world from nothing (*creatio ex nihilo a deo)* and that God is distinct from the world. If "God is the totality of reality," as maintained in this philosophy, one will continue to struggle with the emergence of the synthesis in Dialectical Incarnation and the problems of pantheism. One will move from "finding God *in* all things," to "finding God *is* all things."

It is important to understand another position which deals with the relationship of the infinite God with the finite world; this position is known as *panentheism.* Coming from the same Greek words as pantheism, panentheism means "all in God" in contrast to "everything is God." Rahner helps us clarify the distinction between the two when he states that

> this form [i.e., panentheism] of pantheism does not simply identify the world with God in monistic fashion (God, the 'All') but sees the 'All' of the world 'within' God as an interior modification and manifestation of God, although God is not absorbed into the world. [5]

This doctrine would be considered false if it denies, as classical pantheism is claimed to do, creation from nothing and the distinction of the world from God. The challenge is to maintain that God created the world from nothing, that God is distinct from the world and that the world did not merely become absorbed in God. Is this possible? Is Rahner a panentheist or pantheist? Or neither? This book challenges one to "see" in this dialectical pantheistic manner where "fuller being" is within the infinite horizon in which one stands.

When Teilhard de Chardin came to recognise the fullness of the mystery of Christ as the totality of Incarnation and the discovery of a "real pantheism" he states that Incarnation is:

> the principle of universal vitality . . . a perennial act of communion and sublimation, aggregates to himself the total psychism of the earth . . . gathered everything together and transformed everything . . . *God shall be all in all.* This is indeed a superior form of 'pantheism' without trace of the poison of adulteration or annihilation: the expectation of perfect unity, steeped in which each element will reach its consummation at the same time as the universe. The universe fulfilling itself in a synthesis of centres in perfect conformity with the laws of union. God, the centre of centres. [6]

If it was difficult for early Christian Church philosophers and theologians to grasp the mystery of the hypostatic union where the divine and human are one, it is as difficult, if not more, to grasp that God and All, the totality of reality, are one. The total distinct otherness of God expressed in the condition of the possibility of humanity and creation remain as one, incarnate God/ Nature, which is not separate but is dialectically united as true unity in diversity. One must, in the prophetic words of Teilhard,

> overcome the [dichotomy] which paralyses us, and make up our minds to accept the possibility, indeed the reality, of some *source* of love, and *object* of love at the summit of the world." [7]

When one begins to accept this possibility and see that *all* is

> effectively 'one with God,' this state is obtained not by identification (God becoming all) but by the differentiating and communicating action of love (God all *in everyone*). And that is essentially orthodox and Christian. [8]

This is the dialectical pantheism of Dialectical Incarnation, in which, through incarnation, one is able to believe fully and more completely that love is divine, human and the totality of reality, as one union.

As one recognises the "superior form of 'pantheism,'" to which Teilhard de Chardin referred, it is interesting and important to note that Rahner calls panentheism a "form of pantheism." The distinction between the two is that the former, i.e., panentheism, is understood as meaning all reality is part of the being of God. This understanding of panentheism makes it easier to make reality distinct from God but it lessens the fullness of being in all of reality by making it a part of God and absorbed in God.

Hegel has been called both a panentheist and pantheist. He is the former, because, for him,"Absolute Spirit always overcomes the other and draws it into union with itself." [9] The self-identity of God, as Absolute Spirit, absorbs

God's otherness and, therefore, the fullness, and distinctiveness of what is other than God is lost.

Both Hegel and Rahner begin with the exigency of a being that moves from itself (thesis) to "otherness" (antithesis) as a moment in its self-realization (synthesis).[10] This exigency is a necessity, for as Rahner's philosophical theology of symbol states: "being is itself symbolic, because it *necessarily* 'expresses' itself."[11] Hegel also states that the dialectic is "the principle through which alone immanent condition and necessity enters into the content of reality."[12] Hence, both Hegel and Rahner claim that being necessarily expresses itself. For Rahner, as for Hegel, God is God's Self in the total otherness of God. The challenge is to demonstrate that the otherness of God remains totally itself in this unity, in the same way the early Christian Church philosophers and theologians needed to maintain Jesus' total humanity within his total divinity. It is here that the mystery and the truth of the hypostatic union, as explained by Rahner, clarifies the concern, when he states

> two correlated elements of the one [hu]man, elements which are inseparable from each other and yet *are not reducible* to each other . . . To make this distinction is of paramount importance and significance, for only in this way do one's eyes remain open to all the dimensions of the one[hu]man in all their immense and indeed infinite extent.[13]

If one can accept the hypostatic union as the early Church metaphysical philosophers proclaimed and, as Rahner explains, then the otherness of God, i.e., external reality, is not absorbed and reduced to God, as it is in panentheism. Rahner must keep the dialectical otherness of God distinct and not absorbed into God.

In this new understanding of pantheism nature is freely created from nothing and gratuitously graced. It is not a pantheism in which creation is seen as an emanation from God; rather creation is an intense communion of God and human beings-in-the-world. It must be understood as dialectical and incarnational. As philosophical and theological concepts, there is nature and grace, understood as distinct but never separate. In the existing world, which God freely created and in which humanity exists, there is no such thing as "pure nature." The world, humanity, "all in all" is incarnate with God's actual, indwelling presence.

In developing a new understanding of the truth of pantheism as dialectical, one needs to understand the use of the copula *is*, as Rahner clarified in the "is" formulas, when explaining the hypostatic union in incarnation. When one says that "God is the totality of reality" one is not making a *real* identification but an *existential* identification and definition. "Peter is a man" is a real identification. "Peter is an artist" is an existential identification. Similarly, when understanding this new dialectical pantheism, God must be understood as the God of the existential identification, experienced in Dialectical Incarnation, not some generic notion of God, like "God is divine;" "God is One;" "God is omnipotent," etc. "God is the Incarnate Logos" is an existential identification, like the statement "Peter is an artist." God's transcendence is in direct proportion to God's immanence. Because of the free gratuity of God's creative love, one cannot say it is God's essence that God created humanity and the world, for this would be "real identification." However, one can say that God is absolutely intrinsic to humanity-in-the-world and all creation in the same way that "Peter is his art." With this understanding of God and the existential understanding of the "is" in relation to God, one can say that God is "the totality of reality." With this understanding, love and creation remain free. Peter did not necessarily have to be an artist, he could have been a plumber or a lawyer, or even a "lazy bum," but he had to be something. It is in freedom that he became and artist and now he *is* his art. So too, God had to be something existentially and that something is creation and humanity-in-the-world. Now God *is* the "totality of reality."

The dialectical nature of Rahner's pantheism avoids being a monism as found in classical pantheism. Since it is not a monism, one could say it is a dualism, a "dualism" of creator and creature. To this problem Rahner says:

> what constitutes the relationship between the 'esse' of God and the 'esse' of the creature . . . this relationship when we consider that the creation of finite being by God does not presuppose nor, properly speaking, even create, the difference between God and the creature, but rather, from the standpoint of God, that God himself through his own being precisely *is* this difference in himself. Taking this as our starting-point, it would once more be possible to attain to an immanence of God in the world or an immanence of the world in God.[14]

Accordingly, dialectical pantheism is a "dualism" only in the sense that there remains the distinction of God in contrast to humanity in the world, which is a difference which originates from God and has its ground in God. Conversely, the pantheism of Dialectical Incarnation is a "monism" only in the sense that "all is all' and "God is the totality of reality." But, in understanding the use of the copula "is," the total immanence of God does not diminish God's total transcendence.

We can no longer understand God, or perceive God, as a particular individual, even a supreme one, who exists alongside of the world, related to the world in a wholly external fashion.[15] Mark Lloyd Taylor states:

> The moment of truth in pantheism must be affirmed, namely, that God and the world are not parts within a larger whole, the totality of reality. God, in some real sense, must be the totality of reality, for the God-world difference is not a categorical, but a metaphysical or transcendental, difference. Or, as Rahner

says, God *is* the difference between God and the world. This difference is internal to God, for God is the final horizon that makes possible all categorical differences. [16]

The "truth in pantheism," to which Taylor refers, is explained by Rahner: Pantheism could therefore be called a sensitivity to (or better, the transcendental experience of) the fact that God is the absolute reality, the original ground and the ultimate term of transcendence. This is the element of truth in pantheism. [17]

Since Teilhard de Chardin says, "everything is the sum of the past . . . nothing is comprehensible except through its history," [18] this book has demonstrated the evolutionary, historical foundations of the past with a strong influence of Rahner's philosophy and theology.

In light of this mystery and in defence of dialectical pantheism, it is necessary to recall two earlier statements as one groans in the evolution of "the totality of reality." The first is Hegel's reminder that "the proposition . . . is so paradoxical to the imagination or understanding, that it is perhaps taken for a joke [for it] is one of the hardest things thought expects to do." [19] Second, it is Teilhard's prophetic challenge "to see" so as to have a "vision [which is] fuller being." [20] In the strife and struggle necessarily present in the dialectical process, one needs to be open to the fact that God's creation is God's otherness; not a part of God, not absorbed by God, but is God intrinsically and existentially. Rahner states that "[t]he world receives God, the Infinite and the ineffable mystery, to such an extent that [God Godself] becomes its innermost life." [21] Rahner continues:

> The divine Logos himself both really creates and accepts this corporeality—which is part of the world—as *his* own; [God]brings it into existence as something other than himself in such a way, therefore, that this very materiality expresses God, the Logos himself . . . For we are quite entitled to conceive what we call creation as a part-moment in that process of God's coming-into-the-world by which God actually, even though freely, gives expression to himself in his Word . . . to think of the creation and of the Incarnation, not as two disparate, adjacent acts of God '*ad extra*' which in the actual world are due to two quite separate original acts of God, but as two moments and phases in the real world of the unique, even though internally differentiated, process of God's self-renunciation and self-expression into what is other that himself. [22]

One thus reaches "the real crux of the problem which runs through the whole of our reflections," [23] representing the history of the world and of the spirit to ourselves as the history of a self-transcendence into the life of God—a self-transcendence which, in this its final and highest phase, is identical with an absolute self-communication of God expressing the same process but now looked at from God's side. [24]

Rahner continues:

> Hence, if the reality in which God's absolute self-communication is pledged and accepted for the whole of humanity and thus becomes 'present' for us (i.e., Christ's reality) is to be really the final and unsurpassable divine self-communication, then it must be said that it is not only posited by God but is God himself.[25]

In this last statement, "not only posited by God but is God himself," Rahner is clearly referring to incarnation. However, it is incarnation which becomes "human reality," for Rahner continues to say that the "pledge itself cannot be anything else than a human reality which has been absolutely sanctified by grace."[26] Moreover, it is not merely humanity but also the world that becomes incarnation's reality, because "this event of the indissoluble unity of God and world in Jesus is also a pledge of salvation for the whole of humanity."[27]

In light of this "indissoluble unity of God and world in [incarnation]," we can understand Rahner's claim that,

> the creation, considered as the constitution of the non-divine 'out of nothing' is revealed as the prior setting and condition for the supreme possibility of [God] imparting of [God]self 'to the outside world' to be realized, a self-bestowal in which [God] does not constitute some other being, different from [God]self, but imparts [God]self, and thereby effectively manifests [God]self as the *agape* that bestows itself.[28]

Rahner goes on to say:

> We have attempted to perceive a more radical theological significance in the modern understanding of the world as a world of becoming that exists in a constant process of self-transcendence. The world can really be a world of becoming a unity of spirit and matter that belongs to it, and in a linear process of history in which an ever higher degree of self-transcendence is achieved, precisely because the mystery most interior to it, and a such precisely elevated above it, is the absolute being of God, whose basic act (an act which also includes God's creativity) is the self-bestowal of God upon that which is not divine.[29]

We have now moved to an evolutionary and elevated understanding of God and the world. We no longer simply "find God in all things," but rather "find God is all things" intrinsically and existentially. This is so not because the world is absorbed into the divine, but because of the dialectical nature of a transcendent, loving God, who communicates God's self in the expression of this communication to the creature, as God's self.

THE EXPRESSIONS OF DIALECTICAL INCARNATION IN
EASTERN PHILOSOPHY[30]

The most important characteristic of an Eastern philosophy's world view is the awareness of the unity and mutual interrelation of all things and events. The experiences of all phenomena in the world are manifestations of a basic oneness. Everything is interdependent and inseparable incarnations of one cosmic whole. Everything is a different manifestation of the same ultimate reality.[31] Reality is seen as the essence of the universe, underlying and unifying the multitude of things and events one observes. As such, Eastern religions fall under the umbrella of natural philosophy and theology.

With these common elements among Eastern philosophy and religious expression, there is an already natural similarity with Dialectical Incarnation. To begin with, Eastern thought did not fall victim to a dualistic perspective of the world the way Western philosophy has. With the transcendent and immanent unity of Hinduism and the understanding of an oneness within plurality and its infinite manifestations or incarnations, one can quickly identify how Brahman and the *Aum* will serve as the condition of possibility for an expression of Dialectical Incarnation. So too, the *Tao*, with its dialectical nature, continues to demonstrate how Eastern philosophy coincides with the philosophy of this book. The ultimate essence of Eastern philosophy cannot be separated from its multiple manifestations. With an underlying premise, already established through certain Western philosophers, we now turn to an Eastern perspective, followed with that of African and Caribbean expressions.[32]

Hinduism

Hinduism is not a philosophy in a strict sense of the word, nor is it a defined religion. Hinduism is rather:

> a large and complex socio-religious organism consisting of innumerable sects, cults and philosophical systems and involving various rituals, ceremonies and spiritual disciplines, as well as the worship of countless gods and goddesses.[33]

Hinduism understands that the infinite number of things and events that surround the human are merely different manifestations of the one and same ultimate reality. This reality is called *Brahman*, which is the unifying concept of Hinduism. Brahman clarifies Hinduism's essentially monistic character, despite the fact that it is frequently called polytheistic in that Hindus identify numerous gods and goddesses. The truth is that all these gods are but reflections of the one ultimate reality.[34]

The incarnation of *Brahman* in the human person is *Atman*. Similar to the Western philosophers already discussed in understanding the Self, *Atman* and *Brahman* are one. The individual and ultimate reality are one. So too, a basic recurring theme in Hindu mythology is that God becomes the world which, in the end, becomes God again.[35] One falls victim to *maya* when one confuses the different forms of divinity with reality, without recognizing the how *Brahman* unites all these forms. *Maya* is frequently understood as meaning that the world is an illusion, but actually, the illusion is in one's "seeing," that is, in one's point of view of reality. If one considers the shapes, structures, things and events around them as reality, then one is "under the spell of *maya*" when one does not recognise the unity which Brahman manifests. "*Maya* is the illusion of taking these concepts for reality, of confusing the map with the territory."[36] Seeing the world in the form of a dualism is *maya.*

The world of *maya* is constantly changing, in that all forms are relative and fluid. The dynamic force underlying all of reality is *karma. Karma* in understood as "action" and is the active principle of the all reality where everything is connected with everything else. In the words of the *Bhagavad Gita,* "*Karma* is the force of creation, wherefrom all things have their life."[37] The intention of life is to be free from the spell of *maya. Maya* keeps the human thinking that one is separated from one's environment and that one can act independently. Under this spell one is bound by *karma.* When one is free from the bond of *karma* one finally realizes that there is a unity and a harmony of all nature, including oneself, and one acts accordingly. The *Bhagavad* Gita makes this point very clear:

> All actions take place in time by the interweaving of the forces of nature, but the [person] lost in selfish delusion thinks the he [or she] himself [or herself] is the actor. But the [person] who knows the relation between the forces of Nature and actions, sees how some forces of Nature work upon other forces of Nature, and becomes not their slave.[38]

When one is free from the spell of *maya,* and one has broken the bonds of *karma,* one realises that all the phenomena one perceives with one's senses are actually part of the same reality. This means that one experiences everything concretely and personally, including ones' Self, as one with *Brahman.* This experience of liberation is called *moksha,* and it is the very essence of Hinduism.[39] Hinduism offers innumerable ways of attaining this liberation, such as the Vedanta nonpersonal, metaphysical means, or the "path" of *yoga,* or the personal devotion to a god or goddess.

The most sacred symbol in Hinduism is the symbol *Aum.*[40] Volumes have been written in Sanskrit illustrating the significance of this mystic philosophy. The goal, which all *Vedas* declare,[41] which all austerities aim at, and which humans desire when they live a life of continence, is the Aum. Aum is indeed *Brahman*. Aum is the highest. The Aum is the first manifestation of the unmanifest Brahman, the single Divine Ground of Hinduism, that resulted in the phenomenal universe. Brahman is the ultimate reality and is understood as the "soul," or inner essence, of all things. Brahman is infinite and beyond all concepts. Essentially, all the cosmos stems from the vibration of the sound "Aum" which serves as an expression of manifestation of this one reality of Brahman .

Gods and goddesses are sometimes referred to as *Aumkar*, which means "Form of Aum" and implies the limitlessness that represents the vibrational whole of the cosmos. In Hindu metaphysics, the manifested cosmos, coming from Brahman, has name and form, and the closest approximation to the name and form of the universe is Aum, since all existence is fundamentally composed of vibration.

The Aum of Hinduism is uniting the material perception of the world with the nonmaterial, spirit or idea perception of the world. [42] *Maya* has humanity perceiving reality in a dualistic manner and it is this illusion from which humanity must free itself so as to attain *moksha*.

Hindus, as well as Buddhists, have understood this reality for millennia. Hinduism challenges one to "see" with fuller vision and fuller being. The Aum of Hinduism is the symbol representing the vibrational oneness of all reality. The Aum is both physical-like and idea-like. It is the oneness of this synthesis of two poles which humans have too often separated. The Aum is one, as a synthesis of two poles, with its matter-like and idea-like concepts.

In *advaita* philosophy, the Aum is frequently used to represent three subsumed into one. It implies that our current existence is *mithya*, or "slightly lesser reality." In order to know the full truth, we must comprehend beyond the body and intellect and intuit the true nature of infinity. This Divine Ground is imminent yet transcends all duality and cannot be described in words. This metaphysical symbolism resembles the dialectical nature found in much of Western philosophy. When moksha, or any other similar experience of liberation, is attained, one is able not only to see or know existence for what it is, but to become it. In attaining truth one simply realizes the fundamental unity of all of reality. [43] When one gains true knowledge, there is no split between knower and known: one becomes incarnational knowledge/consciousness itself. In essence, Aum is the signifier of the ultimate truth that all is one. With an understanding of reality as Brahman and its manifestation in the Aum, we can come to recognise how Hinduism expresses the philosophy of Dialectical Incarnation. [44]

Buddhism

Hinduism is not the only Eastern philosophy that offers such support. Buddhism, and the Chinese philosophies of Confucianism and Taoism also continue to express the oneness of all reality, but the latter are more formally descriptive of the dialectical nature of this one reality. Thus, we now move to Buddhism and the later expressions of the *Tao* and the *yin/yang.*

With Hinduism, one can find myth and ritual. With Buddhism, one can find psychology. Siddhartha Gautama, a Hindu living in the middle of the sixth century B.C.E, is the historical Buddha and the acknowledged founder of Buddhism. His philosophy was not directed at the origin of the physical world nor at the nature of Divinity; rather, he was concerned specifically and exclusively with the suffering and frustrations found in the human condition. He offers to the world a type of psychotherapy rather than a metaphysics. He incorporated into his philosophy the Hindu concepts of *maya, karma* and *moksha,* with a "dynamic and directly relevant psychological interpretation" of them.[45]

Buddhism eventually evolved into two main schools, the Hinayana and the Mahayana. Although these philosophies may have developed into a high intellectual level, there is always the intention, especially in the latter, of not losing itself in abstract speculative thought. In Eastern mysticism, the intellect is understood as merely a means to clear the way for the "awakening." The essence of this mystical experience is to go "beyond the world of intellectual distinctions and opposites," as found in much of Western thought, and "to reach the world of the unthinkable, where reality appears as the undivided and undifferentiated 'suchness.'"[46]

A more complete understanding of Buddhist thought can be understood in the *Avatamsaka* school which is rooted in the *sutra* of the same name. The importance of this particular *sutra* is made evident in the enthusiastic words of D.T. Suzuki.

> As to the Avatamsaka-sutra, it is really the consummation of Buddhist thought, Buddhist sentiment, and Buddhist experience. To my mind, no religious literature in the world can ever approach the grandeur of conception, the depth of feeling, and the gigantic scale of composition as attained in this *sutra.* It is the eternal foundation of life from which no religious mind will turn back athirst or only partially satisfied.[47]

This astonishing piece of sacred literature expresses the dialectical nature of Buddhism and its central theme of "unity in diversity." When Buddhism spread across Asia and developed in China and Japan, the difference between the Buddhism of China and of Japan, on one side, and of India, on the other, was so great that

> they have been said to represent two poles of the human mind. Whereas the former are practical, pragmatic and socially minded, the latter are imaginative, metaphysical and transcendental . . . the two poles combined to form a new dynamic unity.[48]

Chinese Thought

Buddhism arrived in China around the first century of the Common Era. At that time the culture and character of China was already more than two thousand years old. Similar to the contrast between Indian and Chinese/ Japanese mentality, so too, within Chinese philosophy, there emerged two complementary aspects. In general, Chinese people are practical and highly organised in their social consciousness. They were concerned with life in society, human relationships, moral principles and government. Complementary to this aspect of Chinese thought is the more mystical and transcendent aspect of the Chinese character. The aim of this aspect of Chinese philosophy is to transcend the world of society and everyday, ordinary life so as to reach a higher level of consciousness. This is the plane of the Chinese sage and philosopher aimed at enlightenment and mystical union with the universe. However, this aspect of Chinese philosophy does not remain exclusive to the transcendent, spiritual realm but is equally concerned with worldly issues. The true philosopher or sage unifies within him or herself the "two complementary sides of human nature—intuitive wisdom and practical knowledge, contemplation and social action."[49] These two characteristics are associated with the images of the sage and of the king. Fully realised human persons, "by their stillness become sages, by their movement kings."[50]

These two aspects of Chinese philosophy emerged, in the sixth century C.E., into what are identified as Confucianism and Taoism. The former, deriving its name from Kung Fu Tzu, or Confucius, was the philosophy of social organization, of common sense and practical knowledge. The latter, whose originator is Lao Tzu, was concerned with the observation of nature and the discovery of its Way, or the *Tao.* For the Taoist, human happiness "is achieved when one follows the natural order, acting spontaneously and trusting one's intuitive knowledge."[51] The dialectical nature of Chinese thought is demonstrated by how these two trends represent opposite poles which are always seen as poles of one and the same human nature, and thus complementary.[52]

The Chinese philosophers understood reality as a "unity in diversity" in which there is an ultimate reality that underlies and unifies the multiple things and events found in the world. Accordingly, there are

> three terms—'complete,' 'all-embracing,' 'the whole.' These names are different, but the reality sought in them is the same: referring to the One thing.[53]

This "One thing" of reality is the *Tao.* The *Tao* can be defined as 'path,' or 'road' (*Taoism*). The way of the *Tao* is the way of Nature and of ultimate reality. *Tao* is often described as a force that flows through all life. It is a process of the universe. A happy and virtuous life is one that is in harmony with the *Tao*, with Nature.

The original cosmic sense of the *Tao* understood it as the ultimate, indefinable reality, similar to the Hindu understanding of *Brahman*. It differs from the Hindu interpretation by its intrinsically dynamic and dialectical quality which is the essence of the universe. For the Chinese, the *Tao* is the "cosmic process in which all things are involved; the world is seen as a continuous flow and change."[54]

The *Tao*, like Dialectical Incarnation, needs the material objective world to be. Conscious experience and the objective, changing, material world are both the conditions of the possibility for the *Tao* and for Dialectical Incarnation. Synthesized together they form one reality.

The *Tao* is the one thing that exists and connects the many things. *Tao, Nature*, Reality are One and humans have evolved from Nature, i.e., from *Tao*. Humans ultimately depend upon Nature for survival. Humans are connected to the Reality, to *Tao*. One must be wise and able to evolve within one's cultural knowledge, so as to live in harmony with Nature, with *Tao*. Humans are integral elements within the totality of reality.

As an understanding of the *Tao* continued to evolve, Confucianists went beyond the original cosmic sense and spoke of the *Tao* as the *Tao* of man, or of human society, recognizing it as the right way of life in a moral sense.[55] Humanity must come to a greater understanding that the moral life, societal life, human life necessarily and directly involves all of Nature. Until we understand what we are as humans, what matter is in its fullness, and how humanity is connected to the universe, it is impossible for humanity to be wise, and to be able to evolve cultural knowledge that enables us to live in harmony with Nature (*Tao*). This is the task of *Aum*, this is the task of *Tao* and this is the task of Dialectical Incarnation's "One Love."

The *yin* and *yang* represent all the opposite principles which one observes in the universe. Within *yang* there are the principles of maleness, the sun, creation, heat, light, heaven, dominance, etc. Within *yin* are the principles of femaleness, the moon, completion, cold, darkness, material forms, submission, etc. Each of these opposites produces the other: heaven creates the ideas of things under *yang*, the earth produces their material forms under *yin*, and vice versa; creation occurs under the principle of *yang*, the completion of the created thing occurs under *yin*, and so on. This production of *yin* from *yang* and *yang* from *yin* occurs cyclically and constantly, so that no one principle continually dominates the other or determines the other. All opposites that one experiences, e.g. health and sickness, wealth and poverty, power and submission, can be explained in reference to the temporary dominance of one principle over the other. No one principle dominates eternally; all conditions are subject to change into their opposites.[56]

This cyclical nature of *yin* and *yang*, the opposing forces of change in the universe, means several things. First, all phenomena change into their opposites in an eternal cycle of reversal. Second, the one principle produces the other, all phenomena have within them the seeds of their opposite state, that is, sickness has the seeds of health, health contains the seeds of sickness, wealth contains the seeds of poverty, etc. Third, even though an opposite may not be seen to be present, since one principle produces the other, no phenomenon is completely devoid of its opposite state. One is never really healthy since health contains the principle of its opposite, sickness. This is called "presence in absence."[57]

> The dynamic character of *yin* and *yang* is illustrated by the Chinese symbol called *T'ai-chi,* or "Diagram of the Supreme Ultimate." This diagram is a symmetric arrangement of the dark *yin* and the bright *yang*, but the symmetry is not static. It is a rotational symmetry suggesting, very forcefully, a continuous cyclic movement: "The *yang* returns cyclically to its beginning, the *yin* attains its maximum and gives place to the *yang*." The two dots in the diagram symbolize the idea that each time one of the two forces reaches its extreme, it contains in itself already the seed of its opposite.[58]

Similar to how Leibniz understood reality as one and many within a harmony of love, so too Chuang Tzu states that "[l]ife is the blended harmony of the *yin* and *yang*."[59]

For both the East and the West, reality is comprised of a unity of seeming opposing poles. This is not a separation of entities, but rather a new understanding of the dialectical nature of reality. The Taoists from the East, and philosophers such as Spinoza, Leibniz, Teilhard de Chardin, and Rahner from the West, can testify that changes in physical reality can be seen as an interaction between dialectical opposites: *yin* and *yang*, matter and spirit, one and many, transcendence and immanence, divine and human. The recognition of the oneness of the universe can be found in both East and West mystical experiences and also in the recent discovery of modern physics. There is a unity of all things which is noticeable in the atomic level of matter and also in the subatomic realm of particles.[60] Fritjof Capra summarises for us how all reality is One from an East's, West's and physics' perspective.

> In ordinary life, we are not aware of the unity of all things, but divide the world into separate objects and events. This division is useful and necessary to cope with our everyday environment, but it is not a fundamental feature of reality. It is an abstraction devised by our discriminating and categorising intellect. To believe that our abstract concepts of separate 'things' and 'events' are realities of nature is an illusion . . . . As we study the various models of subatomic physics we shall see that they express again and again, in different ways, the same insight—that the constituents of matter and the basic phenomena involving them are all interconnected, interrelated and interdependent; that

they cannot be understood as isolated entities, but only as integrated parts of the whole.[61]

THE "I-N-I": DIALECTICAL INCARNATION EXPRESSED THROUGH RASTAFARI [62]

African Philosophy: A Precursor to Rastafari[63]

To make reference to an "African Philosophy" implies that there is something specific and distinguishable within a particular philosophy which gives it its identity. One speaks of European philosophy, Indian philosophy, German philosophy and so on. What makes "African Philosophy" African? It is a great challenge to be able to specify common components of African philosophy when this continent is so vast with seeming endless ethnic groups and cultures. It would seem to be more appropriate to refer to African Philosophies. Nevertheless, as one moves on in offering an expression of Dialectical Incarnation as found in Rastafari, with its African roots, one will garner from the multiple positions present in the diversity of African philosophies those particular elements which support the thesis.[64] To begin with one must examine pertinent understandings of African metaphysics or, at least, aspects of metaphysical thinking which emerge from Africa.

Metaphysical discourse in Africa is holistic in nature and within reality everything interacts with each other.[65] "There is a principle concerning the interaction of forces, that is, between God and humankind, between different people, between humankind and animals, and between humankind and material things."[66] One can recognise that reality is a totality. What is important for our philosophy is that "this system shows an almost unbreakable interrelation between God . . . the living and nature, . . . the living person takes a central place."[67] The human person of African philosophy is a fundamental part of nature in that the human person is a natural being. More than taking "central place" the African person sees himself or herself as the "centre of creation."

> The interactions and intercommunications between the visible created order and the invisible world of God, spirits, and ancestors are possible only through human beings, the ontological mean between beings acting above and below them. . . . .the human being in the African-world view is the centre of creation.[68]

One should already begin to recognise how the understanding of the Self in African philosophy is helpful in supporting Dialectical Incarnation and the understanding of the Self as the "centre of the circumference" of God, Nature and other human beings. As such, there can be seen a strong influence on the

I-n-I relationship of Rastafari. However, it should be noted that reference to African philosophy in this philosophy is merely to serve as a precursor to Rastafari. It would be an injustice to the dept and full meaning of African philosophy to categorically incorporate it into the philosophy of Dialectical Incarnation even though the similarities with the I-n-I are present.

Besides the centrality of the Self in African philosophy, so too, the rejection of dualism is another supporting agreement. Teffo and Roux explain that

> dualisms which are the stock-in-trade of Western metaphysics, such as that between the natural and the supernatural, and others such as those between matter and mind/soul/spirit, do not appear in African metaphysics. [69]

Within Dialectical Incarnation, the human person is an incarnational being comprised of an intrinsic union of matter and spirit. Likewise, African metaphysics also holds that "spiritual entities have material qualities; there is no radical or categorical difference between the spiritual and the material." [70] Chukwudum Okolo also testifies that within African thought the Self is a "psycho-physical being, and incarnate spirit, made up of two principle elements, namely, 'body' and 'soul.'" [71] The body and the soul are not seen as independent entities, but as elements of one incarnational being where body and soul are the conditions of the possibility of being human. Not only is the Self the "centre of creation" as an "incarnate" being, but the Self is also intrinsically in relation with others. It is the community which is the condition of the possibility of the individual. Reference is made again to the significant statement of J.S. Mbiti, "I am because we are; and since we are, therefore, I am." [72]

Before moving on to Rastafari, there is one last similarity which should be identified in African philosophy, i.e., the understanding of God in the world. God is not separate from the world.

> Together with the world, God constitutes the spatio-temporal 'totality' of existence . . . the natural-supernatural dichotomy has no place in African conceptualisation of the universe. [73]

In summary, African philosophy is a precursor to Rastafari, and to Dialectical Incarnation, for three reasons. First, African philosophy understands the Self as the centre of the universe and is intrinsically in relation with others. Secondly, it breaks down Western dualism; and, thirdly, African philosophy recognises the oneness of God in the world.

Rastafari and Its Beliefs

Rastafari is an indigenous African rooted philosophy of Jamaica, yet it has interesting influences of Hinduism and East Indian thought. [74] According to

Ajai Mansingh and Laxmi Mansingh, Rastafari is recognised as a "mystical response to inner spiritual urges for God-realization in time and space."[75] Besides being strongly influenced by African philosophy, Rastafari is also an "interesting combination of East and West; it derives its basic concepts, rituals and codes from Hinduism, while claiming historical connections with Christianity."[76] This is why Rastafari is an expression of Dialectical Incarnation and where we now continue.

The basic oneness of the universe is the central characteristic of Eastern philosophy and of mystical experiences found both in Eastern and Western realms alike. This unity of all reality can be grasped through a recent manifestation of the ultimate reality, namely Rastafari. It is this through the complexity and fluidity of Rastafari and the dialectical relationship of I-n-I that this book now turns in offering a concrete, historical and categorical expression of the dialectical oneness of God, Nature and the human person.[77]

Rastafari is called a variety of things: cult, movement, religion. Leonard E. Barrett has described the Rastafari as a messianist-millenarian cult—messianist because of their belief in the person of Haile Selassie, and millenarian because of the expectation of an imminently good future on earth.[78] Others describe Rastafari more as an escapist movement than a revolutionary one.[79] Consequently it is not easy to summarize the beliefs of such a heterogeneous group as the Rastafari. But in the search for the unity in diversity of God's creation and cultures, there will be a focus on those aspects which can support the philosophy of Dialectical Incarnation. i.e., God, humanity and Nature.

At the heart of the contemporary Rastafari experience of reality is a relational sense of Self, which is expressed by the term I-n-I. At first instance, the "I" connotes the sense in which the Self is inextricably linked with symbols of divine agency. This expression thus proclaims the collapse of the radical dichotomy between creator and creature, and between heaven and earth. Bob Marley, the great Prophet of Rastafari through his Reggae music, expressed the complete rejection of a disjunction between God and humanity in some of his lyrics indicating that God is a living human person.[80]

When one refers to oneself in the first person singular as I-n-I, there is virtual equation between oneself and God. The linkage of Jah, that is, God, and the human also implies a further relation to other selves. Jah is manifest to all persons; therefore, all persons are joined to one another by virtue of their unity with Jah. The expression of "I-n-I" thus connotes a three-fold relationship between the individual Self, Jah, and other selves within nature. The "I" of the Self is fundamentally related to the "I" in Sellassie I (the Roman number I or first is entirely disregarded and instead understood as the first person singular.[81] One Rasta expresses it as:

> I-n-I is an expression of a total concept of oneness . . . so when Ras Tafari
> speak of himself as 'I' he means it in a sense of total uplifting of oneself, total
> dignity of one's self and expresses that so his fellow brethren is the same as
> himself. He says 'I-n-I' as being the oneness of two persons. So God is with all
> of us and we're all one people in fact. [82]

In addition to this unity, the expression of I-n-I is reflective of the redis-
covery and reassertion of one's dignity in an oppressive context. One can
clearly see the influence of Marcus Garvey's thought here. It is not merely
one's unity with other selves and divine agency, but it is also an emphasis
that it is a fully autonomous "I" which stands in this relation. The I-n-I of
Rastafari is thus the centre of the circumference of Nicholas of Cusa and it is
the Self within the infinite horizon of the universe and God of Rahner. The I-
n-I is the breakdown of the dualism which separated the immanent from the
transcendent. The I-n-I of Rastafari is an expression of the One Love of
Dialectical Incarnation.

Of particular importance for I-n-I is Rastafari's life-style, which is called
"livity." The concept of livity represents a new integrating ethos, whereby
one's actions are expressive of one's genuine, essential nature as an I-n-I,
which is opposed to individualism and domination of the environment and
nature as taught in colonialism. A Rasta seeks to live in full harmony with
nature and the environment, this is the harmony of Love of which Leibniz
spoke. The word used for such existence is "I-tal" (vital), demonstrating an I-
n-I's concern to live authentically in relation to nature in a pure, organic way.
Livity, which is I-tal living, is expressed in a Rastafari's appearance, diet, use
of herbs, process of reflection, modes of production and aesthetic activity. [83]

Another fundamental aspect of Rastafari is reincarnation. The Rasta's
understanding of this notion is different from the Hindu doctrine of death and
rebirth. For Rastafari, it is *re*-incarnation, which is a continual repetition of
incarnation. "The God-man is incarnated in many times and many places for
those who have eyes to see him, and death has no place in the process." [84]

According to some, the root of this Rastafari belief is the ancient African
belief in immortality and in the cyclical nature of the universe: "Whatever
goes around, comes around." [85] Each person eventually gets his or her just
reward, somewhere along the road of life, which is very long for each Spirit.
Some doctrines of re-incarnation stress the "transmigration of soul," which is
the belief that a person's soul or spirit must progress by taking in turn every
earthly form—from gas to mineral, and on through plant and animal to
human, "till all the 'lessons' of mortal life has been learned." [86] It is said that
the "transmigration of soul" was the accepted doctrines of the early Christian
Church, but it was eventually dropped by the Roman Catholic Church. [87]

Rastafari has revived this theory and has provided a tangible framework
in which the Mystic unity and connectedness of Jah God's creations manifest

themselves. Rastas see themselves as re-incarnations of earlier personages, even of Christ. All of humanity is the incarnation of God. Each person is a particular incarnation of the oneness of Jah and creation. In fact, Christ and the ancient prophets can never die for "Jah Jah Lives";[88] they live on by becoming re-incarnated into other bodies. Many Rastafari say that there has been 71 appearances of God in human bodies, with His Imperial Majesty, Selassie I as the 72nd and last re-incarnation. This means for them that Haile Selassie, Jesus, Solomon, David, Moses, Joseph, Aaron and all the other God-human were one and the same Spirit (Forsythe 89). The important aspect of this notion of re-incarnation is the unity which it is trying to maintain; a unity of all of God (Jah), with humanity and nature through evolution and history. One remembers that "Christ is the *Alpha* and the *Omega*," and Dialectical Incarnation is the One of "all and all," God, Nature and humanity.

The concept of "dread" is something one needs to understand so as to have a full grasp of the meaning of Rastafari. The term is often interchangeable with "Rasta" and can be described as a "composite summarizing symbolic expression." Rex Nettleford explains that

> [a]ll the responses known to Jamaican history . . . psychological withdrawal, black nationalism, apocalyptic exultation, denunciation and the bold assertion of a redemptive ethic . . . were, as it were, invoked by the Rastafarian and made to take form in one grand and awesome—"dread"—expression.[89]

Following the notion "dread" is the concept of "Babylon" for the Rasta. It is "Babylon" which symbolizes the negative or "fallen' condition from which "I-Lect" (Elect) have fled. This theme is echoed by all of Rastafari and is frequently expressed in their chants and songs.[90]

The Rastafari imagery of Babylon is the "first-person gut-level experiences of alienation and frustration under slavery, colonialism and their legacies."[91] This concept is not imposed but has grown out of the deep feeling and experiences of dismembered beings. Babylon is the psychic image sustained by real life experiences: busted hopes broken dreams, the blues of broken homes and disjointed tribes of people trapped by history. It is an image of fire and of blood, of being on the edge, in limbo, in the wilderness, in concrete jungles surrounded by jungle animals of all shapes and sizes, particularly by 'wolves in sheep's clothing.'[92]

Babylon is thus a sense of desolation in which a person feels disjoined and alienated with the plans of creation (removed from the *Alpha).

> The body in this reversed order rules the head, and the horizontal now becomes the vertical, and the line put by Jah between Man and Woman is blurred.[93]

Jimmy Cliff's popularizing Psalm 137, "By the rivers of Babylon," is a clear expression of this fallen condition and the Rasta's desire to return to "Zion." This falleness, this dread is when the human person is living outside the harmony of love which Leibniz popularized and which is the core of Dialectical Incarnation.

"Zion" is another central theme for Rastafari. Rastas will eventually move out of Babylon, but the "fires of 'hell' must precede the soothing waters of Zion." Zion is the Sun Vision, the Great Magnet.[94] "Zion" is Biblical in origin and Rastafari continues to use it in this tradition. Zion is the "City of David," the "eternal city," the "city of God," because it is there that the Israelites kept the holy ark of the covenant. Those that were born there, like Solomon, are said to be blessed:

> The Lord loves the gates of Zion more than all the dwelling places of Jacob. Glorious things are spoken of you, O city of God . . . And of Zion, it shall be said, 'This one and that one were born in her,' for the most High himself will establish her.[95]

Zion also symbolises peace: His abode has been established in Salem, his dwelling place in Zion. There he broke the flashing arrows of the bow, the shield and the sword, and the weapons of war.[96]

One Rasta chant says of Zion: "No sin can enter in Mount Zion so bright and fair; No sin can enter there forever." Bob Marley sees Zion as "the kingdom of Jah where Lion-man shall reign."[97]

It is increasingly evident that Rastafari is not a single, clearly organized religion or movement. It offers a variety of beliefs within a search for unity between God, creation and humanity. There is a sense of fluidity amidst the diversity of cultural and religious expressions. The initial "doctrine of faith" has been continually expressed in two basic concepts, the divinity of Haile Selassie and the repatriation to Africa for Blacks, which expresses redemption. However, this body of beliefs is still developing.

Rastafari and Incarnation

When referring to the humanity and divinity of God, Rastafari insists that reference to God must take on historical moment and expression. God as Reality must take on a particular expression. God must be experienced within the context of human life; God must be found in particular incarnations. History has philosophical and theological importance for Rastafari for it is through history that God acts. Thus close attention is given to local events found in the media and through which they find signs that might indicate the immanent victory and unification of God and all of reality.[98] History is linear, as compared to the earlier notion of re-incarnation that was cyclical.

History, is life, a journey, a pilgrimage to the Promised Land, to the harmony of One Love found in the totality of reality.

With the Rastafari emphasis on history, a Rasta recognizes that God is very much present in the world, not outside it. God is in the "internal land-scapes of the human experience, not [in] external far-off places."[99] Africa, as Zion, is within the true Rastafari, not across the ocean. For the Rasta, "God is not only Man, he is *a* Man, and He cannot be worshipped in spirit if he is to be worshipped in truth. God is not a 'duppy'; he is spirit-in-body."[100]

Before moving from the understanding of Rastafari to a new understand-ings of incarnation it is important to also realize the Rastafari concept of Original Sin and sin itself. Within the whole framework of the positive self-identity of black people, originally stressed in Marcus Garvey's movement and now fundamental to Rastafari, the sense of guilt or of shame, which Original Sin evokes, does not have place within their belief system. Rastafa-ri, like Dialectical Incarnation, rejects the notion of Original Sin. Original Sin can only serve to perpetuate that self-doubt, that lack of self-confidence, and the acceptance of an imposed sense of inferiority which have plagued Black men and women in exile. There is clearly a need for redemption in the inexorable unfolding of a divine purpose in bringing justice to the oppressed. "But there is no room for repentance, for 'I-man' has done no Original Wrong. Rather, the Original Wrong was done to I-man."[101]

The self-confidence of the Rasta is because of the "incontrovertible fact" that he or she is in direct communication with God. The original state of all humanity and of the ManGodness of the Rasta no longer makes him or her vulnerable to the evils of his or her Babylonian captivity. The exploited slave now recognizes that he or she becomes the centre of the cosmos, the centre of the circumference of God and the universe. This anthropocentrism of Rasta religious and philosophical thought suggests affiliations with the established religious thought, but it would be a mistake to suggest that Rasta draws this indiscriminately from religion, specifically from Christianity. Everything in the Rasta's exterior existence had denied him or her the capability of an intimacy with Jah and of having any self autonomy.[102] The Rasta now starts his or her awareness of himself or herself in the world, as one with "Original Grace," united through incarnation and the harmony of love found in the universe.

Because of the exterior existence of the Rasta which kept him or her oppressed from his or her actual blessed, dignified, material-supernatural existential nature, sin is not merely an individual or personal matter. It is a structural one. As a result, Rastafari resists and prophecies against nations, corporations, empires and races which prevent them from being fully human and fully alive.

A Rastafari Understanding of Incarnation

In Karl Rahner's understanding of the "anonymous Christian," *every* human person is constituted by virtue of God's self-offer in grace and, therefore, every human person is characterized as a "supernatural existential." How similar this is to the ManGodness of the Rasta.[103] Moreover, a human person is living out his or her freely given, graced being, marked by a supernatural existential, when he or she really accepts *himself or herself completely*.[104] When the human person accepts himself or herself, he or she is actually accepting "[incarnation] as the absolute perfection and guarantee of his [or her] anonymous movement towards God."[105] Finally! The black people of the world, as experienced by Rastas, are able to recognize and accept themselves *completely* with dignity in their full blackness as humans.

In understanding the total and complete sense of incarnation present in all of evolution and in history, it is important to recognise that universal grace is given to all humanity *prior* to any reference to a revealed and exclusively Christian understanding of incarnation. Rahner states:

> In an *ultimate* sense God is equally near everywhere. . . . We live in a world in which each and everything is inter-dependent, in which every event is in some way important for every other, at least if it comes later in time . . . in an appeal to the 'cosmic Christ' . . . the pre-existing Logos of God can be conceived without difficulty as a creative, sanctifying, reconciling and divinizing force operating in the world and in history . . . The eternal Logos of God gives himself to the central core of human freedom . . . for the self-communication of the divine Logos to the world is conceived not as a single event within history but as the ultimate dynamic orientation which operates universally and is the ground of the whole of history.[106]

Through the help of philosophers and theologians, like Rahner and many others, who think similarly, all people can begin to recognize and believe that all "are one" through the incarnation present in evolution and history.

In this comprehensive understanding of incarnation, one can be more open to recognize that divinity is clearly Godself in Rastafari. The question is whether people, other than Rasta, can be open to this and actually discover more about God and the world. One now has the ability, and therefore the responsibility, to "see" that God is love and the totality of reality.

Rastafari has clearly not defined itself in any rigid and fixed manner. By its very nature it remains an open and fluid incarnation. Even the basic "doctrinal" belief that Haile Selassie is divine is understood differently. It is the Twelve Tribes, of which Bob Marley was a member and one of the larger sects within Rastafari, which now accepts the entirety of Christian Scripture. They also emphasize Jesus of Nazareth and hold that it is through him that all people are saved.[107] Nonetheless, members are still alienated from the established church and continue to feel the impact of Babylon. Rastas challenge organized Christians as to what they see as the hypocrisy of those,

> Christians who claim to practice love while justifying many forms of oppression of those who uncritically accept many aspects of Westernisation in the name of their faith yet condemn indigenous black forms of expression as un-Christian.[108]

In closing, and within the " developing doctrinal" belief of Rastafari's understanding of Haile Selassie as divine (that which is the theological element that causes the division within Christianity), one can recall how the people of the Old Testament had already grasped Rahner's combined theories of the supernatural existential and anonymous Christianity. They were able to hear God saying:

> Before they call I will answer (Isaiah 65:24),
> . . . I call you by your name,
> I surname you, though you do not know me.
> . . . I gird you, though you do not know me,
> that [humanity]may know, from the rising to the setting of the sun
> that, apart from me, all is nothing.[109]

NOTES

1. William L. Reese, *Dictionary of Philosophy and Religion* (Amherst: Humanity Books, 1996), 546.

2. Schubert Ogden, *The Reality of God* (New York: Harper & Row, 1966), 61ff.

3. Karl Rahner and Herbert Vorgrimler, *Dictionary of Theology* (New York: Crossroad, 1985), 360.

4. Ibid. OT and NT refer to the *Old Testament* and *New Testament* of the Judeo-Christian *Bible*. Ibid.

5. Ibid., 359.

6. Tielhard, *The Phenomenon of Man* (New York: Harper & Row, 1975), 294.

7. Ibid., 267. I place "dichotomy" for Teilhard's "'anti-personalist' complex."

8. Ibid., 310.

9. Thomas Pearl, "Dialectical Panentheism: On the Hegelian Character of Rahner's Key Christological Writings," *Irish Theological Quarterly* 42 (1975): 120.

10. Ibid., 127.

11. Karl Rahner, "The Theology of Symbol" in *Theological Investigations*, IV 9: 229.

12. G.W. Hegel, *Encyclopaedia of the Philosophical Sciences, The Logic* (Oxford: Clarendon Press, 1984), 147–48.

13. Karl Rahner, "Christology Within an Evolutionary View of the World" in *Theological Investigations,* V 8: 164.

14. Rahner, "Christology in the Setting of Modern Man's understanding of Himself and of His World" in *Theological Investigations,* XI 9: 224.

15. Mark Taylor, *GOD IS LOVE: A Study in the Theology of Karl Rahner* (Atlanta: Scholars Press, 1986), 227.

16. Ibid.

17. Karl Rahner, *Foundations of Christian Faith: An Introduction to the Idea of Christianity* (New York: Crossroad, 1992), 63.

18. Teilhard, *The Future of Man* (New York: Harper & Row, 1964), 12.

19. Hegel, *Encyclopaedia of Philosophical Sciences,* 71.

20. Teilhard, *Phenomenon of Man,* 31.

21. Rahner, "Christology Within an Evolutionary View of the World" in *Theological Investigations* V 8: 172.

22. Ibid., 177–78.

23. Ibid., 178.

24. Ibid., 178–79.

25. Ibid., 183.

26. Ibid.

27. Ibid., 20: 217.

28. Rahner, "Christology in the Setting of Modern Man's understanding of Himself and of His World" in *Theological Investigations* XI 9: 220.

29. Ibid., 225–26.

30. As mentioned in the Preface, this philosophy offers an introductory explanation to these philosophies so as to demonstrate the various expressions possible. A more expansive discourse on both Asian and African philosophies will have to be done when structural limits are not of concern.

31. Fritjof Capra, *The Tao of Physics: An Explanation of the Parallels between Modern Physics and Eastern Mysticism* (Boston: Shambhala Publications, 1991), 130.

32. Similar to the use of African philosophy and Rastafari in demonstrating similarities with Dialectical Incarnation, the use of Oriental philosophies does not mean that the terms of references are identical. The understanding of the Self among these philosophies is different. The similarities emerge in recognising the unity of all reality and that bi-polar difference can that still remain one.

33. Capra, *The Tao of Physics,* 85.

34. Ibid., 87.

35. Ibid.

36. Ibid., 88.

37. Ibid.

38. Ibid., 88–89.

39. Ibid., 89.

40. *Aum* is also spelled as *Om*. I will be using *Aum* because the three letters better represent the nature of the dialectic, which has three components, and the nature of the symbol, which has three curves.

41. The *Vedas* are a collection of ancient scriptures written by anonymous sages, the so-called Vedic "seers." There are four *Vedas,* which include the *Rig Veda,* the *Bhagavad Gita,* the *Upanishads* and other scriptural texts.

42. As will be elaborated later, in quantum mechanics and its wave function theory, it has been discovered that "physical" reality must be both idea-like and matter-like. The world is not as it appears and is not substantive in the usual sense of the word.

43. Capra, *The Tao of Physics,* 89.

44. Ibid., 130–31.

45. Ibid., 93.

46. Ibid., 94.

47. D.T. Suzuki, *On Indian Mahayana Buddhism* (New York: Harper & Row, 1968), 103.

48. Capra, *The Tao of Physics,* 99.

49. Ibid., 101.

50. Ibid.

51. Ibid., 102.

52. Ibid.

53. Ibid., 104.

54. Ibid.

55. Ibid.

56. Richard Hooker, *Yin and Yang, Chinese Philosophy* (http://richard-hooker.com/sites/worldcultures/GLOSSARY/YINYANG.HTM).

57. In having discussed the Ionian cosmologists early in Chapter One, this dialectical understanding of reality was being explained by Anaximenes own philosophy. See Hooker, *Chinese Philosophy.*

58. Capra, *The Tao of Physics*, 107.

59. Ibid.

60. Ibid., 131.

61. Ibid.

62. For a more complete theological and Christological understanding of incarnation in Rastafari see Martin J. Schade, "Christ the *Alpha* and the Rasta: A Reflection on Christology Within the Emergence of Rastafari" in *Caribbean Journal of Religious Studies* 17.1 (1996): 38–64.

63. Much more could be offered in demonstrating the importance of African philosophy for both Rastafari and Dialectical Incarnation when a word limit is not of concern. My apologies come with my brief and introductory discussion of African philosophy within the thesis. A more expansive discourse in this very important area of philosophy will be the objective in future research and publication.

64. In discovering the African roots of Rastafari I have also discovered that I could expand the African influences much more than offered in this thesis. In this philosophyI mention only those fundament aspects which indicate its influence on Rastafari as it is an expression of Dialectical Incarnation.

65. P.H. Coetzee and A.P.J. Roux, eds., *The African Philosophy Reader* (New York: Routledge, 1998), 138.

66. Ibid.

67. Ibid.

68. Coetzee and Roux, *The African Philosophy Reader,* 2nd ed. (New York: Routledge, 2003), 211.

69. Coetzee and Roux, *The African Philosophy Reader*, 1st ed., 138.

70. Ibid., 146.

71. Coetzee and Roux, *The African Philosophy Reader*, 2nd ed., 214.

72. Ibid., 213.

73. Coetzee and Roux, *The African Philosophy Reader*, 1st ed., 140.

74. For two informative articles which discuss the Hindu and East Indian influence on Rastafari and Jamaica see Ajai Mansingh and Laxmi Mansingh, "Hindu influences on Rastafarianism," *Caribbean Quarterly,* 1986, Monograph, 96–105; and Ajai Mansingh and Laxmi Mansingh, "The Impact of East Indiana on Jamaican Religious Thoughts and Expressions," *Caribbean Journal of Religious Studies*, 10.2 (April 1989): 36–52.

75. Mansingh and Mansingh, *Hindu Influences,* 110.

76. Ibid., 112.

77. I will not refer to Rastafarian*ism* because "No ism, no schism" is a Rastafari proverb, usually quoted to deny that there exists a religion called "Rastafarianism." Rastafari is not just another sect, or ideology, but is reality itself, ultimate and invisible. No ism, no schism. See "NO ISM, NO SHISM: The Rastafari Movement and Orthodox Christianity" by Norman Redington (Printed version of talk given at the 4th Conference on African-American and Ancient Christianity, Kansas City, MO, January 31, 1997).

78. Theo Witvliet, *A Place in the sun: An Introduction to Liberation Theology in the Third World* (New York: Orbis Books, 1985), 113.

79. Ivor Morrish, *Obeah, Christ and Rastaman: Jamaica and its Religion* (Cambridge: James Clark, 1982), 84.

80. Jack A. Johnson-Hill, *I-Sight: The World of Rastafari* (Metuchen, NJ: The Scarecrow Press, 1995), 23.

81. Esther Sellassie Antohin, "The phenomenon of Ras Tafari," Master's thesis (2004), http://www.angelfire.com/ak/sellassie/page5.html.

82. Johnson-Hill, *The World of Rastafari,* 23.

83. By the tern "natural" Rastas appear to mean everything in creation that has not been significantly tampered with or altered by humans.

84. Joseph Owens, *Dread—The Rastafarians of Jamaica* (Kingston: Sangster's Book Stores, 1976), 141.

85. Dennis Forsythe, *Rastafari: For the Healing of the Nation* (Kingston: Ziaka, 1983), 88.

86. Ibid.

87. Ibid.

88. Ibid., 88–89.

89. Owens, *The Rastafarians of Jamaica,* viii.

90. Ibid., 70.

91. Forsythe, *Healing of the Nation,* 91.

92. Ibid.

93. Ibid.

94. Ibid.

95. G. Herbert, Bruce May and M. Metzger, eds., *New Oxford Annotated Bible with the Apocrypha* (New York: Oxford University Press, 1977), Psalm 87:4–5.

96. Ibid., Psalm 76:2–3.

97. Forsythe, *Healing of the Nation,* 97.

98. Owens, *The Rastafarians of Jamaica,* xv-xvi.

99. Ibid., xvi.

100. Ibid.

101. Ibid., xv.

102. Ibid.

103. Ibid.

104. Karl Rahner, "Anonymous Christians" in *Theological Investigations*, VI 23: 394.

105. Ibid. When Rahner refers to "Christ," he means that Christ is the total incarnation of God in the world.

106. Rahner, "The One Christ and the Universality of Salvation" in *Theological Investigations,* XVI 13: 204–6.

107. Ian Boyne, "Jamaica: Breaking Barriers Between Churches and Rastafarians," *One World* 86 (May 1983): 33–34.

108. Ibid.

109. Herbert et al., *New Oxford Annotated Bible*, Isaiah, 45:4–6.

Chapter Four

Current Perspectives in Dialectical Incarnation

THE PAST AND THE PRESENT: UNDERSTANDING DIALECTICAL INCARNATION

The Ionian cosmologists started the evolutionary discovery of Dialectical Incarnation by the very question they asked and tried to answer: "What is the one stuff of the universe." In the hope to find that one stuff, hylozoism reveals that all of reality is alive, that inorganic matter is an illusion. Pythagoras understood that the substance of all things was number and expressed in music. The universe came forth out of chaos, seeking harmony and acquiring form. Pythagoras identified the cosmos as the harmonious order of reality. Heraclitus then opens one's vision to recognise that all of reality is in flux. Reality is a unity in diversity. One must be grateful to Aristotle for making it evident that there is never matter without form, nor form without matter. Plotinus needs to be appreciated in his recognition that external reality is one with God. Although Dialectical Incarnation is not an emanation, the desire to identify the cosmos with God is to discover Dialectical Incarnation. Nicholas of Cusa adds his contribution to Dialectical Incarnation in his understanding that God is all things through the mediation of the universe. He understands God dialectically, in that God is the *maximum* and the *minimum*, God is the centre and the circumference of the universe and God is the *coincidentia oppositorum*. Within a deeper analysis of what Nicholas offers in and through the incarnation of God, it becomes the human Self, the most significant incarnation, that is actually the centre of the universe; it is the Self in the world, in the cosmos, that is now understood as the otherness of God as the totality of reality. Giordano Bruno revived the doctrine of hylozoism and proclaimed that matter and spirit are two aspects of a single substance in which all opposites and all differences are reconciled. He offers the distinction, but not the separation, of the two dialectical aspects of God and nature as *natura naturans* and *natura naturata*. For Bruno, God and nature are understood as One.

Spinoza goes on to elaborate this theme and he unites the divine with the human. He understands the human person's nature as inherently striving for perfection and to be in harmony with the oneness of God. Like Bruno, Spinoza understands God and nature as one, but has developed the role of the human person as the centre of the universe, perfecting human nature within the entire nature of God and the world. Spinoza's contribution to Dialectical Incarnation is tremendous, but he is not the true prototype, because his philosophy ends up being an idealism, since he fails to "see" the full nature of incarnation in the world. Also, as explained earlier, he treats human passion as a burden that needs to be controlled, rather than a positive element in the nature of the human person. The passions and emotions of humanity are what make the human person so uniquely particular and so free. Granted, humanity must understand one's passions, but they must be recognized as being part of the very striving of humanity, the *conatus* of the human person.

G.W. Leibniz's contribution to this philosophy is that he reminds us that Dialectical Incarnation is a vastness of particular expressions. Spinoza highlights the monism and ideality of this philosophy, Leibniz highlights the pluralism and materiality of this same philosophy. Leibniz works endlessly in establishing his harmony of love, where there is a true unity in a plurality of diversity found in monads. One cannot forget the plurality and the diversity present in all of nature, all of God, and all of the "one stuff" of the universe.

Hegel's and Marx's contribution to this philosophy is that together they necessitate an identification of the synthesis of the two poles of idealism and materialism. With each philosopher understanding his own thesis as the ultimate "one stuff" of the universe, there is a failure to recognise a need in synthesising the two poles. In retrospect, the need to synthesize the dualism of the past entails developing a new vision so as to see the fullness of all reality. Kant is praised for bringing his antinomies into the world of reality, but he fails to bring the dialectic to the "thing in itself." Hegel brings the dialectic to the inner structure of the world, understanding that the totality of reality is an organic whole, which is seeking its *telos* in the Absolute, the *Geist*, which is Spirit. Unfortunately, the dialectic remains strictly idealistic. Marx demystifies the transcendence of the dialectic and gives it a historical materialistic expression. Marx takes the dialectical structure of Hegel and is able to identify the superstructure in the material, historical world. Both Hegel and Marx make tremendous contributions toward the philosophy of Dialectical Incarnation, but each is lopsided. Marx claims to put the dialectic on its "proper" side, inverting it so as to stand correctly within the totality of reality, but the dialectic remains lop-sided because his dialectic is exclusively material. Dialectical Incarnation balances the dialectic strife which has always been explained as a separation of spirit from matter. Hegel and Marx are each noble examples of the thesis, antithesis process within the dialectic, but together, they omit a synthesis for the ideal and material reality of all.

Pierre Teilhard de Chardin consistently promotes a new sense of *seeing*.[1] As stated, "the whole of life lies in that verb"[2] and "*nothing* here below is *profane* for those who know how to see".[3] Teilhard de Chardin razes the barrier which has separated spirit and matter, God and the world. He constantly testifies to the harmony of love found in all of creation, where "God-Love reaching self-fulfilment only in love…is nothing more nor less than a 'phylum of love' within nature".[4]

As a scientist and theologian, Teilhard is able to recognise and witness the unity of God and the world, spirit and matter. He calls all people "to see God everywhere, to see Him in all that is most hidden, most solid, and most ultimate in the world".[5] It is not surprising, then, that this intrinsic union of the world becomes even more evident when one examines recent discoveries of the New Physics and how Quantum theory reveals that there a basic oneness found in the entire universe.[6]

Karl Rahner's contribution to the philosophy of Dialectical Incarnation can be best discovered through the metaphysics he offers in demonstrating that the "incarnate word is the absolute symbol of God in the world".[7] It is the "dynamic unity-in-difference [that] is the pattern for the systematic coherence of Rahner's thought pattern".[8] Through his philosophy and theology of symbol he is able to formulate the metaphysics of the universe where God is love and the totality of reality. It is his insight of the human person as a "supernatural existential" that confirms the philosophy of the Self as the centre of the "infinite horizon" of the universe. Matter and spirit are the condition of the possibility of the incarnate world, in which the incarnate God unites the diversity of the world by God's own ground of being.

There are numerous recent journal articles which testify to the necessity of examining the predominant tenets within the philosophy of Dialectical Incarnation.[9] The first concern is finding a synthesis between seeming opposing poles. This is certainly addressed by Chin-Tai Kim in his article "Transcendence and Immanence." He states that

> the ideas of transcendence and immanence are not mutually exclusive but mutually determinative. All theologies and metaphysical systems that posit an ultimate reality must show its double aspect as both transcendent and immanent.[10]

After defining both terms and offering a historical development and use of them, he specifies that his interest is to "raise philosophical issues – issues about the nature and possibility of, not about the fact, of incarnation". He goes on to say

> the notion of incarnation is paradoxical. In becoming incarnate, in assuming forms of created being, the deity becomes for itself a being other than itself; the incarnating God is identical with, and at the same time different from, the incarnated God; the eternal, infinite non-corporeal being is, and simultaneously is not, temporal, finite and corporeal...A dialectical interpretation of Incarnation thus seems to be the one that recommends itself the most. Hegel did not invent dialectic; he only developed a dialectical system. The idea of dialectic had prefigurations in traditions East and West. [11]

With this dialectical understanding of reality Kim recognises that transcendence and immanence "are two fundamental polar modalities...[which] are relational notions that relate the ground with the ground of beings". [12] If we are philosophizing the nature and possibility of the incarnate God in the world, Kim makes it clear that the

> old parochial picture of philosophy as a self-sufficient comprehension of reality should be discarded...A maximal reflectivity of human thought, if any such is possible, must consist in a synthesis, or more modestly, an attempt at a synthesis, of fragmentary disciplinary visions. [13]

It is this very synthesising of seeming opposing poles of philosophy that has evoked the philosophy of Dialectical Incarnation, which relates the ground (Nature), with the ground-of-beings, that is present in the totality of reality.

In the attempt to find a synthesis between seeming opposing poles another recent article proposes a "Double-Aspect Monism." This theory proposes that the mind and the body are different components of a single neutral substance. In this metaphysics "neither mind nor body exists separately as such but instead there is only one kind of stuff with mind and body as its manifestations". [14]

Although the attempt is being made to synthesise, this theory falls short in comparison to Dialectical Incarnation, because it limits "objects" to only living bodies. Hylozoism and Quantum Physics have revealed that all matter has "mind." This is a form of panpsychism. Panpsychism pertains to all material objects, whereas dual-aspect monism applies merely to objects that are living bodies. Caroll Nash explains that in being monistic

> dual-aspect theory shares with idealism and materialism the attractiveness of there being only one substance which may afford it greater comprehensibility, explanatory economy and aesthetic simplicity. It may be superior to idealism in its acknowledgment of physical happenings and to materialism in its recognition of mental events. [15]

Caroll Nash has offered a way to resolve the mind/body problem with a synthesis of two poles. However, as has been demonstrated, her theory is unable to include the "totality" of all reality. For Dialectical Incarnation, all the earth is incarnate and alive not just "living bodies." With the failure of Double-Aspect Monism we must thus search for another alternative attempt in uniting our seeming opposing poles of spirit and matter.

The dualism of the Western world-view has posed significant problems, because it has fostered problematic and hierarchically arranged aspects of the world into bipolar categories, i.e., human versus nature, culture versus nature, male versus female, symbolic versus material, reason versus emotion, mind versus body, civilized versus primitive, and production versus reproduction. According to Sherrie Steiner-Aeschliman, these bimodal categories represent reifications rather than accurate depictions of reality.[16] Dualism encourages actors to favour one side of the dualism over and against the other. The denigrated categories are said to be exploited in the service of the prioritised categories and an understanding of a holistic, united reality is lost. The lopsided nature of Hegel and Marx remains even within dualism because one category is favoured over the other.

Although dualism can be problematic, Steiner-Aeschliman indicates that accepting monism does not resolve the problem. Simply argued, monism does not resolve the problems found in dualism and is not the sole alternative to dualism. Another world view is possible, one that incorporates monistic and essential dualistic components directly into an understanding of the cosmos and the humans who act in it.

A possible alternative is immanent dualism. By using the term "immanent" one is indicating that there is a world view that draws "attention to shared histories, experiences and realities".[17] In contrast to holism, which suggests a "unity of experience", "immanent dualism is pluralistic".[18] Steiner-Aeschliman states that

> [t]he purpose of describing this world view is to provide a framework for understanding patterns of organization of the world not yet adequately recognized. It describes patterns of organization as interfaces of symbolic and material processes, and suggests a basis for the societal reorganization of late industrialism in response to global environmental change.[19]

When trying to grasp the meaning of immanent dualism one discovers that it is "multidimensional and may be described using a metaphor of voices".[20] If one views science as a "voice of the material world," then religion would then be "a voice of the symbolic world".[21] Immanent dualism, similar to Dialectical Incarnation, synthesizes these two bimodal perspectives and envisions a "world view where there is constant conversation between religion and science." In immanent dualism the two retain "their distinct voices while engaging in dialogue and interdependent integration of thought".[22] Immanence suggests that "the divine and the material are self-referential, connected, united and indivisible in a creative and diverse reality", while dualism "refers to the way in which the divine and the material are distinguishable".[23] The article continues by explaining that

> the unity of immanence and dualism in one world view emphasizes how dialogue between religion and science includes within a single paradigm both similarities and differences—a paradigm that lies between absolutism and relativism, insisting that the cosmos is both rationally intelligible yet inherently contingent.[24] Immanent dualism is a processual and multidimensional world view (i.e., pluralistic, historical, narrative and evolving) rather than mechanistic, linear and unidimensional.[25]

Immanent dualism attempts to do what Dialectical Incarnation does by indicating that there are distinctions in reality, yet those distinctions are not separate. The former recognises the "similarities and differences in one world view in a manner that produces unique distinctions which cannot be made by either monism or dualism" alone.[26] As immanent dualism seeks a "totalizing world view," it "promotes diverse development of both theology and science" while it struggles from having a lop-sided leaning toward either. "Immanent dualism promotes the complementarity rather than the compartmentalization of science and religion".[27] Compartmentalization separates science and theology against each other as polar categories in a way that they do not interact. However, [c]omplementarity brings the unique perspectives of science and religion together and "seeks to understand how both can be a faithful and consistent insight into the same reality".[28]

Dialectical Incarnation, as has been demonstrated earlier, could be called a type of "monism," in that all of reality is one substance. It could also be called a type of "dualism," in that it maintains the distinction between two opposing poles. However, the fact is that Dialectical Incarnation is neither a classical monism nor a classical dualism, it is a synthesis of a dialectical reality. The theory of Immanent Dualism is to be praised for its attempt in synthesising monism with dualism, but it fails because it remains a dualism. Although complementarity is operative, it separates two distinct poles. Hence, one must move on in the quest to find different perspectives in explaining and confirming the philosophy of Dialectical Incarnation.

ALFRED NORTH WHITEHEAD: PROCESS PHILOSOPHY

When seeking support, and/or critique, from contemporary philosophers for the philosophy of Dialectical Incarnation, one must examine Alfred North Whitehead's (1861-1947 C.E.) process philosophy. In doing so, one can quickly discover similarities in the two perspectives of reality. Process philosophy is a metaphysics and an understanding of reality, just as is Dialectical Incarnation. The concern of process philosophy is primarily with understanding and explaining the totality of reality within certain terms of reference. Accordingly, natural existence consists in terms of "processes" rather than "things", that is, process philosophy "sees" ways of change rather than "fixed entities". It looks at the synthesis of "Becoming", rather than the poles of "Being" and "Non-being". Change is not an illusion, but is the foundation of metaphysical reality since process constitutes the essential aspect of everything that exists. Change of every sort, i.e., physical change, organic change and psychological change, is the pervasive and predominant feature of the real world. If change is "Becoming," as it is, the similarity with Dialectical Incarnation is already identified, for in the later, it is the "change" of the process of synthesis which is the essential aspect of all reality.

Like Dialectical Incarnation, process philosophy began with the Pre-Socratic philosophers, especially with Heraclitus of Elea, who is universally recognized as the founder of process philosophy.[29] Heraclitus identifies the "one stuff" of the universe as fire. Fire is constantly changing and is extremely short lived, yet, for Heraclitus it is still the basis of all reality. "This world-order . . . is . . . an ever living fire, kindling in measures and going out in measures."[30] The substantial "one stuff" of the totality of reality is not material, rather the "one stuff" is a "process" and that "process" is "fire". Heraclitus did not see reality as a composite of things but rather as a process of constant change. Philosophy, and specifically metaphysics, must no longer understand nature as consisting of permanent things, i.e., substances. The totality of reality is not comprised of things but rather of fundamental forces and processes. Process is fundamental. A river is not static, but a constant movement. The sun is also not a static entity but a blazing fire. Nature is process, activity and change. Heraclitus understood reality as ever flowing. Even Plato, who favoured the enduring and changeless "ideas" existing in a realm wholly removed from material reality, came to locate his exception by explaining that the material, concrete and changing things *participate* in the changeless and eternal Forms of the *real* world.

Whitehead initially called his metaphysics the "Philosophy of Organism" or "Organic Realism." In its evolution it became known as process philosophy. In his explanation of the "Category of the Ultimate," Whitehead uses a concept which is central to his school of thought, namely *concrescence*. Concrescence unites the terms of "creativity," "many," and "one." It is constructed from the prefix *con*, symbolizing "we", *cre* from "create" and *scence* from sense, or the "scene", that which is seen. The "production of novel togetherness" of all "occasions of experience" is the ultimate notion embodied in the term "concrescence".[31] The present is given by a concrescence of subjective forms. Humans are multiple individuals, but there are also multiple individual agents of consciousness operant in the construction of the given. Whitehead's "subjective forms" complement "eternal objects" in his metaphysical system. Eternal objects are Plato's archetypal forms. In *Process and Reality*, Whitehead proposes that his "organic realism" or "organism" be used in place of classical materialism. [32]

The metaphysics of process philosophy proposes that the ingredients of the "one stuff" of the universe are "occasions of experience". What people commonly think of as concrete objects are actually successions of "occasions of experience". Occasions of experience can be collected into groupings of many smaller occasions of experience. [33] According to Whitehead, everything in the universe is characterized by experience, and this is not the same as consciousness. The mind-body duality does not create a problem because the "mind" is simply seen as a highly developed kind of experiencing.

GOD AND THE WORLD

The final chapter of *Process and Reality* is titled "God and the World". This aspect of process philosophy is of principal importance for us. As we will discover, Whitehead clearly views the world from a dialectical perspective. The predominant dialectical influence is his fundamental process of Becoming, which is the synthesis of Being and Non-Being. The dialectical process is one of constant strife between seemingly opposing entities. Whitehead testifies to the reality of God and the World as being comprised of seeming contradictions. He states:

> It is as true to say that God is permanent and the World fluent, as that the World is permanent and God is fluent.
> It is as true to say that God is one and the World many, as that the World is one and God many.
> It is as true to say that, in comparison with the World, God is actual eminently, as that, in comparison with God, the World is actual eminently.
> It is as true to say that the World is immanent in God, as that God is immanent in the World.
> It is as true to say that God transcends the World, as that the world transcends God.
> It is as true to say that God creates the World, as that the World creates God.
> God and the World are the contrasted opposites in terms of which Creativity achieves its supreme task of transforming disjoined multiplicity, with its diversities in opposition, into concrescent unity, with it diversities in contrast. In each actuality there are two concrescent poles of realization. [34]

For many theologians, the God of scholastic Christian theology is a strictly spiritual, individual being, removed from any sense of time and place. God is outside any type of change and process. Process theologians and philosophers, on the other hand, take a fairly radical (however, not heretical) position of understanding God as having an active role in the spatio-temporal framework of the natural world. Dialectical Incarnation accepts this but claims more: God does not merely take an active role, but *is* the natural world and its spatial-temporal frame. Process philosophy envisions God as having a foothold within the overall process of reality, because this reality is, in fact, God's own creation. Process philosophy has God actively participating in the processes of the world, but this does not make God into a physical or material object or being. For Dialectical Incarnation, God is material and therefore physical, in the literal understanding of both terms. God is *carne,* God is flesh.

Although process philosophy is not a dualism, it certainly favours only one side, and that one side is the process of experience and the occasions of experience. In process philosophy, God is not part of the physical reality the world, but God does participate in the process of the world – everywhere touching, affecting, and informing its operations. This is so, because, for process philosophy, there is no "physical" reality other than occasions of experience. There is no matter in process philosophy. While not located in the physical world, God is still involved in the processes of the world. For process philosophers and theologians God does not control the world but merely influences it.

This is where any similarity stops and the definitive difference with Dialectical Incarnation emerges. For the latter, God is love and the totality of reality, not merely a persuading participant in the ongoing synthesis of a spiritual and material, transcendent and immanent, divine and human, world. In Dialectical Incarnation God needs and requires matter and humans so as to be God and matter and humans need God (as transcendent) so as to be matter and humans. This is not the case with process philosophy.

Process philosophy admits and "needs" particular concrete experience. Whitehead understands that humanity's concrete experience of the world is the instantiation of the composition of our general processes or experiences. A concrete process is always an instantiation of a general process. It is axiomatic in process philosophy that "to be a process is to be a process of a certain specifiable sort".[35] However to be particular, concrete and to be "physical" is not to be material for process philosophy, as it is for Dialectical Incarnation. Whitehead's God does "need" humans to be God, but not in the complete manner in which God needs humans and materiality in Dialectical Incarnation. Whitehead explains:

> Opposed elements stand to each other in mutual requirement. In their unity, they inhibit or contrast. God and the World stand to each other in this opposed requirement. God is the infinite ground of all mentality, the unity of vision seeking physical multiplicity. The World is the multiplicity of finites, actual-

ities seeking a perfected unity. Neither God, nor the World, reaches static completion. Both are in the grip of the ultimate metaphysical ground, the creative advance into novelty. Either of them, God and the World, is the instrument of novelty for the other.

In every respect God and the World move conversely to each other in the respect to their process. God is the primordial one, namely, [God] is the primordial unity of relevance of the many potential forms; in the process [God] acquires a consequent multiplicity, which the primordial character absorbs into its own unity. The World is primordially many, namely, the many actual occasions with their physical finitude, in the process it acquires a consequent unity, which is a novel occasion and is absorbed into the multiplicity of the primordial character. Thus God is to be conceived as one and as many in the converse sense in which the World is to be conceived as many and as one.[36]

Understood as such,

He [God] is the unlimited conceptual realization of the absolute wealth of potentiality. In this aspect, [God] is not *before* all creation, but *with* all creation. But, as primordial, so far is [God] from 'eminent reality,' that in this abstraction [God] is 'deficiently actual'-and this in two ways. [God's] feelings are only conceptual and so lack the fullness of actuality. Secondly, conceptual feelings, apart from complex integration with physical feelings, are devoid of consciousness in their subjective forms.[37]

For Whitehead, God's "sorrow," God's "feeling" is eminently related to humanity's feeling. It is humanity's "foolishness" in this incomplete, actual World, that brings about the "sorrow" of God and thus God "needs" humans to realize God's vision and complete God's actual occasions. But this is where God and the World remain. Whitehead speaks anthropomorphically and cannot grasp the fullness of Dialectical Incarnation. The God of Dialectical Incarnation does not "feel" with these human emotions. God is the not merely the "ground of all mentality" and God is not *"with"* all creation." Rather, God *is* these feelings, God *is* the ground of all mental and material reality, and God *is* all of creation. Process philosophy and theology sees God's relationship to the world in terms of a process of influence. God is not of the world but has an all-pervasive influence upon and within it. The God of Dialectical Incarnation is more than a process of influence for God is the totality of reality.

It is true that for process philosophy the actuality of reality is a synthesis of seeming opposing poles. Although this format in understanding reality is similar to that of Dialectical Incarnation, the "substance" of that reality differs. With this distinction, the God and the World of Whitehead's process philosophy falls short in being the God and the World of Dialectical Incarnation because of the understanding of the objective, material world.[38]

When establishing the foundation of the philosophy of Dialectical Incarnation it has certainly been beneficial to examine process philosophy and to recognise the number of similarities. Nevertheless, in the end, it is the understanding of the material, physical world that separates the two philosophies and which is the core of the difference. Dialectical Incarnation needs matter and wants matter to be the "all in all." Whitehead, with his strong empiricist' influence cannot give proper credit to that which deserves the credit, namely the *materiality* of physical entities. The format is very good but the content of that format is lacking an essential element. Process philosophy intentionally proceeds without the reality of the material world, and although it must be given high tribute and recognition, it offers only partial truth of the "all" of reality. For process philosophy, what a thing is consists in what it does. Material substances do nothing for Whitehead because they are not "occasions of an experience" and are only understood as "process linked terms."

This particular critique of process philosophy is documented in P. F. Strawson's influential *Individuals: An Essay in Descriptive Metaphysics.*[39] In it he explains that processism will eventually fail because physical objects, in particular, material bodies are necessary the individuality or particularity of any viable metaphysical position.[40] Strawson states that "we find that material bodies play a unique and fundamental role in particular identification".[41] As he sees it, processes will not do as basis for particular identification because: If one had to give the spatial dimensions of such a process, say, a death or a battle, one could only have the outline of the dying man or indicate the extent of the ground the battle was fought over.[42]

Strawson maintains that materiality is a necessary precondition for having knowledge of any particular entity.

Strawson's argument runs as follows:

> (P 1) For objective and identifiable particulars to be knowable, some items must be distinguishable from other co-existents, and reidentifiable over time.
> (P 2) These conditions can be met only by material objects, i.e., particulars with material bodies.
> (P 3) Processism rejects the existence of material bodies.

Therefore processism is untenable in metaphysics.

Whitehead's process philosophy, although insightful in the understanding of process in all reality, fails to see that the fullness of reality requires the inclusion of materiality in general, and material bodies in particular. Process is synthesis of two seeming opposing poles and process philosophy uses materiality only as an idea for process, but not as a distinct element of reality.

LOGICAL POSITIVISM AND DIALECTICAL INCARNATION

Besides being the forefront hallmark advocate for process philosophy, Alfred North Whitehead also co-authored with Bertrand Russell (1872-1970 C.E.) *Principia Mathematica*. With the contemporary developments in logic and the foundations of mathematics occurring within philosophy, another philosophical movement emerged, viz. Logical Positivism. Without going into great detail it would be amiss not to make reference to it and ask the question, "What would a Logical Positivist say with regard to the philosophy of Dialectical Incarnation?" This question is especially significant, because Logical Positivism rejects statements about metaphysics, theology and ethics as being unverifiable. These academic disciplines are not a part of serious cognitive thinking. To have meaning, a given statement has to be connected to either empirical data or analytic truth. Logical Positivism aims at connecting philosophy more closely to science, and vice versa. The ultimate basis of knowledge rests upon public experimental verification rather than upon personal experience. It sees metaphysical statements and theological doctrines not as false but meaningless. The "great unanswerable questions" about substance, causality, freedom, and God are unanswerable because they are not genuine questions at all. Logical Positivism holds the position that all genuine philosophy is a critique of language; and its result is to show the unity of science. All genuine knowledge about nature can be expressed in a single language common to all the sciences.

Positivists believe that all knowledge is based on logical inference from simple "protocol sentences" grounded in observable facts.[43] If science is the centre of attention for Logical Positivism, a methodology of science finds it difficult to reconcile itself with metaphysical statements or theological speculations because these concepts are usually encapsulated, closed and dogmatic and it would be a waste of time to foster any form of valid argumentation. Metaphysical statements and theological doctrines are neither verifiable nor confirmable, hence they are rejected. This could be true if metaphysics is viewed as merely transcendental and abstract assertions, like "The Absolute is beyond time", or if theology was strictly confined to formally established dogmatic principles, like "God is Triune". Dialectical Incarnation has indicated that neither is the case. The metaphysics of our philosophy is very much interwoven with science, especially physics, and its theology is open to the "infinite horizon" of the world. Neither is encapsulated nor dogmatic and to confine all philosophy and theology to only that which is scientifically verifiable is limiting both. Dialectical Incarnation, like the *Aum* of Hinduism, the *Tao* and Rastafari is fluid and inclusive.

The main tenets of Logical Positivism pertain to the meaningfulness and verifiability of statements. Accordingly, a proposition is empirically significant only if it is verifiable. A proposition is verifiable only if it is confirmed by observation or can be deduced from other propositions which are verifiable. Therefore, statements that are not verifiable are cognitively meaningless although they may possess emotive meaning.

At the beginning of the *Tractatus*, Ludwig Wittgenstein (1889-1951 C.E.) wrote, "The world is all that is the case. The world is the totality of facts and not of things."[44] The Vienna Circle, the founders of the movement of Logical Positivism, shifted verificationism onto Wittgenstein's "picture theory of meaning" so as to postulate, what they called, the Verification Principle.[45] Within the realm of theology their greatest challenge toward religion was in their rejection of metaphysics.[46]

According to A.J. Ayer (1910-1989 C.E.), the principle of verifiability is a criterion of meaning that requires every empirically significant statement to be capable of being verified. Statements whose truth or falsehood cannot be verified or that are not tautological are meaningless. Statements that have no literal meaning may have an emotional meaning, but they do not express propositions that can be analytically or empirically verified. Analytic statements are tautologies (they are true by definition, necessarily true, and true under all conditions). The truth of analytic statements depends only on the meaning of their constituent elements, and it does not depend on confirmation by empirical testing.[47]

Synthetic statements (including empirical propositions) assert or deny something about the real world. The validity of synthetic statements is not established merely by the definition of the words or symbols that they contain. If a synthetic statement expresses an empirical proposition, then the significance of the proposition is established by its empirical verifiability. Statements that are not significant cannot be expressed as propositions. Every proposition is either true or false, because every empirical proposition asserts or denies something about the real world.

In short, a statement is factually meaningful if, and only if, it is empirically verifiable in theory or in practice. A statement is literally meaningful if, and only if, it expresses a proposition.[48] Literal meaning is a property of statements that are either analytically or empirically verifiable.

Ayer also makes a distinction between verification in practice and verification in principle. The theoretical or practical verifiability of a proposition depends on whether the proposition is verifiable in principle or verifiable in fact. Propositions for which we do not have a practical means of verification may still be meaningful if we can theoretically verify them.

The implications which the Verification Principle has for those who argue for the existence of God, or promote a philosophy like Dialectical Incarnation should be obvious. The statement "God is love and the totality of reality" is unverifiable and unfalsifiable. One cannot say, according to the verifiability principle, that it is true or false. Accordingly, God is not a "fact" which is observable or measurable. One can not observe God, nor empirically measure God in any direct way. Logical Positivism recognises that theology might be considered by many people to be a science (Aristotle and the Scholastic philosophers and theologians called it the "queen of sciences"), but to say that God is an object which can be observed and studied the way in which one can observe other human beings or any physical entity is to misapprehend the nature of things.[49] God *qua* God is not observable. Therefore, the statement, "God is love and totality of reality" has no meaning from a Logical Positivist's perspective. Any metaphysical or theological use of the word "God" is void of meaning and "... as it is not given a new meaning, it becomes meaningless".[50] Arguing for or against the existence, or non-existence is nonsensical. The debate is usually divided into theism, atheism, agnosticism and now non-theism. In non-theism God is merely a human linguistic construct. These terms or positions have emerged from the postulation that the mere statement "God exists" has some form of meaning. The theist will say the statement is true. The atheist will say that the statement is false. The agnostic may say it is true or may say it is false. The fact is that one cannot tell. Finally, the non-theist will say that the statement is true under certain conditions.[51] If Logical Positivists claim that the statements that "God exists" or that "God is love and the totality of reality" are meaningless, then these very positions are also meaningless. As a result, Logical Positivists are neither theists, atheists, agnostics nor non-theists. They have dismissed the argument concerning the existence of God entirely.

Regardless of any attraction Logical Positivism may have for an anthropocentric perspective of religion and related concerns, there are still other implications when maintaining the Verification Principle. When Logical Positivism rejects metaphysics, for example, one cannot, therefore, say anything about ethics nor offer an ethical foundation upon which one would live. Ethical sentences do not express propositions; as such, ethics is understood as emotive. Ethical claims have meaning only insofar as they offer something which could in fact be observed, empirically tested and thereby be verified. A statement like "It is good" is verified only by observing the behaviour of the person who says it, and consequently one has moved into a form of ethical relativism. The statement "It is good" refers to nothing with permanence nor to anything beyond the mere occasion of the claim. To make the statement "It is good" is saying nothing more than saying "Wow!" Ethical statements have no cognitive content; they are merely functional and emotional.

The Verification Principle has already been criticised in two major ways. The first criticism is that the theory cannot "practice was it preaches." When asking the question "What is the meaning of 'meaning'?" one is making a metaphysical statement because there is a meaning which goes beyond the statement. The second criticism is the problem of verification, itself. If statements are meaningful only in so far that the content of the statement can be verified, what does one do with "quarks" and "black holes." Scientists "verify" that there are such entities, yet they are not observable? In response to this criticism, Logical Positivists has allowed for what they call "indirect verification." This type of "verification" is not through direct observation, but then one is on a slippery slope. If scientific laws cannot be proven true via concrete observation, but are permitted via indirect verification, then theological, metaphysical and ethical statements must also be allowed to have meaning. For an outsider, it is difficult to understand how the Verification Principle can be liberal and therefore open enough to include scientific statements but closed and rigid enough to exclude metaphysical, theological and ethical ones.[52]

It would seem obvious from what has been explained that Logical Positivists would reject Dialectical Incarnation. "God is love and the totality of reality" is not verifiable from a scientific observational analysis, because of its infinite horizon in understanding and explaining God and the world.

In response, an advocate of Dialectical Incarnation would indicate that science has evolved and continues to evolve. The science of the new physics is able to verify certain things which are not observable. Quantum mechanics has demonstrated that atomic physics cannot predict what will happen when it delves into the subatomic world. Science, as it was understood before quantum mechanics, would say that it can predict certain things happening, e.g., the apple is always going to fall from the tree. As such, Newtonian physics would say, "If such and such is the case now, then such and such is going to happen next." Quantum mechanics says, "If such and such is the case now, then the *probability* that such and such is going to happen next is ...(whatever it is calculated to be)." Scientists of the new physics can never know with certainty what will happen to the particle that they are "observing." All that they can know is the probabilities for it to behave in certain ways.[53]

Gary Zukav explains it well. Contrary to Newtonian physics, quantum mechanics tells us that our knowledge of what governs events on the subatomic level is not nearly what we assumed it would be. It tells us that we cannot predict subatomic phenomena with any certainty. We only can predict their probabilities.[54]

If Logical Positivists contend that theology or religion is meaningless because it is unverifiable, I again turn to what Gary Zukav says.

> Acceptance without proof is the fundamental characteristic of western religion. Rejection without proof is the fundamental characteristic of western science. In other words, religion has become a matter of the heart and science has become a matter of the mind. This regrettable state of affairs does not reflect the fact that, physiologically, one cannot exist without the other. Everyone needs both. Mind and heart are different aspects of *us*.
> The Wu Li Masters know that "science" and "religion" are only dances, and that those who follow them are dancers. The dancers may claim to follow "truth" or claim to seek "reality," but the Wu Li Masters know better. They know that the true love of all dancers is dancing.[55]

The advocate of Dialectical Incarnation would say to the Logical Positivist: your logic is correct, your means of observing and measuring is correct, your verifying is correct, to the extent that you can verify the things you do, but you fail to *see* beyond the mere empirical world. Reality is dialectical and empirical observation is not the sole manner in which one can offer a proper philosophy of that reality. Reality is supernatural even though one can empirically observe only the natural.

THE NEW PHYSICS

In quantum mechanics and its wave function theory, it has been discovered that "physical" reality must be both idea-like and matter-like. As such, the world is not as it appears.[56] The world is not substantive in the usual sense of the word. But the world is not completely idea-like either. The Copenhagen Interpretation of Quantum Mechanics states that what humanity perceives to be physical reality is actually one's cognitive construction of it. Within the purpose of breaking down the illusion of a dualistic world present in the philosophy of Dialectical Incarnation, it is worth quoting a physicist himself. Henry Stapp makes it clear.

If the attitude of quantum mechanics is correct, in the strong sense that a description of the substructure underlying experience more complete than the one it provides is not possible, then there is no substantive physical world, in the usual sense of this term. The conclusion here is not the weak conclusion that there *may* not be a substantive physical world but rather that there definitely is not a substantive physical world.[57]

This claim that the "physical" world is not physical was first labelled as preposterous, totally remote from experience and thus it was discarded.[58] Too, the experimental evidence itself is incompatible with our ordinary ideas about reality. But physicists are merely the newest members of a sizable group which have always held such views.

It is interesting that this new physics, and its quantum theory, has also been a significant contribution to process philosophy. The traditional understanding of an atom is based on the principle that atoms cannot be cut up or broken into smaller parts. "Atom-splitting" is, therefore, a contradiction in terms. According to this interpretation, it is here that the downfall of classical atomism was brought about by the dematerialization of physical matter in the wake of the quantum theory. Quantum theory teaches that, at the micro level, what was normally understood as a physical "thing", is itself no more than a "statistical pattern, a stability wave in a surging sea of process".[59] Fritjof Capra, as did Gary Zukav earlier, explains it as such.

At the sub-atomic level, matter does not exist with certainty at definite places but rather shows 'tendencies to exist', and atomic events do not occur with

certainty at definite times and in definite ways, but rather show 'tendencies to
occur'. ...All the laws of atomic physics are expressed in terms of these
probabilities. We can never predict an atomic event with certainty; we can
only say how likely it is to happen.
Quantum theory has thus demolished the classical concepts of solid objects
and of strictly deterministic laws of nature. At the subatomic level, the solid
material objects of classical physics dissolve into wave-like patterns of probabilities, and these patterns, ultimately, do not represent probabilities of things,
but rather probabilities of *interconnections*... Quantum theory thus reveals a
basic *oneness of the universe*. It shows that we cannot decompose the world
into independently existing smallest units. As we penetrate into *matter*, nature
does not show us any isolated 'basic building blocks', but rather appears as a
complicated *web of relations* between the various parts of the *whole*.[60]

Quantum theory has not brought about the demise of matter, as process
philosophy wants to believe. Rather, it has brought what is traditionally
labelled as "matter" to a more holistic understanding. Quantum theory has
shown that what we call "matter" is really more than "things" and "solid
bodies." The condition, or the concept, of matter is one aspect, and a necessary aspect, in understanding incarnation. The conditions of the possibility of
spirit and matter are united as one. There is no such thing as prime matter as
Aristotle testifies. Hylozoism has indicated that all matter is alive. What
quantum theory is indicating is that "solid material objects" have a sense of
non-material wave-like patterns. The similarity to process philosophy is evident. The difference from Dialectical Incarnation is that process philosophy
does not recognise matter in any form. Dialectical Incarnation, and quantum
theory, admits of matter but understands matter in a broader, more complete
perspective. Matter is spiritual and relational, not merely comprised of solid
objects.[61]

The significance of quantum theory is that the universe is one and is
based on relations and interconnections. All of reality is a web of oneness.
The distinctions between particulars and waves, between matter and spirit
and between nature and humans, can be made conceptually, but all of reality
is actually one. This is why "particulars can be waves at the same time" and
that in "atomic physics, we can never speak about nature without, at the same
time, speaking about ourselves".[62]

When a philosophy interprets and teaches that the new physics has demolished matter, as process philosophy does, one needs to understand Albert
Einstein's (1879-1955 C.E.) theory of relativity. Einstein's general theory of
relativity thus completely abolishes the concepts of absolute space and time.
Not only are all measurements involving space and time relative; the *whole*
structure of space-time depends on the distribution of *matter* in the universe.[63]

The significance of the new physics for our philosophy continues in the recognition that the reality of nature and physics is dialectical, or paradoxical. Capra explains:

> Every time the physicists asked nature a question in an atomic experiment, nature answered with a paradox, and the more they tried to clarify the situation, the sharper the paradoxes became. It took them a long time to accept the fact that these paradoxes belong to the intrinsic structure of atomic physics, and to realize that they arise whenever one attempts to describe atomic events in the traditional terms of physics...The subatomic units of matter are very abstract entities which have a dual aspect. Depending on how we look at them, they appear sometimes as particles, sometimes as waves; and this dual nature is also exhibited by light which can take the form of electromagnetic waves or of particles. [64]

Gary Zukav continues when he explains how the nature of reality is both "idea-like" and "matter-like." The physical aspect of reality is far from abolished. Quantum theory has given humanity a "complete description" of reality. The wave function of the new physics is a description of *physical* reality. That which the wave function describes is both "idea-like" and "matter-like". [65] The world does not appear in a manner in which the wave function of quantum theory is dematerialising physics. On the contrary, "the wave function represents something that partakes of *both* idea-like and matter-like characteristics". [66]

Whitehead and process philosophy have demonstrated that the physical is not material. Dialectical Incarnation and quantum theory, on the other hand, state that the physical is both "matter-like" and "idea-like." Besides confirming the dialectical nature of reality, Zukav's explanation of the new physics also confirms that all reality is one and we cannot separate that which "appears" to be isolated entities. When describing the notion of "Development in isolation," which is used in quantum mechanics, he explains that it is *we* that create the separation. The "isolation" is only an idealization for observational purposes of the "region of preparation" and the "region of measurement." One may call this situation "'isolation', but in reality nothing is completely isolated, except, perhaps, the universe as a whole (What would it be isolated from?)". [67] When describing how this situation happens Zukav demonstrates that a "photon" seems to be isolated from the fundamental unity, but it is only appearing "isolated" because *we* are studying it. He explains: Photons do not exist by themselves. All that exists by itself is an unbroken wholeness that presents itself to us as webs (more patterns) of relations. Individual entities are idealizations which are correlations made by us. [68]

Henry Stapp goes on to elaborate that according to quantum mechanics the physical world is...not a structure built out of independently existing unanalyzable entities, but rather a web of relationships between elements whose meanings arise wholly from their relationships to the whole.[69]

Everything in the universe, including and especially humans, are actually parts of one all-encompassing organic pattern and no one part of the pattern is ever really separate from it or from each other.[70]

The new physics has supported the fact that all of reality is one, and that in that oneness there are the dialectical aspects that are matter-like and idea-like (matter and spirit) and inseparable. But there is more wisdom being discovered by the new physics that also supports Dialectical Incarnation's understanding of the Self as the centre of the universe. After centuries of trying to understand the nature of the world and its infinite horizon, scientists are still perplexed with their discoveries. "We are not sure," they tell us, "but we have accumulated evidenced which indicates that the key to understanding the universe is *you*".[71] The distinction between the "in here" and "out there" upon which science was founded is becoming blurred. This new vision is not only different from the way scientists viewed the world three hundred years ago, it is its opposite. The new physics informs us that an observer cannot observe without altering what he or she sees. Observer and observed are interrelated in a real and fundamental sense.[72]

NOTES

1. For a more elaborate and complete understanding of Teilhard's use of "seeing", see John A. Grim and Mary Evelyn Tucker, "An Overview of Teilhard's Commitment to 'Seeing' as Expressed in his Phenomenology, Metaphysics, and Mysticism", *Ecotheology: Journal of Religion, Nature & the Environment,* 10.2 (August 2005): 147–64.

2. Pierre Teilhard de Chardin, *The Phenomenon of Man* (New York: Harper & Row, 1975), 31.

3. Teilhard, *The Divine Milieu* (New York: Harper & Row, 1968), 66.

4. Ibid., 5. For a complete analysis of Teilhard's understanding of incarnation and love see Robert Faricy, "The Exploitation of Nature and Teilhard's Ecotheology of Love", *Ecotheology: Journal of Religion, Nature & the Environment* 10.2 (August 2005), 181–95.

5. Teilhard, *The Divine Milieu,* 46.

6. Fritjof Capra, *The Tao of Physics: An Explanation of the Parallels between Modern Physics and Eastern Mysticism* (Boston: Shambhala Publications, 1991), 68.

7. Karl Rahner, "The Theology of Symbol" in *Theological Investigations* (Baltimore: Helicon Press, 1966), IV 9:237.

8. Donald W. Musser and Joseph L. Price, eds., *A New Handbook of Christian Theologians* (Nashville: Abingdon Press, 1996), 376.

9. One will see a vast variety of discussions which evolve around some of fundamental aspects of Dialectical Incarnation in the works cited.

10. Chin-Tai Kim, "Transcendence and Immanence," *Journal of the American Academy of Religion* 55.3 (Autumn 1987): 537.

11. Ibid., 541.

12. Ibid., 545.

13. Ibid., 548.

14. Carroll B. Nash, "Double-Aspect Monism," *The Journal of Religion and Psychical Research* 19.2 (96): 68.

15. Ibid., 70.

16. Sherrie Steiner-Aeschliman, "Immanent Dualism as an Alternative to Dualism and Monism: The World View of Max Weber," *Worldviews: Environment Culture Religion* 4.3 (2000): 235. The pagination of this article is not exact. The hard copy was not available and the electronic copy does not have the pages.

17. Ibid., 243.

18. Ibid.

19. Ibid., 244.

20. Ibid., 241.

21. Ibid., 244.

22. Ibid.

23. Ibid.

24. Ian Barbour, *Religion in an Age of Science: The Gifford Lectures* (San Francisco: Harper Collins, 1990), 84.

25. Steiner-Aeschliman ("Immanent Dualism", 244-45) makes reference to Barbour, *The Gifford Lectures,* 1.

26. Ibid., 245.

27. Ibid.

28. Ibid. Steiner-Aeschliman quotes Richard H. Bube, *Putting It All Together: Seven Patterns for Relating Science and the Christian Faith,* 168.

29. Alfred North Whitehead, *Process and Reality: An Essay in Cosmology* (New York: The Free Press, 1978), 208–9.

30. G.S. Kirk, J.E. Raven and M. Schofield. *The Presocratic Philosophers* (Cambridge: Cambridge University Press, 1990), 217.

31. Whitehead, *Process and Reality*, 21.

32. Ibid., 309.

33. Ibid., 287–88.

34. Ibid., 348.

35. Nicholas Rescher, *Process Philosophy: A Survey of Basic Issues* (Pittsburgh: University of Pittsburgh Press, 2000), 121.

36. Whitehead, *Process and Reality*, 348–49.

37. Ibid., 343.

38. Mark Taylor's *God is Love* goes through the process thought of Rahner in comparison to Whitehead and Charles Hartshorne in Chapter XI. His critique elaborates the thesis's general critique of saying that Whitehead's process philosophy lacks a necessary objective physical element of reality.

39. P.F. Strawson, *Individuals: An Essay in Descriptive Metaphysics* (London: Methuen & Co., Ltd, 1964.)

40. Ibid., 15–30.

41. Ibid., 56.

42. Ibid., 57.

43. Protocol sentence is a sentence consisting of an observation describing directly given experience. See A.J. Ayer, ed., *Logical Positivism* (New York, London: The Free Press, 1959), Chapter Nine, "Protocol Sentences", by Otto Neurath, 202; and Chapter Three, "The Elimination of Metaphysics Through Logical Analysis of Language", by Rudolf Carnap, 63; hereafter cited as Ayer, *Logical Positivism.*

44. Ludwig Wittgenstein, *Tractatus Logico-Philosophicus* (London: Routledge Classics, 2001), 5.

45. The Verification Principle was held to show that the meaning of a statement lies in its method of verification. For example, the statements, "All cats are cats," a tautology, and, "2 + 2 = 4," a mathematical fact, are necessary statements. They state nothing beyond the meaning expressed in the content of the statement and can be proved to be true. By contrast a statement such as, "It rained on Tuesday" needs to be empirically tested as to the truth of its content. This statement becomes true only if after testing it, it can be found to be true, e.g. "I saw it raining on Tuesday." Thus the Verification Principle locates sense and meaning with experience. Despite variations on the theme of the Verification Principle this was the distinctive doctrine of Logical Positivism.

46. See A.J. Ayer, ed. *Logical Positivism* (New York: The Free Press, 1959). *Language, Truth and Logic* (New York: Dover Publications, 1952) defines the verification principle of logical positivism. It discusses the uses and applications of the verification principle as an instrument of linguistic analysis.

47. Ayer, *Language,* 6.

48. Ibid., 15.

49. John N. Deely. *Four Ages of Understanding: the First Post–modern Survey of Philosophy from Ancient Times to the Turn of the Twenty–first Century* (Toronto: University of Toronto Press, 2001), 262.

50. Brian Davis. *An Introduction to the Philosophy of Religion* (Oxford: Oxford University Press, 1982), 3.

51. Ayer, *Language,* Chapter 6.

52. Paul Lafitte, *The Person in Psychology* (London: Routledge, 1999), 37. Ayer accepts indirect verification on the ground that direct reference to perception is too harsh a criterion for the propositions of natural sciences.

53. Gary Zukav, *The Dancing Wu Li Masters: An Overview of the New Physics* (New York: Harper Collins Publishers, 1979), 27.

54. Ibid., 28.

55. Ibid., 88. Albert Einstein makes a similar statement: "Human beings, vegetable, or cosmic dust, we all dance to a mysterious tune, intoned in the distance by an invisible piper." (*Saturday Evening Post* , 1929).

56. Ibid., 81.

57. Ibid., 82. Henry Stapp, *Mind, Matter and Quantum Mechanics* (Berlin, Heidelberg: Springer, 2009) quoted.

58. Ibid.

59. Nicholas Rescher, *Process Metaphysics: An Introduction to Process Philosophy* (New York: State University of New York Press, 1996), 98.

60. Capra, *The Tao of Physics,* 68.

61. Scholastic philosophers recognised this when dealing with the mind/body problem and the metaphysics of matter and form. Therefore, they made the distinction between what they called "spiritual matter" and "corporeal matter." Peter John Olivi is a Scholastic philosopher who makes this contrast. See his *Quaestiones in secundum librum Sententiarum* (Bibliotheca Franciscana Scholastica 4–6), edited by B. Jansen (Quaracchi: Collegium S. Bonaventurae, 1922–26). See Q51 appendix, 146).

62. Capra, *The Tao of Physics,* 68–69.

63. Ibid., 64.

64. Ibid., 66–67.

65. Zukav, *Dancing Wu Li Masters* , 81.

66. Ibid., 80.

67. Ibid., 72.

68. Ibid.

69. Ibid. Henry Stapp, "S-Matrix Interpretation of Quantum Theory" in *Physical Review* 3.6 (1971): 1303 quoted.

70. Ibid., 48.

71. Ibid., 92.

72. Ibid.

Chapter Five

Material-Existential Instantiations of Dialectical Incarnation—the Self, Ethics and Culture

UNDERSTANDING THE SELF WITHIN DIALECTICAL INCARNATION: THE SELF

Any philosophy, any theology, and any epistemology of the divine and the world must first begin with anthropology, for it is the human person who is the philosopher, the theologian, the believer, the searcher. Within anthropology, the starting point is the subject, the Self, of that human person, the agent in the search, the active condition in which the world and God is known. All understanding of the world and God is filtered through the Self. There is no other way of observing the world and God except through the Self. The world and "divinity" have no "meaning" outside the Self. In order to understand this philosophy it is paramount to have an understanding of Self. The Self becomes aware of Nature, which is the actual and only means in which the Self may have a glimpse of the mystery of God and the world.

We have discovered that seeming opposing elements, for example, matter and spirit, human and divine, are actually dialectically one. Too often, humanity wants to make the world and God into objects and then describe them. Epistemology inevitably involves metaphysics. When one seeks to know something, that something is an objective reality. That objective reality is explained through an understanding of metaphysics. Epistemology is only one side of any philosophical inquiry. Metaphysics is needed so as to describe the world and the being of God which humans seek to know. The necessary relationship between epistemology and metaphysics is demonstrated through the history of Western philosophy. The question of the Ionian cosmologists mentioned earlier, "What is the one stuff of the Universe?," was both epistemological and metaphysical. Plato's Divided Line is an obvious demonstration of this dualism: he divides the "real" world from the material and "unreal" world. The constant interaction continues in history through obvious examples: Plotinus's emanation and the physical world, the ontological as well as the cosmological arguments for the existence of God, and Descartes's statement, "*Cogito ergo sum.*" In the seeming endless search to know the world and to know God one always has to describe being. The dichotomy between the two are worthy ways of philosophizing reality, but it is crucial to realize that epistemology and metaphysics are only concepts in knowing, describing and experiencing the oneness of all in the totality of reality. Dialectical Incarnation, and the self within this understanding, intends to break down the dualism fortified by Descartes and understand the unity between idea (spirit) and matter, transcendent and immanent, subject and object, epistemology and metaphysics.

The discovery of the Self necessitates a discovery of Nature. A new cosmology has surfaced where not only does epistemology and metaphysics unite but now physics, metaphysics and mysticism are all seen as one reality. Often philosophers feel the need to debate the nature of the world and the nature of God in exclusive, limiting ways. It is now the time to "know" more dialectically, where the opposing force is not an enemy, but a friend. The strong individualism which began with the Modern era must be seen as intrinsically one with a dialectical harmony found with the common good and the total nature of the world. The task at hand is to discover the Self as an incarnational being, a person who is dialectically one with the universe and God. From this understanding, one discovers the nature of the universe and the nature of God more fully, recognizing that God needs the entire universe, all of creation, especially humans, to be God.

Dialectical Incarnation is not a philosophy of the mind, nor is it a philosophy of the body. Either side, alone, is too lopsided. Dialectical Incarnation can be best described as a philosophy of the heart. A philosophy of the heart is a synthesis of body and spirit. Body and spirit are the conditions of the possibility for the heart to love, for the heart to "know" and to feel the harmony of love which is the entirety of the universe, God and Self.

One knows things mentally through the mind, but the mind does not exist without the body. The body, with all its emotions, and the mind, with all its endless capacities, are united in a philosophy of the heart, a philosophy of incarnation, a philosophy of love and relationship. The heart is the symbol of the Self in its being with the world and with the divine. The Self is a particular, individual being. God "needs" these individual beings, that is, humans, as conscious, whole, incarnational entities that are present within the diversity of Nature (the world), expressing themselves as the infinite particularities of the "one love, one heart," which is the totality of reality. Humans are the necessary connection of the human and divine because we can be our own object.

René Descartes started a new movement which began with the *cogito*. The "I" of Descartes is a thinking being, aware of existing. An innate idea of God emerges within this I and the extended world is recognized and confirmed, but as opposing and dualistic. Descartes, with others, started modern philosophy with its individualism and egocentric movement. Descartes was right in starting with clear and distinct ideas of the thinking mind in establishing his philosophy. But the problem is that he started with the I as a thinking being rather than the Self as a whole being. The human person is not just a thinking being when he or she starts his or her earthly, living, thinking existence as a physical, biological, emotional, spiritual and whole being. It is with certainty that the human person is body and soul, and therefore an incarnational being. As an incarnational being one cannot escape one's emotions and one's passions, as Baruch Spinoza clarifies in his *Ethics*; but can be free with them and welcome them as the uniqueness of one's human personhood. Passions are testimonies to one's humanness, but humans, especially many Christians, have interpreted passions as evil. One needs, according to this earlier perspective, to eliminate them from one's human life. The human being is a whole, a body, a mind, and a heart; for any complete and certain knowledge of Nature, of God, and others, it is through the subjectivity of a whole being. Humanity has tried endlessly to rid itself of the "evil" body and share in the idea of God as the Divine Mind.

Within the dialectical understanding of the world and God, one begins with the imperative, "Know thyself!" The Self of the human person is intrinsically in relationship with the other. A psychological and philosophical description cannot omit an understanding of the "Self and the Other." A person is not a subject until he or she knows another so as to be in relationship. D.W. Hamlyn reminds us that "knowledge of oneself is impossible without an awareness of one's relationship to other people."[1] The relationship with the "other-than-self" involves other individuals, the community, the environment, Nature and God as the totality of reality. Tunde Bewaji also speaks directly of this communal nature of the Self when he says:

> Descartes crafted what is intrinsically the psychology of the Western person, centring everything around and about the self, the ego consciousness and the individual identity. He successfully pioneered the making of reality self-determined, knowledge is personal, and morality ego-located. On the contrary, there are other cultures in which it is insane, arrogant and irresponsible to build all "knowledge," reality, morality, social constructs around the lone self. In these cultures, in their primordial expression, the self has no meaning except as socio-culturally constructed. The important morale derivable from the above is represented in the saying *"I am, because we are"*; for there can be no

I had there been no preceding and nurturing *we*—ontologically, epistemologically, psychologically, logically, morally, socially, politically, etc. [2]

One is not a subject until one knows another so as to be in relation. This
displays the relationship with the "other-than-self," which is the community.
Knowledge of another also requires self-knowledge. Mbiti continues the
quote, saying, "I am because we are; *and since we are, therefore I am.*" [3] The
Self and the Other are intrinsically linked, both are necessary to be each.
Once self-knowledge and knowledge of the other are recognised, there is the
need for a "free relationship" with whatever or whoever the other is.

UNDERSTANDING THE SELF FROM
A PSYCHOLOGICAL PERSPECTIVE

Psychology, as a formal academic endeavour, emerged out of philosophy. [4] In
establishing a philosophy of incarnation in the world of today, it is beneficial
to understand the Self from a psychological perspective. This still may not be
an easy task. After all, William James, who is a psychologist, philosopher
and theologian, states that "the most puzzling puzzle with which psychology
has to deal," is the understanding of the Self. [5] A general description of the
Self can begin with the fact that the human Self is reflexive; it can become
the object of its own reflection. The Self can observe itself as a "being in the
world." [6] To reiterate, all understanding of the world is filtered through the
Self. There is no other way of observing the world except through the Self.
Moreover, in one's discovery one realizes that from late adolescence onward,
the Self is stable, it is persistent over time. There is an ongoing, stable unity
amidst the diversity of expressions of one's Self. There is something that
keeps David Hume's "bundle of impressions" together. From this diversity
one can understand the Self as also inclusive; it is a complex of ideas,
functions and experiences. Consequently, due to variety of personal and
interpersonal motives in one's life, the public display often does not match
the Self of which one is privately aware. There are phrases such as "the
authentic self," "the ideal self," "the actual self," "the social self," etc. The
question is "Which one is the genuine self?" One must be able to discover
this true self and understand when it is that one is not "true" to one's self or
to others.

The Self also has a character of uniqueness. The Self is a "consciousness
of a this-which-could-not be-replaced-by-another." [7] There is no other "me"!
Yet, the Self is also a this-in-relation-with-another. We are our relationships.
Erik Erikson's first stage in his psycho-social theory of development identifies the relationship of "trust versus mistrust" as the beginning "crisis" from
which the Self develops. Trusting one's Self and the first "other" in human

experience will be the foundation on which one subsequently relates to all others, the world, religion, God and technology.

The Self as Person: Individualism versus Personalism

Since the modern era, the dominant philosophy of Self has been individualistic, according to which each is basically "out for" him or herself, and so self-interest becomes the motivating power of each person. Individualism has led to an understanding of social life as a struggle among rivals, a "survival of the fittest."

The philosophy of the Self present within the philosophy of Dialectical Incarnation does not lead back to an individualism. With individualism's anti-social elements, its seeming unlimited selfishness, its lack of a genuine solidarity and its exploitation of the less powerful, one must find a remedy in another vision of the human person and the Self.[8] Another philosophy which favours our philosophy is that of *personalism*. Personalism suggests a philosophy centered on the human person. It distinguishes itself from individualism because of its relationship with the common good. The definition of the common good used by the philosophy of Dialectical Incarnation is:

> the sum total of all those conditions of social living—economic, political, cultural—which make it possible for women and men readily and fully to achieve the perfection of their humanity.[9]

Is any movement to centre life on a person taken individually in logical opposition to collective or community interests? For Dialectical Incarnation there is no logical opposition between the true interests of the person and those of the community or society. There is a natural harmony, a harmony of one love, one heart, in the totality of reality. This becomes more evident when one understands the claims of personalism, and the ways it differs from individualism.

Personalism represents a view which underlines the person's dignity prior to any and every social grouping. In the dynamism that characterizes the human person, it sees a call to self-fulfilment through the free expression of transcendent and lasting values. Personalism takes particular account of freedom: the freedom of the individual and the freedom of others. In this freedom it takes no less account of personal responsibility. In personalism,

> [t]he person is a whole, not however in a closed sense, since he [or she] must be open. The person is not a small god without doors or windows like Leibniz's monad, or an idol that does not see, nor hear, nor speak. The person tends by nature to social life and communion.[10]

Personalism maintains a keen awareness of the dignity and rights of the person, and invites everyone to defend them against any type of violation perpetrated against oneself or against others. It proposes that whoever recognizes his or her rights, must also be aware of his or her duties and responsibilities.

Personalism insists on duties towards others, and understands that the fulfilment of these duties also means personal development and self-fulfilment. The person grows as he or she enriches himself or herself through relations with others. These must be open and generously receptive relationships. Without this dynamic, the consequence is what Karl Marx called alienation, that which is both a social isolation and a human degradation.[11] In genuine personalism there is a natural alliance between the person, as an individual human being, and the community.

A personalist point of view does not simply propose "the centrality of the human subject," as is sometimes stated.[12] This could more easily express an individualistic view, but it is inadequate for personalism. Within a dualism between immanence and transcendence, individualism suggests immanence within the concept of the human person; while true personalism always leads to transcendence. Karol Wojtyla says, in his *Person and Community: Selected Essays*:

> In philosophical anthropology, transcendence—in keeping with its etymology *transcendere*—signifies a surpassing (a going-out-beyond or a rising-above), to the extent that this is verifiable in the comprehensive experience of the human being . . . Transcendence is the spirituality of the human being revealing itself.[13]

Personalism does not answer simply to one's Self. One's own inner resources are not adequate to fulfil him or herself. This capacity for self-transcendence leads one on to a new and higher level of existence. As such, personalism transcends any form of individualism, subjectivism, and egoism, because the community and the common good are always intrinsically considered.

In understanding the relationship between individualism and the community, it is worthwhile to hear what Karol Wojtyla also states in his *The Acting Person*. Within the individualist perspective:

> the good of the individual is treated as if it were opposed or in contradiction to other individuals and their good; at best, this good, in essence, may be considered as involving self-preservation and self-defense . . . For the individual the "others" are a source of limitation, they may even appear to represent the opposite pole in a variety of conflicting interests. If a community is formed, its purpose is to protect the good of the individual from the 'others.' This is, in broad outline, the essence of individualism.[14]

The Self of Dialectical Incarnation is a person in the world, a person with and in a community, a person who necessarily considers the common good in all of his or her actions.

The common good, for the individualist, is a concept to be ignored or at most to be understood in materialistic terms, reduced to standards of living and public services. The community and the common good are valued according to economic and ideological parameters, not according to sincerity, loyalty, fidelity, justice and mutual respect. Alasdair MacIntyre informs us that "modern society is indeed often . . . nothing but a collection of strangers, each pursuing his or her own interests under minimal constraints."[15] The tendency in an individualistic society is for persons increasingly to regard each other not only as strangers but as rivals. Everyone is held to be fundamentally selfish and an atmosphere of mutual distrust becomes generalized. To be "only concerned with me" is the only safe philosophy for the individualist.[16]

IDENTITY AS EGO VERSUS THE SELF

The ego can be described as having desires of a possessive or selfish origin. The ego's aims are to defend and strengthen one's self in relation to any perceived threats and needs; it is characterised by the words "me" and "mine."[17] The drives of the ego are suited to survival and growth in the physical and social world.

On the contrary, the Self of Dialectical Incarnation transcends selfish concerns and represents the lasting or inherent truth of the human being. The Self may be inherent in us, yet the manifestations of the Self are frequently covered over by those of the ego which actually hinders self-realisation. With the concern for understanding a comprehensive philosophy which unites humanity, divinity and the totality of reality, it is the Self who must be the agent, not the ego.

In being the agent in the world one must understand the self as a *whole*.[18] The word "oneself" happens to express the intuition of one Self as a unitary, and thus, consistent whole. It is the "I" which persists as the same single Self through time and through changing life circumstances. In our most basic understanding of the Self as a whole one cannot identify the Self merely with the body, for the body does alter greatly through life. Although the Self is not dependent on the body it is never separate from it. To speak of the Self is to speak of an "incarnational being," for it is materiality which gives the Self its particularity. The Self needs *carne*, the Self needs "flesh" or matter to be the Self. As an incarnational being, the Self synthesises spirit with matter. One is reminded that the human Self cannot exist without this synthesis in the same way in which Aristotle maintains that matter can never be without form and form can never be without matter. Yet, this leads us to a problem.

The Problem of Emergence

The problem with identifying the Self brings about the relationship between the mind and the body. A person is composed of both. How are the mental and physical aspects of a person related to one another? From what does the Self emerge? The problem of emergence evokes an attempt in explaining the appearance of consciousness (mind) in a physical being (body). How do the two meet? Did consciousness emerge from a physical realm?

The philosophy of Dialectical Incarnation, in fact, refutes the problem of emergence because reality is not a dualism. It is the dualism of Western philosophy which brings about the problem, because there has been a separation of spirit and matter, divinity and humanity, transcendence and immanence, subject and object. The Self is an intrinsic whole, and consciousness, as subject, is intrinsically and incarnationally united with the external world, as object. The problem of emergence exists only for those who understand reality as being dualistic. This dichotomy of the world is that which the philosophy of Dialectical Incarnation is identifying as an illusion. When one can understand one's Self as an incarnational being, the "problem" of emergence is no longer a problem. The "problem" for Dialectical Incarnation is to philosophically argue that "matter," body *qua* body, is actually the condition of the possibility for incarnation. "Spirit," mind *qua* mind, is the condition of the possibility for incarnation. These seeming separate entities are already emerged. There is no problem of emergence. It is time to understand the previous separation is a lack of "seeing," and a lack of understanding in a new dialectical and incarnational manner.

The dichotomy between the mind and the body has also been critiqued by the well known French Philosopher and Phenomenologist, Maurice Merleau-Ponty (1908–1961). In his *Phenomenology of Perception* he indicates that consciousness and perception cannot be experienced without the physical body. Descartes' *cogito* is no longer adequate. Merleau-Ponty states that "the thinking subject must have its basis in the subject incarnate."[19] The conscious experience of the Self is one where "I become involved in things with my body, they co-exit with me as an incarnate subject."[20] Alex Scott explains this when he says [b]odily experience gives perception a meaning beyond that established simply by thought. Thus, Descartes' cogito ("I think, therefore I am") does not account for how consciousness is influenced by the spatiality of a person's own body.[21]

Merleau-Ponty's phenomenology had discovered what Dialectical Incarnation is proclaiming. The mind and the body, although valid distinct concepts of consciousness cannot be separate in reality and in the perception and experience of that reality. Merleau-Ponty's understanding of the Self is one which is embodied, what he later calls the "incarnate *cogito*." Descartes' dualism of separating the body and the mind cannot account for the way in which human beings encounter and perceive the world. It is understood that our mind is woven into our body, which are in turn woven into the world. Merleau-Ponty reworks Descartes, arriving at his incarnate Cogito, in which mind, body, and world cannot be separated.[22]

Maurice Merleau-Ponty's influence by philosophers such as Karl Marx and Jean Paul Sartre has certainly brought the traditional understanding of the phenomenological experience into more dialectical perspective. Merleau-Ponty's critique of dualism brought forth what he described as "ontology of flesh" and which may be called "dialectical monism." He rejects the

> dualistic analyses of Being . . . and argues in favour of a mutual 'intertwining' (chiasme) of the lived body-subject and the world . . . Being made visible constitutes . . . "the flesh [chair] of the world."[23]

Now that Descartes' dualism of mind and body has been further critiqued it becomes more evident that a new paradigm is necessary. With the insights of Merleau-Ponty it is discovered that the thinking subject, or *cogito*, is unacceptable. The human Self is now an "incarnate *cogito*" and directly interwoven with other incarnate *cogitos* and the world itself. This is the incarnated being and the Self of Dialectical Incarnation of which the problem of emergence is resolved.

UNDERSTANDING THE SELF FROM A PHILOSOPHICAL PERSPECTIVE

The Romantic movement of the 19th century assumes that humanity has a true Self and that life is about discovering and expressing it. On the contrary, the post-modern approach assumes that there is no essential Self at all. The human person is either a product of the environment or the human person creates himself or herself through one's own free choices. Both Romantic and post-modern philosophies are designed to liberate people from various forms of oppression. Yet, the greatest possible form of oppression can be the falling victim to an anthropomorphism of God, superstitious religion and technology.

The temptation is to believe that one's personality and one's actions can be separated. However, the human being is a unity. Humans conform to the values of the crowd. They defend their selves by playing the roles publicly required of them while remaining unaffected at heart. Yet, humans cannot live double lives without being harmed by the separation they create. Writing on post-war Poland, Czeslaw Milosz, in his acclaimed book *The Captive*

Mind, noted that many people had lost the ability to distinguish between their real and their false selves. "A man grows into his role so closely that he can no longer differentiate his true self from the self he simulates."[24] Therefore, it is dangerous to think that one will be unaffected by the games one plays and the world one creates.

An Overview of Understanding the Self in Dialectical Incarnation

It has been stated that the Self is the centre of the philosophy of Dialectical Incarnation. Yet, it is still worthwhile to hear again, briefly, from Nicholas of Cusa and Baruch Spinoza in understanding the Self in the World and God.

One is reminded that according to Nicholas of Cusa, *learned ignorance* distinguishes the learned from the unlearned or uninstructed, while at the same time this *ignorance* elevates the learned to the level of the "wise." It is the Self who recognises his or her "ignorance" when the tendency to anthropomorphise God surfaces. The human Self should not assume a knowledge it does not have outside of him or her Self.

Nicholas of Cusa goes on to recognise the imperative of "Know Thyself" as central to his philosophy. The unknowable mystery of God can only be "known" through the centre which is the subject of awareness but which is also God as God's Self. The centre of an infinite circle is the point of self-awareness of the subject who has the entire cosmos, and Nature, i.e., God, as its "infinite horizon." As Karl Rahner explained, the human person, the Self, is a "Hearer of the Word," because the "Word" cannot be heard without a "hearer."[25] The centre of the circumference must be the Self-in-God who is aware of the infinite horizon. Thus, expanding and elaborating the perspective of Nicholas of Cusa, in Dialectical Incarnation, it is actually the human Self which is the very centre of God and the world. The Self is the "centre of the circumference" because the Self is the link between God and the world. It is stressed again that God needs the subject, God needs the "hearer," and God needs the "knower" so as to be a God who is "essentially love of others" and the totality of reality.[26]

The philosophy of Baruch Spinoza can also be used to highlight the validity of this philosophy. As mentioned in his *Ethics*, the "Mind's intellectual Love of God is the very Love of God by which God loves Himself."[27] The starting point of God or Nature (the world) is a knowledge of the Self. As the progression takes place for Descartes from the *cogito* to the Idea of God, to extension in the world, so too, the progression from the Self, to awareness of God *qua* God, and then to Nature *qua* extension (and also *qua* God), takes place in this philosophy.

Baruch Spinoza's fundamental insight is that God and Nature are an indivisible, uncaused, substantial whole. This is the only substantial whole and outside of Nature (and God), there is nothing. Everything that exists is a part of Nature/God and is brought into being by Nature/God. The Self is the first active, conscious aspect of Nature. The Self makes it possible, then, for God to love Godself objectively in and through Nature and in and through the active, subjective agent, the human person. He states that "[h]e who understands himself and his affects clearly and distinctly loves God, and does so the more he understands himself and his affects."[28]

Spinoza goes on to speak of "those things which pertain to the Mind's duration without relation to the body."[29] Here Spinoza is offering a formal structure which leads to the blessedness to which humans strive and which is to be found in the intellectual and eternal love of God. Spinoza explains that the "greatest striving of the Mind, and its greatest virtue is understanding things by the third kind of knowledge" which is intuition.[30]

Spinoza continues to elaborate this intellectual love of God at the end of *Ethics*. He demonstrates that "[w]hatever we understand by the third kind of knowledge we take pleasure in, and our pleasure is accompanied by the idea of God as a cause."[31] This intellectual love, we understand, is eternal and no love is eternal except intellectual love.[32]

The oneness of human love and divine love is further explained when Spinoza says,

> not insofar as [God] is infinite, but insofar as [God] can be explained by the human Mind's essence, considered under a species of eternity; i.e., the Mind's intellectual Love of God is part of the infinite Love by which God loves [Godself].[33]

The "more perfection each thing has, the more it acts and the less it is acted on; and conversely, the more it acts, the more perfect it is."[34] The more the human subject uses his or her mind as an active, incarnational being, he or she will also know him/herself and the God who is love and the totality of reality.

In summary thus far, one realizes that any endeavour to "know" the world and God must begin with the subject who is the searcher. Descartes' *cogito* is insufficient as a mere thinking being and his dualism is limiting. The starting point must be the Self as an incarnational, critically reflective, loving human person, who is intrinsically one with a dialectical harmony found in the common good and the total nature of the world. The mind and the body are conditions of the possibility of a philosophy of the heart, in which a divided dualism is rejected, and a whole physical, biological, emotional, spiritual, conscious loving Self is welcomed. The Self becomes aware of the external world of Nature, not as a dualistic separation but as a dialectical harmonious one. Humans, created in the image of God, have love for the reason of their existence because God is Love. Love needs particulars to love and someone with whom one is in relationship. The human person, as a transcendental

Self, must have the vision of Teilhard de Chardin in order to see the fullness being found in God and Nature. The Self is intrinsically open to be a "Hearer of the Word" of God and to know God. Humanity must have a "learned ignorance" through which one realizes that the only way one can come to know the world and God is through knowing the Self as the sole knower of God. God *qua* God and Nature *qua* Nature are beyond one's knowledge, therefore to know God and Nature one must see oneself as the centre of the circumference of God-in-the-world and seek the total horizon of God as love and the totality of reality.

THE ETHICS OF DIALECTICAL INCARNATION: A HARMONY OF LOVE

"All human acts are moral acts," claims Thomas Aquinas.[35] Not only is the human Self the centre of the circumference of God, Nature and the infinite horizon of the world, as explained previously, the Self is also the agent in all moral choices and behaviour.[36] It is paramount then, that one examines an ethics within the philosophy of Dialectical Incarnation. Several of the already mentioned supporting philosophers will continue to be important as the philosophy progresses and gleans from other ethical theories and ethicists.

THE BEGINNING OF A HARMONY OF LOVE: NICHOLAS OF CUSA AND BARUCH SPINOZA REVISITED

Philosophical ethics must begin with anthropology. One begins with the moral agent, the subject, who is the Self as the active agent. Within the philosophy of Nicholas of Cusa, for example, the Self is the "centre of the circumference" of God, the universe, and now of the realm of ethics. Nicholas turns to the human mind and its inadequacies when it comes to having knowledge of God and one's role in the world. God is all things through the mediation of the universe. God and the world are inseparable terms, and God is the unity of the possibility of things. Through incarnation, the Self becomes the centre of the circumference of the intellectual natures, the universe and, consequently, of ethics.

The unknowable mystery of God can be "known" only through the centre which is the human Self as the subject of awareness of God. The objective self of God is the human person who is now the subject to God's own infinity. The centre of an infinite circle is the point of self-awareness of the subject who has the entire cosmos and Nature, i.e., God as God's "infinite horizon."

The philosophy of Baruch Spinoza also highlights the validity of a dialectical incarnational ethics of love. Everything that exists is a part of Nature and is brought into being by Nature. The Self is the first active, conscious aspect of Nature. The Self makes it possible for God to love God's self objectively in and through the active, subjective agent who is then called on to love God and Nature. Spinoza confirms the philosophy when we are reminded that "he who understands himself and his affects clearly and distinctly loves God, and does so the more he [or she] understands himself and his affects."[37]

Spinoza offers a formal structure that leads to the blessedness that humans strive for and is to be found in the intellectual and eternal love of God. As indicated earlier, the "greatest striving of the Mind, and its greatest virtue is understanding things by the third kind of knowledge" which is intuition.[38]

This third kind of knowledge proceeds from an adequate idea of [the absolute essence of] certain attributes of God to the adequate knowledge of the essence of things, and the more we understand things in this way, the more we understand God.[39]

With reason, one starts with things seemingly separate from the mind and then, by comparing and contrasting them, one infers other things to be true. With intuition, one starts with what cannot be apart from one's mind. When this is known, the essence of things becomes known directly, not through inferential steps. This knowledge is immediate because there is nothing in between. With reason, something stands between the mediating premises and the conclusion. The human Self is the link between God and Nature and intuition is the most immediate connection between the two. When Spinoza says "proceeds from," it does not mean a procession through time but rather a direct union of object and subject. What "proceeds from," follows without mediation. It is the Mind "Minding" Itself.

Spinoza continues to elaborate this intellectual love of God at the end of *Ethics*. He notes that "[w]hatever we understand by the third kind of knowledge we take pleasure in, and our pleasure is accompanied by the idea of God as a cause."[40] This intellectual love, we understand, is eternal.[41] The more the human subject uses his or her mind as an active, incarnational being, he or she will also know oneself and the God who is love and the totality of reality.

LEIBNIZ'S HARMONY OF LOVE

G.W. Leibniz's philosophy is a "harmony" within the entire cosmos or world. The "God is love" of Spinoza's monism is united with Leibniz's pluralism and harmony so as to become an ethics of a "harmony of love." The two synthesized together bring about a genuine dialectical incarnational system of ethics.

Leibniz's ethics can be understood as a composite theory of the good. His particular system of ethics emerges from 1) Platonism, in which goodness is coextensive with reality or being, 2) perfectionism, whereby the highest good consists in the development and perfection of one's nature, and 3) a form of hedonism, in which the highest good is pleasure.[42] He equates the metaphysical good with reality, moral goodness with virtue and the physical good with pleasure.

Leibniz uses perfection in three different but related ways. The *metaphysical* good consists in the reality of a thing, the degree of metaphysical perfection, which is harmony. The *moral* good involves the development and perfection of a characteristic or set of characteristics fundamental to human nature, what he calls moral perfectionism. This is a form of virtue ethics in which intellectual apprehension of harmony brings about virtue. In other words, the human, i.e., the Self becomes aware of this harmony and as the Self "apprehends" this through reason the Self becomes virtuous.

For Leibniz, "[v]irtue is the habit of acting according to wisdom."[43] When one genuinely loves, one possesses the charity of the wise. Therefore, love is the pleasure one takes in the happiness and perfection of others.[44] Leibniz claims that the more one's benevolence expands to encompass the happiness of more and more "others," the more one grows in justice and virtue, and the more one approaches moral perfection.

In support of the philosophy, Leibniz unites the moral good with the metaphysical good by way of the *physical* good. The physical good unites virtue and harmony ("Leibniz's Ethics"). The harmony of the universe is a precondition for virtue and happiness, but harmony alone is not sufficient. Harmony, as an "objective" reality, is gained by the "knowledge" of the Self. If there were no minds, no Self, the universe would be devoid of virtue and happiness. The Self is the condition of the possibility for knowledge of the universe to be "known." Such knowledge and beauty of all of creation is necessary for happiness. Thus, the Self discovers the objective harmony of love present in the universe and then creates the unison of that harmony by living in "perfection" and virtue.

KANT'S TRANSCENDENTAL SELF
AND THE CONDITION OF THE POSSIBILITY

The Self of a Dialectical Incarnational ethics accepts Kant's transcendental ego as "creator" of the world of space and time (similar to the centre of the circumference of Nicholas of Cusa) with the autonomous source of its own kingdom of ends, its own realm of freedom and duty. Kant's transcendental theory considers the Self an inscrutable subject presupposed by the unity of empirical self-consciousness. Kant moved from an instrumental ethics to an intrinsic one in which the Self is aware of ethics as "good in itself." In bringing the Self to a transcendental level, Kant describes the Self along with the World, and God as being in the noumenal, unknowable realm of existence, while still being the condition of the possibility of an ethics (or a metaphysics, or an epistemology). He stresses the principle of humanity, where every rational being exists as an end in him/herself and not merely as a means to be arbitrarily used by this or that will. In light of this, one moves again to the sense of harmony established by Leibniz. According to Kant, one should act in harmony, in unison with the will of every rational being in making universal laws; one should endeavour to further the ends of others. Harmony is allowing each human person to be all that he or she can be as an active agent within the harmony of the laws present in the "will" and Nature of God and the universe.

The ethics of this philosophy begins with the Self, because it is the human person who is the moral agent. The Self goes beyond the mere thinking being of Descartes' "ego," because the Self is a whole being. The "ego" of Descartes dualism is replaced with a synthesizing position of an incarnational being of body and soul, human and divine. The Self is the centre of the circumference of God's total being and Nature. Ethics begins with the whole incarnational Self. The Self becomes aware (conscious) of the union of God and Nature (Spinoza) in which there is an intrinsic harmony. The Self must recognise this harmony and will thus act in virtue (Leibniz). The Transcendental Self (Kant) is the very condition of the possibility of any ethics whereby the Self discovers the harmony of the human will and of Nature in which there is the categorical imperative to bring all of humanity and Nature to perfection. The Self is in relationship with others (and Nature) and exists in the harmony of love which is the expression of God in and through the particularity of all creation (Leibniz). The Self seeks the common good of all humanity and Nature, for "I am because we are."[45] These are the preliminary points as one continues towards a dialectical incarnational ethics.

THE ANTHROPOLOGICAL ETHICS OF
DIALECTICAL INCARNATION[46]

Karl Rahner offers an existential virtue ethics. Virtue Ethics emphasizes the character of an individual more than the actions of that individual. The goodness of an action derives from the character of the person who performs it, not vice versa. Virtue Ethics began with Plato, but Aristotle is the major inspiration for this form of ethics, especially for contemporary virtue ethics. Thomas Aquinas added to Aristotle's list of virtues by defining "cardinal" virtues which control the appetites (prudence, justice, temperance, fortitude) and "theological" virtues (faith, hope, charity).[47]

In understanding God as "the totality of reality," we have discovered how God, the world and humanity, although united, are comprised of seemingly opposing elements. God is transcendent; God is immanent. The human and the world are nature; the human and the world are graced and supernatural. The human person has a transcendental dimension and a categorical dimension. The world is unity; the world is diverse. The human person is an individual; the human person is a social being. The philosophy expressed as Dialectical Incarnation not only admits of these differing poles within the "totality of reality" but, as already stated, it also recognizes that God is incarnate in this totality, and God's self-communication is effected through this incarnation. One recalls that Rahner states "that the incarnate word is the absolute symbol of God in the world . . . [and] . . . the presence of what God is in himself."[48]

In that the "totality of reality" is incarnate, there is a true unity within diversity and difference. In ethics, there must be a complete regard for the individual human person in the midst of the social dimensions of life. Both sides of the dialectical nature of humanity and the world need to be respected. The human person lives in participation with God, the world and others. As such, the "guiding idea is that participation means unity-in-difference, a sharing through which the uniqueness of the parties is enhanced."[49] Dialectical Incarnation contains the basic tenet of Rahner's thought that the difference is distinct but not separate, united by the incarnate God. A dialectical understanding of the "totality of reality" recognizes, as Paul Ricoeur states, that there is a "tension between two distinct and sometimes opposed claims."[50] An ethics within such a dynamic structure acknowledges that, as the human person remains united with the Self, God and others-in-the-world, there is a dialectical tension, a strife, a creative anxiety, which "may even [and actually should] be the occasion for the invention of responsible forms of behaviour."[51] Therefore, as the human person seeks to live a moral life within the "totality of reality," he or she must be completely open to the difference-in-unity and that there is a positive result which occurs in and through the strife, the tension, which is intrinsic to all reality.

The incarnational aspect of the ethics being proposed here stems from the position offered by Duns Scotus in which creation and incarnation are one act of love. "I say that the incarnation . . . was immediately foreseen from all eternity by God as good more proximate end."[52] Coming from Scotus' position, Rahner continues his inquiry. The point Rahner is proclaiming is fundamental for an ethics of Dialectical Incarnation. In that creation and incarnation are united as one act of God's love, then, "[g]race is God [God]self . . . [and] . . . cannot be thought of independently of the personal love of God" (Rahner IV 7: 177). As such, human love is divine love and is also the incarnate energy of love found in the totality of reality,

That human nature is "always endowed with God [God]self" will certainly affect how "being" moves to "doing." This perspective affects both how one understands oneself, how one understands the "neighbour" one is called to love and how one understands the world in which one lives. One begins with the intrinsically divine original state of the human person and the world rather than the understanding of an intrinsic evil.[53] There is a single, "primal act of God." Not only is creation and incarnation united, but so too is redemption. Redemption and the consummation of the world are all within the one act of God.

John Macquarrie also speaks of consummation as part of a single dynamic work by God, that is "one great action of holy Being." Creating, reconciling, and consummating are "three distinguishable but inseparable aspects" of God's single activity.[54] As human persons walk towards their *telos* in the moral life, they possess an *a priori* condition which establishes their very nature and being. This graced being-in-the-world brings the world-of-being towards consummation. The human person is characterized by a "supernatural existential" by which one is given the "condition of the possibility" to move toward one's infinite horizon. By identifying one's actual human condition, one will better recognize one's given virtues, and thereby

> perfect the fundamental anthropological dimensions of being human that are needed for integrated virtuous behaviour. [These virtues will be] providing the bare essentials for right human living and specific action.[55]

God's love manifests itself, in the first place, as the power that grounds existence. The love and grace from God's self-communication is the "supernatural existential" which enables the human person to transcend finite existence. Rahner conceives human nature as essentially open to God's free disposition. God created the human person as potentiality, invited by God's free action in history, calling us towards our goal and destiny.[56] Paul Tillich also writes: "God is the power of being in everything that is, transcending every special power infinitely but acting at the same time as its creative ground."[57] For Rahner, the human person is a graced event and a transcendental subject because God *is* the very ground of being. God is the foundation for the transcendental being even to be.[58]

Thomas Merton confirms that love is the heart of ethics, because it is the heart of *existence*. He states:

> To say that I am made in the image of God is to say that Love is the reason for my existence, for God is love.
> Love is my true identity. Selflessness is my true self. Love is my true character. Love is my name (Seeds of Contemplation).

One can now understand how God as love is the condition of the possibility in which humanity loves. The human person is called, by one's very nature, to love because it is his or her own existence.

In defining the harmony of one love and one heart in the totality of reality, it is beneficial to understand that the first love of God is frequently understood as God's *agapic* love. This love is described as "sacrificial giving," "unselfish," "God's way to the human," "God's grace," "spontaneous, overflowing, unmotivated love," which "creates value in the beloved."[59] The distinguishing feature of *agape* is that it is "directed to the beloved for the beloved's sake." The object of *agape* is the beloved, its aim is the good of the beloved, and its reason is also the good of the beloved.[60] *Agape* is considered primarily as God's love, for God is *Agape*. Although this type of love is frequently referred to as Christian life, it is actually a universal love for all people. Vacek makes an important point when he states that beyond *agape* love there must exist an *eros*, a self love: "Love of self is, at least in our age, a third 'commandment' alongside love of God and love of others."[61] In the light of the dialectical nature of this philosophy, he further states that "we must live in a dialectical tension of self-affirmation and other-affirmation, each under the grace or vocation that we receive from God."[62] According to Vacek, however, *agape* and *eros* are not enough for a complete ethical life. It is *philia* love that one must come to understand.[63]

Philia is distinguished from *agape* and *eros* by the mutuality that it creates.[64] *Philia* is the love that God established. It is a relational love, a love of friendship. Unlike *agape*, which is only for the sake of the beloved, *philia* is for the sake of the *mutual* relationship the two share with one another. In the ethics of Dialectical Incarnation, it is *philia* that serves as the "heart," for the mystery of God and the mystery of the human person are one in an essential love relationship. The human person understands himself or herself only when he or she realizes that he or she is the one to whom God communicates God's Self in love.[65] Because God is the ground of all being, there is an essential, relational nature with God built into one's own being. Rahner states that "'[n]ature,' therefore, is in the real order willed from the outset for the sake of 'grace,' and 'creation' for the sake of the covenant of personal love."[66] This is *philia*. In an ethics of unity in difference, *philia* is a "power that creates unity and forms the human community ever more extensively and intensively."[67] All human love finds "its culmination and ultimate goal in a community of solidarity with and in God."[68] Josef Fuchs also stresses this *philia* or relational love with God, when he describes morality: "man is not fulfillment of his own self, but total openness to the call of the God . . . given in divine freedom."[69] It is this existential, dynamic, personal morality, offered by Karl Rahner and made explicit by Josef Fuchs, which serves in substantiating an ethics of Dialectical Incarnation. It is the capacity of love, created by God's love, which serves as the heart of this ethics.

UNDERSTANDING CULTURE
IN ESTABLISHING UNIVERSAL ETHICS

In the quest for an all-inclusive, universal ethics it is worth understanding two theories or perspectives which look at morality differently. First, there is a philosophical perspective and theory called *ethical relativity*, which holds that since different cultures have diverse moral beliefs; there is no way to decide whether an action is morally right or wrong other than by asking whether the members of this or that culture believe it is morally right or wrong.[70] Ethical relativism is the view that the people of a particular culture determine the moral status of an act in that culture. What is morally right in one's culture may be morally wrong in another's. For example, homosexuality or polygamy or premarital sexual expression may be acceptable and morally permissible in one culture and morally wrong in another. *Cultural relativity*, on the other hand, is a sociological term indicating the important differences between cultures. While ethical relativism seeks to give an answer to the ethical question, "What actions are really morally right?" cultural relativism only gives an answer to the question, "What actions do different cultures believe are morally right?"[71] Although these theories may seem the same, the former is an ethical theory; the latter is an anthropological and sociological theory.

With immense cultural diversity and plurality in the world, is there a possible common moral thread to which one can look when establishing a universal form of ethics? Can the national motto of Jamaica, "Out of many, one people" become "Out of many people, one ethics?" Dialectical Incarnation offers a universal, single ethics, united as one but expressed in a diversity of manifestations.

As an example of the difficulty in offering a single, universal ethics in light of a diversity of cultures, reference is made to the role of language in culture. When analysing any culture and any ethics within culture, language must be considered. Both the oral tongue and the scribal writ are that by which a people's civilisation and culture is known. Is a child of a particular culture able to freely experience the native tongue of his or her forebears' experience simply to make room for what is consecrated as *the* universal and powerful language?[72] So too, from the experience of our ancestors, who determines *the* universal and powerful ethical code for a people's culture. Again, cultural relativity surfaces as one searches for a universal ethical code within Dialectical Incarnation.[73]

Within the nature of describing Dialectical Incarnation, there is frequent reference to *the* Incarnation of Jesus Christ and the language used is frequently that of a Christian tradition. Yet, the philosophy goes beyond any Christian limit or any other religious limit. The terms used must be understood as having universal meaning, going beyond any particular religious or cultural framework. In that one recognise the diversity and plurality of the world in which one lives and its various religious groups, one cannot turn exclusively to any particular religious ethics, be it Christian, Hindu, Jewish, Islamic or Rastafari. Hence, as one continues this quest it will be with the intention of being an ethics for all denominations, all cultures and all societies. Although incarnation is very much a Christian belief it is in no way exclusive to Christianity. Incarnation is within Eastern philosophies as well as the philosophy of Rastafari. The commandment of love is an all-denominational, universal commandment because the God of all Nature is Love and the totality of reality. Philosophical or secular ethics should be the same as any particular religious ethics in its content. All humans should love not only their neighbour but their enemy as well. Although Christian Scripture may state that one cannot love the God that one does not see without loving the neighbour that one does see (1 John 4:20–21), the philosophy of Dialectical Incarnation must be independent of scripture. [74]

THE NATURE OF NATURAL LAW

Real

Natural law theory has functioned through the centuries as a summary statement for the vision of humanist realism. [75] The fundamental conviction is that what makes things right or wrong is precisely and solely the fact that they help or hurt the human persons that inhabit this world. Realism recognizes that the moral task of the human person genuinely makes a difference; it is not an exercise in futility. Morality is not a game that we play because God wants us to. Whether I do the right thing or not truly affects the quality of life that I live, and that others live, in the midst of the large human community.

Experiential

The assertion of realism leads us to the fact that natural law theory is an expression of ethical "experientialism." This means that since deeds are judged to be right because they are, in fact, good for human persons, the process of moral evaluation is, in principle, a public, measurable, quasi-experimental process. Moral evaluative judgments are conclusions derived from concrete perceptions of human reality and of what truly helps or hurts human persons. To determine an action as right or wrong we sometimes say that it is an attack on human nature. But how do we know that a particular action contradicts that nature? Here only two answers seem possible. Either we know the nature of the human person as a result of some divine illumination or revelation (which we are not doing in that this is a philosophical perspective) or we know it as a result of ordinary human observation, a result of reflection upon the collective experience of human selfhood. It is through human observation that natural law morally evaluates human actions.

Consequential

To hold the real and experiential approach to the discovery of moral values is also to assert that ethical value is consequential. Thus we must speak of "consequentialism." This term, which is much discussed in both philosophical and theological literature, suggests that specific actions are to be evaluated from a moral point of view by considering their actual effects, or consequences, in the arena of human life. As an example, one knows that it is wrong to take money from a neighbour's table because it does injury to the neighbour and perhaps also to the one stealing. It is also harmful to the development of community. Yet, if this person was starving and had no other recourse, natural law morality would be quite prepared to approve of the "theft." Why? Property rights are relative, and in certain cases the neighbour's right to his money must be balanced against the other's right to continue living. In general, this analysis can be expressed in our terms by saying that in the particular case at hand the good consequences of the theft outweigh the bad, and thus the action is morally right. All private property has a social mortgage and consideration of the consequences is what brings us to this ethical conclusion.

Historical

It is one thing to discover what is right and wrong and to isolate what truly helps and hurts other human persons and the self. It is quite another to ask about the general perduring validity of the conclusions reached. The question is the universality and immutability of the natural law. We have humanised the world. We are co-creators. This has been verified by the data of the historical sciences. Palaeontology, cultural anthropology, political science, and history all testify to the difference human beings have made in the world. We have not simply been present in the world; we have not merely interacted with our environment. Our presence has been a creative presence; our interaction has been an evolutionary force. Our culture has changed, and we have changed ourselves. Thus the significance of intellect and freedom, as forces for change in the world, is certified.

The significance of understanding ourselves as intellect and freedom is to highlight the essential historicity of the human person. It is to take note of the central openness of ourselves and our world, of our fundamental capacity (and challenge) to change. But if the world situation of the moral person can change, if we ourselves can change, if, therefore, human nature is not so much a finished fact as it is a project and an experiment, then it follows that the natural law is likewise open to change.

Instead of speaking of the mutability of natural law, one should speak of its historicity. By this term one indicates, not that the natural law *will* change but that it is in principle and of necessity capable of change. This basic principle of historicity within Natural Law is paramount for us as we continue to discover an ethics of Dialectical Incarnation.

Proportional

In understanding natural law as real, experiential, consequential and historical, one now comes to realise natural law is also proportional. Although human beings may want to do good, and avoid evil at all times, it is quite unreasonable to do so. The maxim is clear, but the possibility of living out human lives is not so precise. Human beings are finite and limited. Humanity's best hope is that humans do as much good as possible, and as little evil as necessary.

We humans are also social. There are many of us. Human rights are relative. In the words of an old cliché, "my right to swing my arms ends where your nose begins." Individual rights go as far as the rights of other individuals and the common good. Anything I do must not prevent others from being completely human. As such, the common good is the sum total of all those conditions of social living-economic, political, cultural, religious, etc., which make it possible for women and men readily and fully to achieve the perfection of their humanity. [76] Individual rights are always experienced within the context of the promotion of the common good. In life there are many goods, sometimes complementing each other, but often competing and conflicting with others.

Human beings are also temporal, meaning that all human actions have multiple effects. The consequences of which we have spoken do not present themselves in clear, logical manners. Human actions are many, and one is not always "doing good." Therefore, what is one to do? One ought to do that action which maximises the good and minimises the evil. The "right action" is that which contains the proportionally greatest maximisation of the good and the minimisation of evil. This is humanity's hope in doing good and avoiding evil.

HISTORICAL ROOTS OF NATURAL LAW

Greek Influence

It has been stated that the Stoics emphasised "nature" and the moral necessity for humankind to "conform" to that which is given in nature. For the Stoics, the goal of philosophy was to live the morally good life through right moral conduct. "Don't fool with Mother Nature" could be taken as the moral imperative. Accept what is given in nature because what is the given order of events will ultimately assert themselves according to their own design anyway. This law is objective and exists entirely apart from humankind. Reality is given. One simply conforms to what is there as given. The human person finds that he or she is in a world that is in substance unchanging. If one wishes to prosper and survive, one has to come to terms with reality as it is and accept it.

Roman Influence

Whereas the Greeks emphasised the idea of the "natural" in Natural Law morality, the Romans emphasised the law. Cicero spoke of Natural Law as the innate power of reason to direct and control human activity. To act in conformity with that law discovered and given in nature is to live in accordance to the dictates of human reason.

Where the Greeks tended to be inflexible or fatalistic in their understanding of the world, the Romans tended to be innovative. Where the Greeks tended to focus on the essential and the static of reality, the Romans focused on the empirical and the dynamic. The first approach (Greek) reflects the *Classicist* point of view of the world, whereas the second (Roman) reflects the *Historically Conscious* mentality of the world. The first is a traditional world view perspective, the latter is a contemporary world view perspective. In the Roman Catholic tradition, this shift in point of view was stated in *Gaudium et Spes* when it says, "Thus the human race has passed from a rather static concept of reality to a more dynamic, evolutionary one."[77] In light of these different perspectives on Natural Law, it is important to understand the "physicalistic" vs. the "personalistic" perspectives.

PHYSICALISM VERSUS PERSONALISM

Physicalism, when understanding Natural Law, emphasises and sometimes absolutizes the physical act of the human independently of other human perspectives. Personalism, in contrast to physicalism, emphasises the human person together with his or her acts, inasmuch as these actions extend beyond the biological to include the social, spiritual, and psychological dimensions.

The physicalist interpretation allows moral positions to be taken without ambiguity in every instant the same kind of physical act occurs. Interfering with the faculty of speech or the faculty of reproduction for whatever reason is in itself "evil," because it contradicts the design of human nature.

Tradition has regarded a violation of the natural order as a serious offence, since violation of the natural order is an affront to God. Physicalists say that since the order of nature comes directly from God and is a reflection of God's Eternal Law, it assumes priority over the order of reason which comes more immediately from the human person and only mediately from human nature.

The personalist world-view of contemporary morality does not look on human nature as a finished and static product in which God's will is located, commanding a fixed moral response. Within the limits set by physical laws, which already determine human reality, human reason can and must intervene to bring about something new. From a personalistic perspective, one can rationally discover what Natural Law requires by reflecting on that which is given in human experience within authentic human life and from one's own human potential for self-discovery. When formulating an ethics of Dialectical Incarnation, it is to this personalism that the philosophy is directed.

EXISTENTIAL ETHICS

The starting point for Rahner's existential ethics is the human person, as transcendental subject, freely open to God. By starting here, however, one immediately realizes that the human person is who he or she is by God's self-communication. This self-communication does ground ethics in a rational understanding of faith because, according to Rahner, God communicates the Word of God to a partner in dialogue: "natural moral acts can be obtained only with the help of the [communication] of God's Word."[78] This means that the moral agent received an *a prior* condition, as a supernatural existential, to be able to properly intend any moral action.

This understanding of Rahner's ethics may be seen as a contradiction to the intention of using reason, not faith and revelation, as the condition of the possibility of a dialectical incarnational ethics. Rahner's anthropological focus is not underplayed, however. The human person is always the centre of Rahner's existential ethics, but this person is a "supernaturalized" human person. Rahner is stressing the "graced" event of the person, which will be the condition of the possibility of the life and ethics of the human person in the world. The human person is a divine person and this ethics should begin with this awareness. The separation between divine and human is over.

Going beyond the possible "kernel of truth" in situation ethics and traditional natural law ethics, Rahner broadens the understanding of nature by describing it as *nature of a person*. In the same way the human person is constituted by God's self-communication, so too, nature is "constituted" by the person. In Rahner's methodology, the true grounding structure of the human person lies simultaneously in freedom and nature. God constitutes human nature in freedom and for freedom, a freedom exercised and limited in nature. It is transcendental freedom that makes categorical freedom in the individual even possible. Grounded as such, the human person has a responsibility to discover "God's will" through discernment and, then, to create history. Therefore, the structure of human nature is not static and unchanging; rather, it is dynamic and historical. It is for this reason that existential ethics supplements an *a priori,* fixed and static essential ethics, for the former is within historical reality, namely, the history of God's love and God's call within the particular history of an individual and his or her response. In the ethics of Dialectical Incarnation one's response is to love one's neighbour and as such one essentially and equally loves God. However, before further explicating this fundamental, incarnational "commandment," it is necessary to understand the relationship and difference between essential and existential ethics and Josef Fuchs' *humanum* and *Christianum.*

Within the objective of this philosophy and in demonstrating that there is a no exclusive "distinctively Christian [Hindu, Muslim or Rasta] morality" in its content, one which is basically different from or even in contradiction to a morality concerned with the dignity of women and men everywhere, one must first examine the notion of intentionality, or the intentionality of any religious group. [79] When one understands the human person as being dialectical, and therefore as being both categorical and transcendental, one realizes that human morality must likewise be both. On the one hand, the particular categorical conduct of morality is one in which "categorial values, virtues and norms are realized—values, virtues and norms of different categories, such as justice, faithfulness, and purity." [80] On the other hand, there are "transcendental attitudes and norms, which inform various ethical categories and go beyond them." [81] It is in this transcendental realm that one sees the human person in her or his "entirety," one sees the human person as, to use Rahner's term, a human characterized by a "supernatural existential," and one who is open to the infinite horizon of God's self-communication. In this context, the questions "What is Christian?," "What is Hindu?," "What is Moslem?," etc., and "What is human?" arise more specifically from the question, "are there distinctly Christian [Hindu, Muslim, Rasta, etc.] categorical ways of conduct, or are genuinely human attitudes and life styles in the various areas of life not also those of Christians [Hindus, Muslims, Rasta]"? [82] Simply put, one is first a human and then one is a Christian, Hindu, Muslim or Rasta. It is here that "intentionality" of the human person plays a significant role in answering this question. The question of whether there is a distinctly religious ethics, which is different from a secular ethics, surfaces from another question: is someone first Christian, Hindu, Moslem before one is human? We are first human and ethics is a human endeavour. A religious ethics is formulated from ones motive or one's intention. All people should love their neighbour regardless of the religion to which one subscribes.

INTENTIONALITY

Leading toward a moral perspective, intentionality refers to "a full, personal, enduring decision in each particular situation; hence the permanent, present, and not past act of decision."[83] A universal understanding of intentionality refers to the "living conscious presence in the daily shaping of life and the world" (Fuchs, *Personal Responsibility* 56). This intentionality is the underlying, enduring, permanent awareness of the human person, here and now, who has come to realize who he or she is. Within a perspective of Dialectical Incarnation, one realizes that he or she is constituted by God's self-offer with an intrinsic, radical openness to transcendence, viz. God. One's intentionality is rooted in the awareness of one's supernaturalized existence. Intentionality is characterized by a "supernatural existential," so that it grasps the "totality of reality" found in the complete nature of the human person and the mystery of God. Intentionality emerges from one's being a transcendental subject open to the infinite horizon of the universe. This intentionality is a nonthematic, unreflexive consciousness, because it is transcendental and goes deeper and beyond the categorical levels of awareness. Is this intentionality exclusively Christian, Hindu, Muslim or Rasta?

To answer this question in light of the search for an ethics of Dialectical Incarnation, and how virtue ethics looks at the character of the human person as he or she *is*, it is worthwhile to turn to Rahner's explanation of an "anonymous Christian." Accordingly, a human person is living out his or her freely given, graced existence, marked by a supernatural existential, when he or she really accepts himself or herself completely.[84] When the human person accepts himself or herself, he or she is actually accepting incarnation "as the absolute perfection and guarantee of his anonymous movement towards God."[85] A person who denies his or her concrete being as human, in fact denies the divine, and likewise, denies the fullness of his or her incarnational being. When one denies the divinity within oneself, one also denies their own concrete human Self. In the union of the divine with humanity, through incarnation, all humanity is divinized in humanity's actual nature. The person is constituted as a being, open to the divine precisely as a transcendental being. The intentionality of any ethics, be it a philosophical or a religious ethics, is the intentionality to be a complete human person. The denying of one's own concrete being as fully human is, therefore, the foundation of evil.

This comprehension of intentionality helps in understanding Josef Fuchs' *humanum* and *Christianum*:

> The existentially believing Christian discovers, in the search for a lifestyle which can express his faith, his intentionality, that it is the human person who believes existentially, that therefore this belief must be lived and expressed by

the human person, in the genuine realization of being-human, of the *humanum*.[86]

One is first a human and then a Christian, or a Hindu, Buddhist, Muslim, Rasta, etc., and therefore one cannot separate the *humanum* from the particular religion, as if humanity exists separate from different religions. Rahner continually stresses distinction without separation. Such is the case with the *humanum* and the specific element of any religion within morality. Transcendence is distinct but not separate from immanence. God is distinct but not separate from the world. "Love of God" is distinct but not separate from "loving your neighbour." The body is distinct from the soul but not separate, for the genuine human is a "bodily-spiritual being," i.e., an incarnational being.[87] When one makes a distinction which separates the *humanum* from the *Christianum*, or from an essential aspect of any religion, one makes a distinction which is "based on a misunderstanding of the nature of 'human' morality, but also in a misconception of the nature of God."[88] The ethics of Dialectical Incarnation recognises these theoretical distinctions, but does not separate human morality from the nature of God. It is within the "totality of reality" that "all human acts are moral acts." When one is being fully human, one is also being fully divine, and can be fully Christian, or fully Hindu, or fully Muslim, or fully Rasta or fully any other religion to which one belongs. Being human, and the ethical intentionality of being human, transcends any particular religion and any particular, immanent expression of transcendence.

Identification of true human nature is only "one side of the coin," for now the human has the responsibility to live out his or her transcendental nature. The human person must discover what kind of life is proper to one who is free, and therefore responsible, to the infinite horizon. And this must be lived out in one's existential life in the categorical, historical, concrete world.

The human person is not only conditioned by the "supernatural existential" but is also free. Freedom, according to Rahner, must first of all be thought of as 'freedom of being."[89] The human person is concerned about one's Self and being, regardless of the external world into which one finds oneself. He or she is a person already in relation to himself or herself. Rahner turns to the subject as the starting point of freedom, because subjectivity is the human person's most fundamental experience of himself or herself-in-the-world. This experience of oneself-in-the world provides the human person with an understanding of the divine. In actuality, one's own subjectivity is grounded in the divine. As a "supernatural existential," the human person's subjectivity is grounded in divinity and in the totality of reality, which is entirely incarnate with that same divinity. As such, freedom is "necessarily the freedom of the subject towards itself in its finality and thus is freedom towards God."[90] Freedom, for Rahner, is the "freedom of self-understanding, the possibility of saying yes or no to oneself" and also to the divine.[91]

Freedom "never happens as a merely objective exercise, as a mere choice 'between' individual objects."[92] Freedom is "not the capacity of always being able to do something else."[93] Rather, freedom is self-possession, self-exercise, self-achievement and self-realization. However, freedom is "always a self-realization in the direction of God or a radical self-refusal towards God."[94] Freedom is "to be or not to be," when one discovers one's supernatural existential status of human life. One remains free to be fully human and divine or not to be fully human and divine.

The human person, who is aware of his or her true nature, knows that recognition leads to responsibility. Likewise, freedom also is responsibility. The human person has discovered himself or herself-in-the-world and in history, as subject, as agent and a creator *in* history, not as an object *of* history. The world-of-nature, i.e., the cosmos, is not only divinized but is humanized. Therefore, the human person "on account of his [or her] freedom, . . . is responsible for his [or her] eternal salvation or damnation,"[95] and is also responsible for the world and "neighbor." Human beings are free and therefore responsible for themselves, not only with regard to their finality, but also for the history they create and the social framework which constitutes that history. Humanity is responsible for itself and cannot "exculpate itself by throwing the blame on something other than itself and God."[96] When the human person is truly responsible in his or her self-determination, and in the creating of the social world, it is ultimately done in love. This is because love and divinity are one's nature. "Freedom is always self-realization . . . before God . . . as the capacity of the 'heart,' it is the capacity of love."[97] Love serves as the thread that unifies the many, free activities of the human person and identifies such actions as Christian, as Hindu, as Muslim, as Rasta, either actually or anonymously. Consequently, the distinctiveness of Christian morality, or any other religion's morality, is the recognition and awareness of the fullness and freedom of the human person who is motivated by and inspired through his or her religious element. Moreover, as free human persons, one creates one's history, so too, one determines the content of one's conduct. When one recognizes oneself, as a believer within a faith community, one chooses that external context, one's own concrete, existential "spot" within the "totality of reality," in which one will live a moral life.

In an ethics of Dialectical Incarnation, it is important to look at the *telos*, the goal, of the person-in-the-world and the role of the human person as a moral agent. For a Christian, a Hindu, a Muslim or a Rasta, to have a relationship with God, to love God and to hope for a full consummation with God, is also to consciously and to freely have a relationship with *this world*, to love this world, and to hope for this world. The two relationships are mutually dependent. Once again, this is *philia*, the covenantal love we have with God and the world. This basic proviso within humanity's desire to transform the world so as to have a "new earth" is not different, and adds nothing more than, the statement that "love of God and love of neighbour are one."[98] In this way, human beings become co-creators, and co-redeemers, with God in continuing the evolutionary work of creation and redemption. The world is not merely the material "stage" upon which the Christian, the Hindu, the Muslim or the Rasta, can live out his or her earthly life of virtue so as to consummate one's life in the "new heaven." The incarnate history of the world is the history of salvation, for those seeking salvation. The "kingdom of God," for those believers who use such a term, is the consummation of this world. The immanent consummation of the world is the transcendent consummation of the world.

The self-bestowal of the transcendent God is the immanent factor in the human person's being a creature.[99] This transcendence of the human person is, so to speak, the very "condition of the possibility" to be the immanent creature the human person is and to be the partner and co-creator with God in the on-going creation of the world toward its final consummation. It is God's absolute immediacy, in the human person and the concrete world, that is the principle in the movement and the very goal itself, i.e., the consummation of the world. The actual movement toward this consummation of the world is achieved "in the goal itself . . . the present is sustained by the future itself."[100] From a non-believing, secular perspective, one looks at the world and can say that the world, with the human person, is the means towards its own consummation. From a Rahnerian perspective, the "new earth" is the only earth that is, and it has a transcendent-immanent consummation.[101] Heaven is not another place, but a way of talking about the earth, transformed finally by God, through the human person.

In sum, in the existential ethics prefaced by Cusa, Spinoza, Leibniz and developed by Rahner and Fuchs, and in light of the philosophy of an ethics for Dialectical Incarnation, the human as a Hindu, the human as a Jew, the human as a Christian, the human as a Muslim, the human as a Rasta, and so on, are theoretically distinct but never separate. The world and God, God and the human person, are likewise distinct but not separate. Recalling Rahner's anthropological philosophy and theology, God and the human person's transcendence have an "original unity," and the "two [God and humanity] are mutually dependent on each other."[102] Therefore, a misunderstanding of the difference between God and the world can bring about an unwanted dichotomy. The difference is not the difference within the realm of the categorical, as if one is referring to two categorical realities; rather it is a difference which "comes from God" and is "identical with God."[103] God is different from the world in mystery, because "this difference is experienced in our original transcendental experience,"[104] which is mystery. The difference between God and the world is a unity-in-difference not a difference in two separate dualistic categories. The moral agent should be viewed as being in and looking at the world, with God, so that together they bring the world, with humanity, to its final consummation. As humans sustained by the divine, supernaturalized human beings are proper moral agents, in a world for which they are responsible.

Just as we cannot separate God from the world, so too, we cannot separate the love of God from the love of neighbour. For Rahner the only true way to love God is by loving the neighbour. Rahner states:

> In the case of this unity the important thing is to understand rather that the one does not exist and cannot be understood or exercised without the other, and that two names have really to be given to the same reality if we are to summon up its one mystery, which cannot be abrogated. [105]

Finally, the intentionality to love, a love which is united with a divine love, is the heart and core of dialectical incarnational ethics, as it is for Christian ethics, as well as Hindu, Muslim and Rasta ethics. Human action is moral when the human acts in accordance with the basic law and dynamism of human nature. The human is immoral when the person acts counter to this dynamism of human nature. The "totality of reality" is the complete mutual, *philial*, covenantal love God and humanity-in-the-world have together and in which the human lives a moral life. In the philosophy of Dialectical Incarnation, love is human because love is divine, and together, love is the totality of reality. As such, love, which is always incarnate, is the one stuff of the universe, harmonising all for those who know how to "see."

VIRTUE ETHICS IN DIALECTICAL INCARNATION

In Rahner and Fuchs, one sees a shift from a static, impersonal essential ethics to a dynamic, personal existential ethics, where the human person becomes aware of the entirety of his or her nature as a "supernatural existential" and "transcendental subject," radically open to the infinite horizon and mystery of God and of him or herself. Although neither Rahner nor Fuchs name or describe virtue ethics, they certainly "prepare the way" for such an ethics. How? First of all, existential ethics begins with the human person, the human person characterized by the "supernatural existential," but situated in his or her categorical realities, i.e., the concrete, historical settings of his or her human existence. Similarly, virtue ethics begins with the human person in his or her context, not with rules and acts. One has moved from the static, essential ethics, with its standardized "manuals," used to "judge" an act as morally right or wrong, to an understanding of morality based on the character of a person within the dynamics of history and the acquisition of virtue mediated by temporal and historical reality. A static, essential ethics is one like Kant's Deontological ethics or a physicalistic Natural Law ethics. In comparison it needs be stated that one has not moved to a mere situation ethics. In strict situation ethics the human person, and being itself, is reduced to a particular situation removed from one's supernatural existential nature. Virtue ethics begins with the whole human person, with his or her character, based on the historical conditions and the acquired virtues which help in the transition from "being" to "doing." The "task of virtue is defined, therefore, as the acquisition and development of practices that perfect the agent into becoming a moral person while acting morally well."[106] Simply stated, virtuous people will do virtuous acts.

It is important to have a large overview of virtue ethics in order to determine how it is operative in the ethics of Dialectical Incarnation. In the new shift toward the whole human person as the starting point of ethics, there is the focus on the agent in his or her context with reference to the character traits, the personal commitments and community traditions that condition that context.[107] In light of this greater awareness of the entirety of the human person as a moral agent, virtue ethics incorporates the realization and the role of historical consciousness. As the world became humanised it also became conscious. This consciousness, in the evolution of the world, is historical, and the human person is part of this historical, collective consciousness.

Within virtue ethics, character needs to be understood as historically conditioned. There has been an historical development of the person, and his or her own nature. Virtue ethics helps the human person develop and "walk" towards his or her *telos,* that is, toward the *omega* of a human person-in-community. The ethics of Dialectical Incarnation wants to stress that, as one looks to the human person, one consciously and seriously remembers humanity's original state, humanity's "Original Grace" which exists prior to any reference to a "Fall" into "Original Sin." The ethics of Dialectical Incarnation rejects the notion that humanity has an original evil component. It is Original Grace which represents the human person's basic character. One has this character from the moment of one's conception and through all of creation present in evolution. With Original Grace as one's *a priori* condition, one starts one's ethical journey with the whole person "walking" toward one's *telos.* From this original state one is further conditioned by his or her historical and temporal realties. In this view, Original Sin, for Rahner, is the social, collective dimension of sin in which a person is born. Within humanity's freedom, the human person- in-community has the *responsibility* to remove Original Sin. God did not create "Original Sin," humans did and it is humans who must eradicate this "evil."

One of the most commendable elements of virtue ethics is the return to essential aspects of human life in its original state, that is, the importance and centrality of friendship, emotions and desires. Within the Judeo-Christian tradition that forms much of western history, one is reminded that God called humans into *philia*, the relational love of the covenant. Similarly, one's moral character becomes what it is through the friendship one has with an other.

This friendship necessarily includes sharing one's emotions and one's desires in the love relationship of friendship. Virtue ethics realizes "emotions and desires as ethically central: emotions are intrinsic to certain virtues, and, combined with desires, they witness to the quality of one's character and help direct one's actions."[108]

The anthropocentric nature of virtue ethics demonstrates the similarity it has with Rahner's anthropological existential ethics and the place of the virtue of love. Rahner is very concerned that one understands the human person as the *whole* human person. He states:

> His corporeality, temporality and historicity, final incapacity to catch up with himself by reflection, the unfathomable and adventurous character of his existence, the anticipation of his future in hope or despair . . . all these together are necessarily also the essential traits of *love* for another person. [109]

Virtue ethics begins with the *whole* human person, while it remains an ethics with a teleological character. This ethics is "premised on the notion of a true human nature with a determinate human good or end or *telos*."[110] And, this true human nature embodies human passions. This "teleological scheme" starts with the human person as one happens-to-be and moves to how one could-be if one realized one's essential nature. It is here that the dialectical tension surfaces, because there is a contrast between what-we-are and what-we-could-be. The tension is the process of becoming which takes place, according to Alasdair MacIntyre, as one makes "the transition from the former state to the latter."[111] Within this scheme, the moral agent must continually reflect upon and discern those "conditions," such as "actions, habits, capacities, and inclinations," including one's passions, which direct or lead one toward one's true nature and those that direct one away from that true nature. One's true nature is the human good with a genuine *telos*.[112] Is this not the moral command of Karl Rahner in his anthropocentric ethics? Is this not the command of an ethics of Dialectical Incarnation which states: "Know yourself and be the fullest human person you can be in the world!"? The philosopher/theologian, Irenaeus, as early as the second century, explained that the "Life of [the hu]man is the glory of God; the life of [the hu]man is the vision of God."

Alasdair MacIntyre brings ethics back to its Aristotelian roots. MacIntyre states:

> "The hypothesis which I wish to advance is that in the actual world which we inhabit the language of morality is in the same state of grave disorder as the language of natural science in the imaginary world which I described."[113]

MacIntyre claims that the moral structures that emerged from the Enlightenment were philosophically doomed from the start because they were formed using the incoherent language of philosophical morality. Kierke-gaard, Marx, Kant, and Hume all "fail[ed] because of certain shared charac-teristics deriving from their highly specific historical background."[114] That background is the Renaissance's abandonment of Aristotelianism, and in particular the Aristotelian concept of teleology. MacIntyre believes that an-cient and medieval ethics relied on the teleological idea that human life had a proper end or character, and that human beings could not reach this natural end without preparation. Renaissance science rejected Aristotle's teleological physics as incorrect and unnecessary and this led Renaissance philosophy to then make a similar rejection in the realm of ethics.

As an ethics of Dialectical Incarnation is established, a whole teleological cosmology comes into focus. The nature of the human person, with his or her *telos*, is to be virtuous. The nature of the human person is to recognise one's Self in a harmony of one love and one heart. This is humanity's teleological physics and humanity's teleological ethics.

This notion of *telos* in virtue theory must be understood in a complete manner. It is here that virtue ethics is a process of moving from "being" to "doing." When we are "becoming," in and through our "walking" toward our *telos*, that which is "what-we-can-be," the function or purpose of what-we-can-be, is of essential importance. A person is not just a being, but a being who does something, even if it is just to live. A farmer is a farmer by what he does; a mother is a mother by what she does. One knows another, not by what he or she is, but by what he or she does. Virtues are dispositions toward action, not "entities." In virtue ethics, one has as one's end, the human good, and thereby, one does prudent actions, just actions, and loving actions, and by these actions one helps and fosters the virtuous life of others.

The role of function and purpose help define one's human good or *telos*. One recognizes that the content of the human good is not static, but that the *telos* of virtue, actions and moral life is constituted by action, practice, and the exercise of virtues. The human good, toward which we are "walking," consists of a way of living which is "enabled by and consistent with the various virtues."[115]

A corollary to this first content of the human good is that the virtues that lead us to the *telos* are also components of the *telos*. Virtues are instruments and means to lead one to his or her end. But they are also much more, because they are integrated to the end, the human good, and the *telos*. This is exactly what Rahner is saying when he speaks of the *telos*, or goal, in the consummation of the world. Rahner states that the actual movement toward the consummation of the world is achieved "in the goal itself . . . the present is sustained by the future itself."[116] To be a virtuous person is one's goal, but the virtues are that which "sustain" one on one's journey toward one's goal. The movement or the "walking" in ethics is contained in and sustained by the goal itself. As God says "Be holy as I am holy," so too, God can say "Be 'becoming' as I am 'becoming.'" If holiness is the goal, holiness is also that which sustains one in becoming holy. If God is Grace, it is Original Grace which sustains one in one's "walking" toward one's goal, namely, God. Virtue ethics is an ethics of becoming. The ethics of Dialectical Incarnation is an ethics of becoming, because the God, who is the "totality of reality," "though unchanging 'in [Godself],' can become something 'in another.'" Rahner explains that

> [t]he mystery of the incarnation must lie in God himself; in the fact that he, though unchanging 'in himself,' can become something 'in another.' The immutability of God is a dialectical truth like the unity of God."[117]

The reality that the human good is both individual and corporate is another dialectical aspect of both virtue ethics and Dialectical Incarnation. The human person is an individual, but the human person is also, and essentially, a "social being." The human person is who he or she is by the relationships he or she has; "I am because we are." The human person needs others in his or her moral growth. From early pregnancy, in the womb of the mother, to birth and childhood, to and through adulthood, there is a need of relationships in order to be all that one can be. Even in solitude, one is not alone for one is with one's God. In general, "the best life for human beings is social."[118] An ethics must maintain a concern for the individual "human good," while it also maintains a concern for the collective "common good."[119] In the ethics of Dialectical Incarnation, human dignity is recognized and protected only in community with others. Any individual private possession must be understood as having a "social mortgage."[120] This is the *philia* relational and therefore social aspect of love, which is the heart of this ethics.

Another virtue of importance in our proposal of an ethics is the virtue of *epikeia*. In existential ethics, in virtue ethics, and in the ethics of Dialectical Incarnation, there is the stress on the dignity, role, character and responsibility of the human person in view of the human/common good. The virtue of *epikeia*[121] offers to the human person his or her full dignity as moral agent who is responsible for the common good. According to Thomas Aquinas, *epikeia* is as an expression of justice.[122] Josef Fuchs indicates that "situating *epikeia* within justice shows that it is not a dispensation from the law but that it is the correct application of an inherent limited law oriented toward serving the public good."[123]

Timothy O'Connell provides a definition of *epikeia*, which captures well the understanding of Aquinas:

> *Epikeia* is the virtue (power, skill, habit) by which . . . persons discern inner meaning of any human law so as to intelligently obey it in the majority of cases and to reasonably violate it in the proper exceptional case. *Epikeia* is the virtue by which [humans] deal humanely with the reality of human law.[124]

This virtue is important for this philosophy, because it is based on the living out of the cardinal virtues already mentioned, and because it truly offers to the human person recognition of his or her creative freedom and responsibility as a moral person. Moreover, it confirms another very significant element of ethics, namely, the role of conscience.

In order to bring to closure the contribution of virtue ethics to the ethics of Dialectical Incarnation, it is important to look specifically at certain virtues and their role in ethics. In doing so, one must take into account genuine "claims of culture and the uniqueness of individuals."[125] In this approach of incarnating virtues in the concrete, historical context of a person, one is not trying to "preconceive a definitely excellent person . . . an ideal expression" of such a person; rather, we "need simply to identify the minimal conditions that must be met to call any person virtuous."[126] In their existential ethics, Rahner and Fuchs speak of the "condition of the possibility" to live towards one's *telos,* i.e., the infinite horizon within concrete historical "categories." Virtue ethics speak of the incarnational "condition," whereby the cardinal virtues serve as providing the bare essential for right human living and specific actions . . . [and] provide a skeleton both of what human persons should basically be and at what human action should basically aim."[127]

The original cardinal virtues of Plato are justice, courage, generosity and temperance. In stead of calling them cardinal virtues, Aristotle identified certain virtues which are "needed by all people at all times." These virtues are generosity, courage, honesty and loyalty. In James Keenan's own proposal of cardinal virtues, he identifies the relational character and nature of the human person. As such, and unlike Thomas Aquinas' structure of virtues, he presents his own list: justice, fidelity, self-care and prudence.[128] Keenan understands the first three virtues as "distinctive" and not as "auxiliary to the other."[129] The fourth, i.e., prudence, "determines what constitutes the just, faithful, and self-caring way of life."[130] It is these cardinal virtues which serve as the "condition" for the human person to seek the *telos* of the human good, which is also the common good of the individual in the community. Beyond these cardinal virtues, which are necessary for being a morally upright person, there are other virtues which are the "stuff that we should practice in order to realize" genuine love and which help us "to strive to become fully alive human beings."[131] This other list includes such virtues as hospitality, humour, sympathy, and wisdom,[132] but the particular virtue of *gratitude* is paramount in an ethics of Dialectical Incarnation. "Sin" is, in many ways, a lack of gratitude. The first sin of Adam and Eve, within the perspective of the Judeo-Christian scriptures, was a lack of gratitude for having and being all that they had and were. They wanted the one thing they did not have, to be God.[133] Adam and Eve wanted to be God *qua* God, not recognising the divinity intrinsic to their own nature. In our offer of an ethics, gratitude must be an underlying virtue. In recognizing one's true "supernaturalized" nature, in perceiving one's "condition of the possibility," in being aware of one's "infinite horizon," one must be grateful, and as such one will utilize the gifts given to him or her. Then one will freely and responsibly act in such a way that all people may be able to "be" and "do" that which is possible in moving toward the *telos* of the human/common good.

CONSCIENCE

In the ethics of Dialectical Incarnation it is conscience which brings one to the end. Although this ethics has been argued from an all-denominational, rational perspective, an important Roman Catholic encyclical, *Gaudium et Spes*, will be used so as to describe the nature and role of conscience in the human person's responsibility to be a moral agent in his or her everyday existence.

> Deep with his conscience man discovers a law which he has not laid upon himself but which he [or she] must obey. Its voice, ever calling him to love and to do what is good and to avoid evil, tell him inwardly at the right moment; do this, shun that. For man has in his heart a law inscribed by God. His dignity lies in observing this law, and by it he will be judged. His conscience is man's most secret core, and his sanctuary. There he is alone with God whose voice echoes in his depths. By conscience, in a wonderful way, that law is made known which is fulfilled in the love of God and of one's neighbour. [134]

With conscience as the human person's sanctuary [135] with God, one realizes that, as one "walks" towards one's *telos*, one must, as Rahner says,

> return to the transcendental experience of our orientation towards the absolute mystery . . . takes place in the unconditional obedience to *conscience*, and in the open and trusting . . . moments of prayer and quiet silence. [136]

With all that is said and done, if one listens to the sanctuary of God within one's Self, one will be the moral, virtuous, loving, material-supernatural-existential person one is created to be and called to do. By explicating an anthropocentric existential ethics of Dialectical Incarnation one has come to a better recognition of the role of humanity in the world. A philosophy of Dialectical Incarnation in no way passes responsibility to God. It is humanity's responsibility, within humanity's freedom, to consummate the world. As it is only through one's humanity that one comes to know one's divinity, it is only through humanity that we come to know the "totality of reality." It is only through the expressions of one's humanity that one can dialectically proceed from "finding God *in* all things" to "finding God *is* all things."

A CULTURAL INSTANTIATION OF DIALECTICAL INCARNATION: *RIDDIM OF CREATION*

Hegel offers the internal structure of the dialectic as an organic whole. Marx offers the external superstructure of the dialectic as material and historical. Dialectical Incarnation offers a material-supernatural existential structure as an incarnational "occasion of an experience" in the *riddim* of creation. [137]

Paul Tillich argues that humanity's deepest concern drives one into confrontation with a reality that transcends one's own finite existence. Although humans create their destiny, they do so in a dialectical manner, in which one goes beyond one's own, finite limited Self. Karl Rahner frequently makes reference to this manner of thinking in his use of the "supernatural existential." To speak of transcendence, is to indicate that one "goes beyond" what simply is, toward what can be.

Like Rationalism and Humanism, existentialism has given great value to the power of the human person in his or her engagement in the world. However, like process philosophy, it lacks an essential component, namely, the dialectical other of our subjectivity, i.e., the objective material body and world. We are not simply "beings-in-the-world," as Martin Heidegger calls the human person, we are incarnational beings in an incarnational world, intrinsically composed of both subject and object, idea-like and matter-like, soul and body. Incarnation is our being, incarnation is our reality, incarnation is our existence and incarnation is our essence.

RIDDIM OF CREATION: DIALECTICAL INCARNATION IN MUSIC AND CULTURE

For Dialectical Incarnation, there is no longer a separation of sacred and profane. Nothing is profane; all is sacred in its origin, when viewing the world in which humanity lives. One recognizes that the transcendent is also immanent. A concrete, historical, incarnational event and expression is found in Bob Marley's song, "One Love." Marley proclaims to the world that all is "One Love! One Heart! Let's get together and feel alright!" Humanity is one with itself, with nature and with the world. Humanity's own material "supernatural existential" is how humans exist in a harmony of love. As such, Dialectical Incarnation now offers another incarnational and existential expression of the "Dialectical 'One Love, One Heart.'"

When one looks at the history, the cultural expression, the very nature of daily life, Jamaicans, as well as all Caribbean people, are a people of song and dance. It is this instantiation of Jamaica, and therefore of the Caribbean, which will be used to offer a philosophy and theology of culture and symbol, incarnationally expressed in the musical piece, *Riddim of Creation*. As Paul Tillich says, "[philosophy and] theology must use the immense and profound material of the existential analysis in all cultural realms."[138] Therefore, the "profound material" of song and dance will be used to demonstrate a philosophy and theology of the Caribbean people and beyond, manifesting oneness of all reality.

It is often suggested that music be used as a means to convey religious, philosophical and social messages. But the reality is that most often the music of a people is already expressing what is going on within the culture of the society. Music is the heart beat of a society and culture. Hence, one needs to have the vision to see the oneness of the plurality found in society and all of reality. Paul Tillich says that one must confront the material of all cultural realms with the answer implied in the religious, philosophical or social message. This statement indicates that one does not merely study philosophy, theology or sociology and any academic discipline, but one *does* philosophy, theology and sociology. One does this by allowing all cultural realms to express themselves as one discovers the transcendent message they evoke in their own immanent realm. A religious, philosophical or social message, then, is not imposed upon a people, but rather is evoked from the culture of the people. It is through this understanding of incarnation, coming from below, that *Riddim of Creation* is offered as a cultural symbol of the divine and transcendent within the Caribbean person's co-operative response.

Riddim of Creation is a musical expression in the form of a "Liturgy," for the magnificence and splendour of all of creation, its growing pains, its struggles, its evolution and all involved in creation's ongoing birth.[139] As one examines the different aspects of the evolution of this musical piece, one needs to be reminded that one must search for "the immense and profound material of the existential analysis in all cultural realms."[140] This is because there is no longer the separation of the sacred and the profane.

With incarnation and "revelation" from below, nothing is profane; all is sanctified in its origin. The starting point is Original Grace, not Original Sin. Divinity, or grace, is received at the moment of creation and at the conception of the human person. The incarnation of God in the world begins to take on the cultural expression of the people who exist in the diversity of God's creation, which is then expressed through the diversity of races and creeds found in the world. In this manner, one looks at the Caribbean person in a culture of song and dance, so as to discover a philosophy and natural theology that has evolved, rather than one which has been imposed.

In identifying the nature of the Caribbean people, it is interesting that a philosophy and natural theology of song and dance had already emerged from the culture of the people of Israel. At the very end of the Book of Psalms it states:

PRAISE THE Lord! Praise God in [God's] sanctuary; praise God in God's mighty firmament!
Praise [God] for [God's] mighty deeds; praise [God] according to God's exceeding greatness!
Praise [God] with trumpet sound; praise [God] with lute and harp!
Praise [God] with timbrel and dance; praise [God] with strings and pipe!
Praise [God] with sounding cymbals; praise [God] with loud clashing cymbals!
Let everything that breathes praise the Lord! Praise the Lord! [141]

A general philosophy and natural theology of culture is transnational and all-denominational, while at the same time particular and culturally national or ethnic. This is "unity in diversity." One can discover meditations where all of creation, with humanity as its hallmark, yearns to sing and dance for God and with God. Significant meditations, which indicate that God and Nature, together, express a culture of song and dance, are the following. [142]

To dance in the sky
and sing praises to the life all around . . . oh mother earth, SING!
The earth sings a song of gladness.
The earth sings a song of praise. (Nancy Wood)
Sing to Life a new song!
Sing to Life, all creation
Sing of compassion . . .
Declare among the nations: "All is God" (Rabbi Rami M. Shapiro)
The earth reveals God's eternal presence . . .
Life comes forth by God's creative will . . .
A divine voice sings through all creation.

One can grasp a philosophy and theology of culture, along with that of symbol, when they come *from* a people's culture; when song and dance symbolise one's "ultimate concern," i.e., one's God, one's Nature.

A PHILOSOPHY AND THEOLOGY OF CULTURE

According to Paul Tillich, religion is being ultimately concerned about that which is and should be one's ultimate concern. It is not a theoretical understanding, but more of an existential one. This existential concept of religion is therefore the disappearance of the gap between the sacred and profane, the religious and the secular realm. In this philosophy and theology, all of creation, all of culture begins by being sacred. Tillich states that the unconditional character of this concern implies that it refers to every moment of one's life, which certainly involves song and dance. It refers to every space and every realm of one's existence. The universe and all of creation is the sanctuary of the divine.

Every work day is a day of the Lord, every supper a Lord's supper, every work
the fulfilment of a divine task, every joy a joy in God. In all preliminary
concerns, ultimate concern is present, consecrating them. Essentially the religious and the secular are not separated realms. Rather they are within each
other.[143]

   In this non-separation of the sacred and the profane or secular, every song
and every dance is a song and a dance of God, for God and with God, who is
one's ultimate concern. Unfortunately, this is not what is actually the situation in the world. Humanity continues to want to separate. The secular element, as does the sacred, tends to make itself independent and to establish a
realm of its own. Humanity's predicament is the situation of the "estrange-
ment of [hu]man from his [her] true being. One could rightly say that the
existence of religion as a special realm is the most conspicuous proof of
[hu]man's fallen state."[144] One knows in the history of the world how religions divide and separate. Nevertheless, this is not to say that one, i.e., sacred
or profane, religious or secular, swallows the other. One can refer to and
make a distinction from the sacred and the profane, the religious and the
secular, in theoretical terms, but these different elements are always understood as distinct but not separate.
   This understanding of having distinction but not separation also involves
religion and culture. According to Tillich, religion is the "meaning-giving"
substance of culture, and culture is the totality of form in which the basic
concern of religion expresses itself. Religion is the substance of culture;
culture is the form of religion.[145] With this understanding one prevents a
dualism of religion and culture. "Every religious act, not only in organised
religion, but also in the most intimate movement of the soul, is culturally
formed."[146] In one's non-separation of the two, every cultural act can be and
is a religious act, if one allows it to be that. In this specific focus, cultural
song and dance are religious and are sacred. They are the cultural forms in
which religion, philosophy and theology actualise themselves.
   When it is said that the "form of religion is culture," this becomes most
obvious in the language used by religion. According to Tillich, every language, including that of the Bible, is the result of innumerable acts of cultural
creativity. Language is the expression of humanity's freedom from the given
situation and its concrete demands. As Tillich states:

There is no sacred language which has fallen from a supernatural heaven and
been put between the covers of a book. But there is human language, based on
[hu]man's encounter with reality, changing through the millenia, used for the
needs of daily life, for expression and communication, for literature and poet-
ry, and used also for the expression and communication of our ultimate concern. In each of these cases the language is different. Religious language is
ordinary language, changed under the power of what it expresses, the ultimate

of being and meaning, the expression of it can be narrative (mythological, legendary, historical), or it can be prophetic, poetic, liturgical. It becomes holy for those to whom it expresses their ultimate concern from generation to generation.[147]

The particular expression of language, for our purpose, is song, and the manner in which this song is expressed is dance. It is holy because it reflects one's inner desire to praise and thank God, one's ultimate concern. The important point to make is that it emerged from the culture, from the people, not brought down from above. Song and dance reflect and reveal divinity's very being in the world.

One principle which must be emphasised is that religious art is the principle of artistic honesty. There is no one particular sacred artistic style, all is sacred. Artistic style is honest only if it expresses the real situation of the artist and the cultural period to which he or she belongs. According to Tillich, one can participate in the artistic styles of the past in so far as they were honestly expressing the encounter which they had with God, humanity, and world.

A summary of the philosophy and theology of culture is that incarnation and "revelation" come from below, not from above. Incarnation is the alpha of evolution whereby the religious and philosophical message can be understood as emerging from the culture of a people without an external imposition. This culture, i.e., the form of religion and the form of philosophy, expresses itself in human language, actualised in and through different artistic styles, i.e., song and dance, and expresses the people's encounter with God, humanity and the world.

PHILOSOPHY AND THEOLOGY OF SYMBOL[148]

One is reminded that,

> it is only to be expected that no theology [nor philosophy] can be complete without also being a theology [and philosophy] of the symbol . . . in fact the whole of theology [and philosophy] is incomprehensible if it is not essentially a theology [or philosophy] of symbol.[149]

As already stated, a symbol is dialectical, because it possesses its own integrity, while at the same time a symbol represents and points beyond itself to something which is *other* than itself and makes that other present. A symbol is not merely a sign or an indicator, nor a substitute for some absent reality. Rather, a symbol is a unity in plurality. Riddim of Creation is the music of no one religion, so it can be the music (unity) for all religions (plurality). This understanding of unity in difference is not a limit of a symbol, but a perfection of itself. Therefore, a symbol's identity is directly proportional to its difference. It possesses itself, its own identity, by giving itself away from itself to the other. A symbol posits the other as its own reality and by doing so truly becomes itself, in a real sense, for the first time. Every incarnation, as particularity in the world (these are infinite), is a symbol of God. Incarnation, from the particularity of each sub-atomic particle to the wholeness of the universe, are symbols in that they point beyond themselves to something which is other than themselves and make the other present.

A real symbol, as we understand Rahner, makes present that which it symbolises. God is not merely an agent in the world but is the very ground of the whole world process and the unity amidst the complexity and multiplicity of humans in the world. God is active in the world, in and through God's symbol, God's incarnations. With this brief revisit of a philosophy and theology of symbol, offered by Rahner, one can begin to understand how cultural expressions of humanity can truly be representing God's own realty.

Paul Tillich also offers a philosophy and theology of symbol, one that is less metaphysical and more existential in its application. Nevertheless, the philosophies and theologies of Rahner and Tillich are similar. Tillich states that a "symbol represents something that is not itself, for which it stands and in the power and meaning of which it participates."[150] Every symbol opens up a level of reality for which non-symbolic speaking is inadequate. He says that

> the more we try to enter into the meaning of symbols, the more we become aware that it is a function of art to open up levels of reality; in poetry, in visual art, and in music, levels of reality are opened up which can be opened up in no other way. Now if this is the function of art, then certainly artistic creations have symbolic character.[151]

In the example of art, there is no other way that a painting, a musical piece, a sculpture, any visual or auditory artistic expression, can be mediated except through the concrete artwork itself. The art then becomes a symbol of something beyond the external, visual expression. As one remembers, symbols open up levels of reality.

> But in order to do this, something else must be opened up—namely, levels of the soul, levels of our interior reality. And they must correspond to the levels in exterior reality opened up by a symbol. So every symbol is two-edged. It opens up reality and it opens up the soul.[152]

With this understanding of the function of symbols, it becomes clear that symbols cannot be replaced by other symbols. Tillich explains that every symbol has a special function that is just *it* and cannot be replaced by more or less adequate symbols. Signs can be replaced, but not symbols.

One last aspect of an understanding of symbol must be asked. "Out of what womb are symbols born?" Paul Tillich states that they come

> out of the womb which is usually called today the "group unconscious" or "collective unconscious," or whatever you want to call it—out of a group which acknowledges . . . its own being. It is not invented intentionally. [153]

The important point is that the meaning of a symbol is not created nor invented. It is really discovered because it is an incarnation from below. When one looks at the collective unconscious group called the Caribbean people is one open to the symbol of their expression of culture found in song and dance? The intention of this philosophy is to have eyes that can see, and hearts that can love, so as to recognize the incarnation of God in the evolution of creation with its diversity of cultural expressions.

When dealing with a philosophy and theology of symbol it is important to look, even briefly, upon the nature of religious symbols. Religious symbols do exactly the same thing as all symbols, they open up a level of reality, which otherwise is not opened at all, which is hidden. Religious symbols open up to the dimension of reality that is the ground of every other dimension and every other depth. It is the level below all other levels, the level of being itself, or the ultimate power of being. Accordingly, the dimension of ultimate reality is also the dimension of the holy. Religious symbols are, therefore, symbols of the holy. They participate in the holiness of the holy. But, participation is not identity; they are not themselves *the* holy. Religious symbols are taken from the abundance and diversity of "material" which experienced reality gives us. Consequently, everything in time and space can be and has become, at some time in the history of religion, a symbol of the holy. In our understanding that there is no separation between the sacred and the secular, this is only naturally so, because everything in the world, everything in creation, rests on the ultimate ground of being, that which all religious symbols represent.

In speaking about this ground of being and the focus of this philosophy one is reminded that incarnation is the unifying element of all creation, with its diversity. This diversity of creation is expressed in and through the different cosmologies, peoples, cultures and consciousness of faith, which is then found in the diversity of religions. The revelation of the religious message of God incarnate is not only or primarily found from above, but truly comes from below, as well. The incarnation of God in the world, that is, Dialectical Incarnation, is one's very ground of being, one's very ground of existence. When the Caribbean people and their cultures are observed and reflected upon, one is now more open to discover the incarnation of God given through them and their expression of life. This recognition of symbol allows a people's expression of song and dance to be truly representing their ultimate concern, namely God. Therefore, the song and the dance of the Caribbean people are symbols of the holy.

RIDDIM OF CREATION: A SYMBOL OF THE HOLY

According to Paul Tillich,

> [symbols] have the tendency (in the human mind, of course) to replace that to which they are supposed to point, and to become ultimate in themselves. And in the moment in which they do this, they become idols . . . [this]we will call "demonization."[154]

So as not to demonise the symbol of song and dance, it is important to maintain one's adherence to the doctrine of creation and its relation to God, the ground of being and one's ultimate concern. A reminder of the doctrine goes as such: God is creator. God freely created. God freely created from nothing. God is distinct from creation. And humanity is the hallmark of creation. So as not to fall victim to demonization, one needs to constantly hold firm to these five aspects of the unity of God, creation and humanity. Humanity, although distinct from the Creator, is not separate from the Creator and therefore expresses itself with the Creator as one unity.

Riddim of Creation: A Liturgy emerged from a personal experience of Caribbean culture and the desire to manifest this experience of the Holy found in the expression of these people through song and dance.[155] From this ground of being there emerged a desire to thank God for the splendour of creation, which, in Dialectical Incarnation, is God's created "otherness," distinct but not separate. But, as Paul Tillich has stated, the womb out of which symbols are born is the collective group who says "yes." When one observes Caribbean people praising their God, it would not be difficult to recognise that song and dance serve as a symbol of the Holy. Song and dance are the primary manners of praising their God. As one segment of the lyrics found in the entrance song of *Riddim of Creation* says, "you are a witness in time, I am a witness in time" the Caribbean collective people must now recognise and acknowledge that the expression of their relationship with God, which is song and dance, is a symbol of the ground of their being. As one recognises and acknowledges this symbol of God, one must continually remind oneself of the five elements of the doctrine of creation so as not to demonise the symbol.

ORIGINAL GRACE PRECEDES ORIGINAL SIN

The philosophy and theology underlying the whole of *Riddim of Creation* is one of creation and incarnation. One is reminded that according, to the position of Duns Scotus, in the beginning, quite independently of the fall of humanity, that the whole of creation was planned with the God-human, that is, Incarnation, in view. Even if humanity had not sinned, the Word (or the *Riddim)*, would still have become human, for the truth is, as has been stated, "[Incarnation] is the supreme revelation of God in this world and the masterpiece of all of God's creation."[156]

The first track of *Riddim of Creation* begins with "In the beginning was the . . . *Riddim,"* and reflects the Prologue of John's Gospel.[157] This scripture passage, and the philosophy and theology behind it, is stating that all of creation, "all things that were made," have received the dwelling of the Word (*Riddim)*, that all of creation is graced (Original Grace) with God. This is why the book of Genesis states that, "God saw all that God had made, and it was very good." The *Riddim of Creation* is expressing musically that God, who is incarnate in the world, is the unity within all diversity of creation. An anthropological philosophical theology should not begin with Original Sin, but with Original Grace, for humans are a "graced event" prior to having a sinful existence. This new perspective, this new viewpoint and this renewed attitude of the human person, will hopefully bring about the much-needed incarnational renaissance.

The *Riddim of Creation* is a symbol, expressed in a Caribbean style of song and dance, representing the Holy for which we wish to be a "witness in time." Therefore, the *Riddim of Creation* takes an incurable optimistic understanding of the world in inviting all people, all creeds, at all times to live in the harmony of love which is the *riddim* and which is the philosophy of Dialectical Incarnation.

In the history of this complex world, there is commonly a cosmological vision in which God, humanity and the world are united.[158] Humanity needs to allow the "revelation" of God to be expressed incarnationally, in and through the people, creeds, colours, cultures and music found in the world.

In incarnational spirituality, it is important to have eyes and ears to "find God in all things." Music is clearly a way to find God. However, the philosophy and theology behind this music goes further, saying that God is expressing God's self through the *Riddim of Creation*, through symbol. This is the incarnational spirituality and philosophy which this music wants to reveal. As such, even though it emerges from a traditional Roman and Anglican liturgical style, it moves to be truly catholic, that is universal. It becomes the catholic music of no one religion, so it can then be the music for all religions.

RIDDIM OF CREATION: A HARMONY OF LOVE

The cultural expression of the Caribbean people of song and dance can be and is a symbol of the Holy, a symbol of one's ultimate concern, God. In addition, however, dance has also become the image to demonstrate the unity of God, creation and humanity. This philosophy started with anthropology. It is the human person as a material-supernatural existential that serves as the condition of the possibility of knowing God and Nature. The human person is able to recognise one' Self as the centre of the universe which is God and Nature, the totality of reality. One can understand God *qua* God, as an object of knowledge, only in and through one's Self, the human person. And the human person as a transcendental subject is able to be open to the mystery and the infinite horizon of God *qua* God, because of the divinity given to the human in God's *a priori* self-communication. A reminder that, if humanity-in-the-world, namely, all of creation, is metaphorically understood as the dance, one can know and observe the dancer, as a dancer, only through the dance itself. Without the dance, the dancer is merely a concept, not a dancer. Likewise, without the dancer there could be no dance. The human person-in-the-world is a material-supernaturalized being of love, who is a particular transcendental subject, because God is the very ground of being, the foundation, for the supernatural and transcendental being to even be. God could not self-communicate without a "hearer of the Word," or a listener of the *riddim*, or dancer of the dance. Because of this essential, relational nature between God and the human-in-the-world, anthropology and theology "are not opposites but strictly one and the same thing, seen from two sides."[159] As such, neither is known without the other, and why it is proper to have begun with anthropology.

To say that humanity is created in the image of God is to say that humans are co-creators with God. As co-creators humans live-out their genuine character by wanting to express themselves within one's own unity with God, through the "material" existential being of song and dance. This has been done through the *Riddim of Creation.* Now that the barrier of dualism is being razed, there need no longer be a separation of the sacred from the profane, in that the totality of reality is actually "One Love! One Heart!"

NOTES

1. D.W. Hamlyn, *The Theory of Knowledge* (New York: Anchor Books, 1970), 246.

2. John Ayotunde (Tunde) Isola Bewaji, *An Introduction to the Theory of Knowledge: A Pluricultural Approach* (Ibadan, Nigeria: Hope Publications, 2007), 108, quotes J.S. Mbiti, *African religions and philosophy* (London: Heineman, 1969). The statement by Mbiti is actually the foundation of Ubuntu philosophy. Ubuntu is very much the philosophy of Incarnation, but this will be elaborated in another book.

3. Chukwudum, B Okolo, "Self as a problem in African philosophy" in *The African Philosophy Reader,* 2nd ed. (New York: Routledge, 2003), 213.

4. Spencer A. Rathus, *Essentials of Psychology* (Fort Worth: Harcourt College Publishers, 2001), 9.

5. William James, *Principles of Psychology* (New York: Holt, 1890), 330.

6. Heidegger's term for this is *Dasein.*

7. Mary Whiton Calkins, "Psychology as Science of Self II: The Nature of the Self," *Journal of Philosophy, Psychology and Scientific Methods* 5.3 (1908): 64–68.

8. Cormac Burke, *Man and Values: A Personalist Anthropology* (New York: Scepter Publishers, 2008), Appendix II (Individualism and collectivism; personalism and community). http://www.cormacburke.or.ke/node/2465

9. Peter J. Henriot, Edward P. DeBerri and Michael J. Schultheis, *Catholic Social Teaching: Our Best Kept Secret* (New York: Orbis Books, 1995), 23.

10. Burke, *Man and Values*

11. Karl Marx, *Karl Marx: Selected Writings,* 2nd ed. (Oxford: Oxford University Press, 1987), 45, 47, 77).

12. Burke, *Man and Values*

13. Quoted in Burke, *Man and Values*

14. Karol Wojtyla, *The Acting Person* (Dordrecht, Netherlands: Springer, 1979), quoted in Burke, *Man and Values.*

15. Alasdair MacIntyre, *After Virtue: A Study in Moral Theory.* 2nd ed. (Notre Dame: University of Notre Dame Press, 1984), 250–52.

16. Burke, *Man and Values*

17. I purposely do not use the upper case "Self" as I normally do because the ego is not the Self.

18. Robert C. Priddy, *The Human Whole: An Outline of the 'Higher' Psychology.* Accessed June 27, 2009. http://robertpriddy.com/P/.

19. Maurice Merleau-Ponty, *Phenomenology of Perception* (London: Routledge Classics, 2002), 225.

20. Ibid., 215.

21. Alex Scott, "Merleau-Ponty's *Phenomenology of Perception*," http://www.angelfire.com/md2/timewarp/merleauponty.html

22. Trevor G Elkington, "Between Order and Chaos: On Peter Greenaway's Postmodern/Poststructuralist Cinema," *Film-Philosophy Journal* 8.1 (January 2004).

23. Anthony Harrison-Barbet, *Philosophical Connections: Merleau-Ponty,* http://philosophos.org/philosophical_connections/

24. R.H Hoyle, M.H. Kernis, M.R. Leary and M.W. Baldwin, *Selfhood: Identity, Esteem, Regulation* (Boulder, CO: Westview Press, 1999).

25. Karl Rahner, *Hearer of the Word: Laying the Foundation for a Philosophy of Religion* (New York: Continuum, 1994).

26. Mark Lloyd Taylor, *GOD IS LOVE: A Study in the Theology of Karl Rahner* (Atlanta: Scholars Press, 1986), 338.

27. Baruch Spinoza, *The Collected Works of Spinoza* (Princeton, NJ: Princeton University Press, 1985), *Ethics,* 612.

28. Ibid., 603.

29. Ibid., 606.

30. Ibid., 603.

31. Ibid., 611.

32. Ibid.

33. Ibid., 612.

34. Ibid., 614.

35. This statement means that any act, behaviour or way of proceeding that a human *intends* belongs to morality. See James F. Keenan, *Virtues for Ordinary Christians* (Kansas City: Sheed & Ward, 1996), 12.

36. The self is more than a subject. The self is a person, intrinsically united with the other.

37. Spinoza, *The Collected Works, Ethics,* 603.

38. Ibid.

39. Ibid.

40. Ibid., 611.

41. Ibid.

42. G.W. Leibniz, Theodicy: Essays on the Goodness of God, the Freedom of Man, and the Origin of Evil (Chicago: Open Court, 1951), 258.

43. G.W. Leibniz, *G.W. Leibniz: Political Writings,* 2nd ed. (Cambridge: Cambridge University Press, 1988), 83.

44. Ibid., 163.

45. John S. Mbiti, Introduction to African Religion (Santa Barbara, CA: Praeger, 1975), quoted in Bewaji, *Theory of Knowledge,* 108.

46. An interesting examination of Incarnation and Anthropology is offered by John Haldane, "Incarnational Anthropology," *Supplement to 'Philosophy'* 29 (1991): 191–211. He is taking a philosophy of the mind perspective dealing with the doctrine of the Incarnation, namely the Jesus, a man, is both totally human and totally divine. It is significant, however, that he is asking the question of the necessary connection of matter and form, and immanence and transcendence and in the end leads the reader to what this theses is actually about, i.e. the synthesis of these two seeming opposing poles. His conclusion is worth quoting:

These final thoughts combine a recognition of present immanence with a prospect of future transcendence. I cannot see that Heidegger's rejection of the latter as an unsettling legacy of Christian theology places him in any better position to explain the former. On the contrary, the only prospect I see for explaining the subjectivity of *Dasein*, and its very existence, involves the sort of incarnational anthropology discussed above.

47. Reference has already been made to Alasdair MacIntyre, a contemporary supporter of virtue ethics. Another strong advocate of contemporary virtue ethics is Philippa Foot, along with Bernard Williams, John McDowell and Rosalind Hursthouse. More will be discussed later in this chapter.

48. Karl Rahner, "The Theology of Symbol" in *Theological Investigations* IV 9: 237.

49. Edward Collins Vacek, *Love, Human and Divine* (Washington, DC: Georgetown University Press, 1994), 21.

50. Quoted in James F. Keenan, "Proposing Cardinal Virtues," *Theological Studies* 56 (1995): 721.

51. Ibid.

52. For Duns Scotus, creation and incarnation are one act of love for God. Teilhard de Chardin goes further and says that creation, incarnation and redemption are all one act of love (quoted in Allan B. Wolter, "John Duns Scotus on the Primacy and Personality of Christ," in *Franciscan Christology* (St. Bonaventure, NY: Franciscan Institute of St. Bonaventure, 1980), 153.

53. The intrinsic evil referred to is the notion of "original sin," which was developed by St. Augustine and became the starting point of so much of Christian theology, especially in the Protestant movement. Original sin basically states that through the fall of Adam and Eve, human nature is now intrinsically damaged, even evil.

54. Joseph J. Kotva, *The Christian Case for Virtue Ethics* (Washington, DC: Georgetown University Press, 1996), 97.

55. Keenan, "Proposing Cardinal Virtues," 714.

56. Robert Kress, *A Rahner Handbook* (Atlanta: John Knox Publishing, 1982), 131.

57. Quoted in Vacek, *Love, Human and Divine,* 97.

58. Karl Rahner, "Theology and Anthropology" in Theological Investigations, IX 2: 28–29.

59. Vacek, *Love, Human and Divine,* 159.

60. Ibid., 162.

61. Ibid., 273.

62. Ibid.

63. Ibid.

64. Ibid., 281.

65. Karl Rahner, *Trinity* (New York: Herder and Herder, 1970), 47.

66. Rahner "Immanent and Transcendent Consummation of the World" in *Theological Investigations* X 15: 281.

67. Vacek, *Love, Human and Divine,* 281.

68. Ibid.

69. Josef Fuchs, *Personal Responsibility and Christian Morality* (Washington, DC: Georgetown University Press, 1983), 62.

70. Manuel Velasquez and Cynthia Rostankowski, *Ethics: Theory and Practice* (Englewood Cliffs, NJ: Prentice Hall, 1985), 5.

71. Ibid.

72. Rex Nettleford, *Caribbean Cultural Identity: The Case of Jamaica* (Kingston: Institute of Jamaica, 1978), 1.

73. It is the purpose of establishing an ethics in this philosophy so as to find a universal ethical "code" which is operative in all cultures, all religions. Immanuel Kant's *Religion Within the Limits of Reason Alone* also is seeking to find that universal code which is void of the limits and divisions that religion brings about. He works to clarify what has been already discussed, i.e. the distinction between natural, philosophical theology and biblical, revealed theology. The ethics of dialectical incarnation is an ethics emerging from the former.

74. One could say that I am making a distinction between the fact that there is a universal ethical form and its particular cultural content. That is the unity in diversity of dialectical incarnation. The cultural religious expressions are the diversity of the one love, the one heart of dialectical incarnation. This will be elaborated when the philosophy moves to an existential ethics.

75. Timothy E. O'Connell, *Principle for a Catholic Morality* (Minneapolis: The Seabury Press, 1978), 144.

76. Henriot, DeBerri and Schultheis, *Catholic Social Teaching,* 23.

77. Austin O.P Flannery, ed., *Vatican Council II, Conciliar and Post Conciliar Documents* (New York: Costello Publishing Company, 1975), #5.

78. Rahner, "The Dignity and Freedom of Man," *Theological Investigations* II.8: 244.

79. For discussion on the question "Is there a distinctively Christian morality?" see Josef Fuchs, *Personal Responsibility and Christian Morality* (Washington, DC: Georgetown University Press, 1983), chapter 4.

80. Ibid., 55.

81. Ibid.

82. Ibid.

83. Ibid., 56.

84. Rahner, "Anonymous Christians" in *Theological Investigations* VI 23: 394.

85. Ibid.

86. This could read "The existentially believing Hindu, Buddhist, Muslim, Rasta." See Fuchs, *Personal Responsibility,* 58.

87. Ibid., 59.

88. Ibid.

89. Rahner, "Theology of Freedom" in *Theological Investigations* VI 13: 184.

90. Ibid., 182.

91. Ibid., 185.

92. Ibid.

93. Ibid., 186.

94. Ibid., 185.

95. Rahner, "The Theological Problems Entailed in the Idea of the 'New Earth'" in *Theological Investigations* X 14: 200.

96. Ibid., 204.

97. Rahner, "Theology of Freedom" in *Theological Investigations* VI 13: 187.

98. Rahner, Idea of the 'New Earth,' X 14: 264.

99. Rahner, "Immanent and Transcendent Consummation of the World" in *Theological Investigations* X 15: 281.

100. Ibid., 282.

101. This is why this world is the best world when we discussed the question given to Leibniz earlier.

102. Rahner, *Foundations of Christian Faith: An Introduction to the Idea of Christianity* (New York: Crossroad, 1992), 68.

103. Ibid., 62–63.

104. Ibid., 63.

105. Rahner, "Reflections on the Unity of the Love of neighbor and the Love of God" *Theological Investigations* VI 16: 232.

106. Keenan, "Cardinal Virtues," 711.

107. Kotva, *Virtue Ethics,* 17.

108. Ibid.

109. Rahner, "Reflections on the Unity" VI 16: 242.

110. Kotva, *Virtue Ethics*, 17.

111. Ibid.

112. Ibid.

113. MacIntyre, *After Virtue,* 2.

114. Ibid., 51.

115. Kotva, *Virtue Ethics,* 20.

116. Rahner "Immanent and Transcendent Consummation" X 15: 282.

117. (Rahner IV 4: 113, 114, n. 3)

118. Kotva, *Virtue Ethics,* 22.

119. The common good was defined earlier in the section of the Self and Person: Individualism versus Personalism.

120. Catholic Church, *Laborem Exercens* (On Human Work), Encyclical Letter of His Holiness Pope John Paul II (Boston MA: St. Paul Editions, 1982), #14.

121. *Epikeia* (Greek: epieikes, reasonable): An indulgent and benign interpretation of law, which regards a law as not applying in a particular case because of circumstances unforeseen by the lawmaker. The lawmaker cannot foresee all possible cases that may come under the law, and it is therefore reasonably presumed that were the present circumstances known to the legislator he would permit the act, e.g., a mother presumes that she may miss Mass on Sunday when there is no one present to care for her baby. Epikeia is not permitted, however, no matter how grave the inconvenience, if violation of the law would render an act null and void, e.g., to presume that marriage may be contracted because of grave inconvenience in spite of an existing diriment impediment.

122. Thomas Aquinas, *Basic Writings of Saint Thomas Aquinas: God and the Order of Creation* (Indianapolis: Hackett Publishing, 1997), II-II q. 120, a. 2.

123. Fuchs, *Personal Responsibility* 257, quoted in Richard M. Gula, *Reason Informed By Faith: Foundations of Catholic Morality* (New York: Paulist Press, 1989), 257.

124. O'Connell, *Catholic Morality,* 190.

125. Keenan, "Cardinal Virtues," 713.

126. Ibid.

127. Ibid., 714.

128. Ibid., 723.

129. Ibid., 724.

130. Ibid.

131. Ibid., 105.

132. Ibid., 106.

133. Ibid., 121.

134. Flannery, *Vatican Council II,* #16.

135. Sanctuary generally means a sacred and holy place.

136. Rahner, *Foundations,* 54.

137. Martin Schade, "Riddim of Creation: An Incarnational Expression of Caribbean Theology" *Caribbean Journal of Religious Studies* 19.1 (1998): 28–38.

138. Paul Tillich, *Theology of Culture* (New York: Oxford University Press, 1959), 49.

139. *Riddim of Creation: a Liturgy* is an album (CD) which I conceptualised and produced. I also directed a liturgical dance by the same name, along with several of Jamaica's leading

artistes and dance companies. These emerged from his participation in the Jamaican culture and with the people over the years.

140. Tillich, *Theology of Culture,* 49.

141. I replaced "God" for "him" and "God's" for "his" in this edited translation. G. Herbert, Bruce May and M. Metzger, eds., *New Oxford Annotated Bible with the Apocrypha* (New York: Oxford University Press, 1977), 150.

142. Elizabeth Roberts and Elias Amidon, eds., *Life Prayers from around the World* (San Francisco: Harper, 1996).

143. Tillich, *Theology of Culture*, 41.

144. Ibid., 42.

145. Ibid.

146. Ibid.

147. Ibid., 47–48.

148. I will be using both Paul Tillich's and Karl Rahner's philosophy and theology of symbol. These positions come from an existential and metaphysical perspective, respectively. In that this philosophy as examined Whitehead's process philosophy and theology, it is significant to mention that Whitehead also wrote on symbolism, *Symbolism, Its Meaning and Effect* (New York: Capricon Books, 1927). Whitehead's analysis of symbolism, in contrast to Tillich and Rahner, corresponds with the educational process of human beings. For Whitehead the symbolism of God includes both bodily and mental activities which disclose the double structure of life based on forgiveness and grace on the one hand, on sanctification and sacrifice on the other hand. The symbol gives rise to thought and unfortunately, stays in that realm, which is in accordance with the thesis' original critique of Whitehead.

149. Rahner, "The Theology of Symbol" in *Theological Investigations* IV 9: 235.

150. Tillich, *Theology of Culture,* 56.

151. Ibid., 56–57.

152. Ibid.

153. Ibid., 58.

154. Ibid., 60.

155. *Riddim of Creation: a Liturgy* is the name of an album (CD) which I conceptualised and produced, as well as a liturgical dance that I directed, with several of Jamaica's leading artistes and dance companies. It emerged from my participation in the Jamaican culture and people through the 29 years living in Jamaica.

156. N.W Wildiers, *An Introduction to Teilhard de Chardin* (New York: Harper & Row, 1967), 132.

157. Herbert, May and Metzger, *New Oxford Annotated Bible*, John 1:1–5, 14.

158. This was elaborated in the earlier chapters, especially the philosophy of Spinoza, Teilhard, African philosophy and Rastafari, among others.

159. Rahner, "Theology and Anthropology" in *Theological Investigations* IX 2:28.

Conclusion

Humanity has entered into a new millennium of evolution. With one's new vision of love as human, divine and the totality of reality, humanity is coming out of the cave with a mind and heart that are united with the divine and the entire cosmos. Humanity is coming to realise that the dualism of Western philosophy and of natural theology is not the paradigm to which one can now adhere. A dialectical and incarnational perspective of reality allows all to be one, in which each particular incarnational being unites with the whole by being a unique incarnation. Every particular sub-atomic neutron, to the entirety of the cosmos as a whole, is intrinsically summoned to be perfect. Each particularity has its perfection to be what it is as unique, and exists so as to be perfect in its particularity. Matter is not a mistake or a less important aspect of the whole. Matter is what is needed for reality to be. Each of the bi-polar components of reality is the condition of the possibility of incarnation. The human person, as the centre of the universe, is able to recognize him or her Self as the synthesis of transcendence and immanence, of God and Nature, of unity and diversity, of spirit and matter. The separation found within the components of the totality of reality must end. Humanity must have eyes that can see and hearts that can love each and everything as a particularity, found in the oneness of all, which is Love. Love is Incarnation. Love needs a beloved "heart" to love. Love needs a particular, and therefore material, beloved. Love, as Incarnation, is the *Alpha* and it is Love, as Incarnation, which is also the *Omega*.

As this philosophy comes to a conclusion, it offers its final contribution in the discovery of Dialectical Incarnation. As has been made manifest through a dialectical historical perspective of Dialectical Incarnation, one can now see how Love, as Incarnation, can be identified as the First Mover because the entirety of the process of incarnation begins with the Lover as subject. Incarnation can be identified as the material cause of the world, because it is the "out of which" that particular being is. Dialectical Incarnation is the efficient cause because incarnate love begets itself and is also the formal cause, because it is the "what it is" of the universe. Incarnation is the final cause because Love, as a harmonious one, is that toward which all of reality moves. Incarnation exists through the condition of the possibility of transcendence, God, spirit and equally through the condition of the possibility of immanence, Nature and matter. Love and incarnation are human, divine and the totality of all. Humanity, divinity and all of matter, together and completely, are a harmony, a phylum of love, found in the totality of the universe. It is the human person, the Self, which is the crucial and necessary link between the two, seeming opposing, bi-polar conditions of the possibility of the incarnate universe. This new "philosophy of the heart" must express itself in the totality of reality so that our world will find its perfection.

Traditional philosophy, through the ontological argument of Anselm, states that "God's essence is God existence." For Dialectical Incarnation all infinite particulars of the totality of reality have as their essence their own existence. Dialectical Incarnation is an equally balanced synthesis of an essentialist's condition of the possibility as it is an existentialist's condition of the possibility. "My essence is my existence," as is "your essence is your existence," as is a particular neutron's essence is its existence. Every human and every particular being of the world can say "I am, who am."[1] Throughout history we humans have been afraid of humanity's divinity. Humanity has condemned itself to an intrinsic evil condition which humanity never actually had. It is time that we humans recognise the divine that we are, and it is time for us to allow God, the divine, to be the human and the Nature, that God, the divine, is. Let us awaken from our slumber and see that we humans are the centre of the circumference of the dialectical One Love, One Heart found in the totality of realty. And, in so doing, let there be peace!

> A human being is part of the whole called the 'universe' by us. We experience ourselves, our thoughts and feelings as something separate from the rest...a kind of optical delusion of consciousness. This delusion is a kind of prison for us, restricting us to our personal desires and to affection for a few persons nearest to us. Our task must be to free ourselves from the prison by widening our circle of compassion to embrace all living creatures and the whole of nature in its beauty. The true value of a human being is determined by the measure and the sense in which they have obtained liberation from the self. We shall require a substantially new manner of thinking if humanity is to survive (Albert Einstein).

NOTE

1. These are the words God says to Moses when Moses asked "Who are you?" in Exodus 3: 14.

Bibliography

Adelmann, Frederick, J. *From Dialogue to Epilogue, Marxism and Catholicism Tomorrow.* The Hague: Martinus Nijhoff, 1968.

Antognazza, Maria Rosa. "The Defence of the Mysteries of the Trinity and the Incarnation: An Example of Leibniz 'Other' Reason." *British Journal for the History of Philosophy* 9.2 (2001): 283–309.

Antohin, Esther Sellassie. "The phenomenon of Ras Tafari," Master's thesis, 2004. http://www.angelfire.com/ak/sellassie/page5.html.

Aquinas, Thomas. *Basic Writings of Saint Thomas Aquinas: God and the Order of Creation.* Indianapolis: Hackett Publishing, 1997.

Aristotle. *The Basic Works of Aristotle.* New York: Random House, 1941.

Ayer, A.J. ed. *Logical Positivism.* New York: The Free Press, 1959.

———. *Language, Truth and Logic.* New York: Dover Publications, 1952.

Ball, Richard A. "The Dialectical Method: Its Application to Social Theory." *Social Forces* 57.3 (1979): 785–98.

Barbour, Ian. *Religion in an Age of Science: The Gifford Lectures.* San Francisco: Harper Collins, 1990.

Barrett, Leonard E. *The Rastafarians Sounds of Cultural Dissonance.* Boston: Beacon Press, 1977.

Berry, Stephan. "On the Problem of Laws in Nature and History: A Comparison." *History & Theory* 38.4 (1999): 121–38.

Bewaji, John Ayotunde (Tunde) Isola. *An Introduction to the Theory of Knowledge: A Pluricultural Approach.* Ibadan, Nigeria: Hope Publications, 2007.

Bielfedt, Dennis. "Can Western Monotheism Avoid Substance Dualism?" *Zygon* 36.1 (2001): 153–77.

Blank, Andreas. "Leibniz's *De Summa Rerum* and the Panlogistic Interpretation of Theory of Simple Substance." *British Journal for the History of Philosophy* 11.2 (2003): 261–69.

Bobro, Marc, and Kenneth Clatterbaugh. "Unpacking the Monad: Leibniz's Theory of Causality." *Monist* 79.3 (1996): 408–36.

Bourman, Stephen Paul. "God moves in." *Christian Century* 119.25 (2002): 9–11.

Boyne, Ian. "Jamaica: Breaking Barriers Between Churches and Rastafarians." *One World,* 86 (May 1983): 33–34.

Bracken, Joseph A. "Bodily Resurrection and the Dialectic of Spirit And Matter." *Theological Studies* 66.4 (2005): 770–82.

———. "Reconsidering Fundamental Issues Emergent Monism and the Classical Doctrine of the Soul." *Zygon* 39.1 (2004): 161–74.

Brink, David O. "Objectivity and Dialectical Methods in Ethics." *Inquiry* 42 (1999): 195–212.

Brown, Stuart. "Leibniz and the Classical Tradition." *International Journal of the Classical Tradition* 2.1 (1995): 68–90.

————. "Soul, Body and Natural Immortality." *Monist* 81.4 (1998): 573–91.

Bube, Richard H. *Putting It All Together: Seven Patterns for Relating Science and the Christian Faith.* Lanham, Maryland: University Press of America, 1995.

Burgess, Andrew. "A Community of Love? Jesus as the Body of God and Robert Jenson's the Trinitarian Thought." *International Journal of Systematic Theology* 6.3 (2004): 289–300.

Burke, Cormac. *Man and Values: A Personalist Anthropology.* New York: Scepter Publishers, 2008, Appendix II (Individualism and collectivism; personalism and community). http://www.cormacburke.or.ke/node/2465.

Burnet, John. *Early Greek Philosophy.* London and Edinburgh: Kessinger Publishing, 1892.

Burns, Robert M. "Divine Infinity in Thomas Aquinas: Philosophico-Theological Background." *Heythrop Journal* XXXIX (1998): 57–69.

Calcagno, Antonio. "The Incarnation, Michel Henry, and the Possibility of an Husserlain-Inspired Transcendental Life." *Heythrop Journal* XLV (2004): 290–304.

Calkins, Mary Whiton. "Psychology as Science of Self II: The Nature of the Self." *Journal of Philosophy, Psychology and Scientific Methods* 5.3 (1908): 64–68.

Capra, Fritjof. *The Tao of Physics: An Explanation of the Parallels between Modern Physics and Eastern Mysticism.* Boston: Shambhala Publications, 1991.

Caponigri, Robert A. *A History of Western Philosophy: Philosophy from the Renaissance to the Romantic Age.* Notre Dame: University of Notre Dame Press, 1963.

Carlin, Laurence. "Leibniz on Conatus, Causation and Freedom." *Pacific Philosophical Quarterly* 85 (2004): 365–79.

Carr, Anne. *The Theological Method of Karl Rahner.* Missoula, Montana: Scholars Press, 1977.

Carr, Paul H. "Does God Play Dice? Insights from the Fractal Geometry of Nature." *Zygon* 39.4 (2004): 933–40.

Case-Winters, Anna. "Rethinking the Image of God." *Zygon* 39.4 (2004): 813–26.

Casey, Damien. "The Post-modern Universal: An Incarnational View." *Pacifica* 16.3 (2003): 257–70.

Catholic Church. *Laborem Exercens* (On Human Work). Encyclical Letter of His Holiness Pope John Paul II. Boston MA: St. Paul Editions, 1982.

Cheng, Chung–Ying. "Ultimate Origin, Ultimate Reality, and the Human Condition: Leibniz, Whitehead and Zhu Xi." *Journal of Chinese Philosophy* 29.1 (2002): 93–118.

Chernoff, Fred. "Leibniz's Principle of the Identity of Indiscernibles." *Philosophical Quarterly*, 31.123 (1981): 126–38.

Chevannes, Barry. *Rastafari Roots and Ideology.* New York: Syracuse University Press, 1994.

Clarke, W. Norris. *The One and the Many: A Contemporary Thomistic Metaphysics.* Notre Dame: University of Notre Dame Press, 2001.

Cockburn, David. "Self, World and God in Spinoza and Weil." *Studies in World Christianity* 4.2 (1998):173–87.

Coetzee, P.H., and A.P.J. Roux, eds. *The African Philosophy Reader.* New York: Routledge, 1998.

————. *The African Philosophy Reader.* 2nd ed. New York: Routledge, 2003.

Coffey, David. "The Whole Rahner on the Supernatural Existential." *Theological Studies* 65.1 (2004): 95–118.

Collingwood, R.G, ed. *The Idea of History.* New York: Oxford University Press, 1993.

Copleston, Frederick. *A History of Philosophy.* New York: Image Books, 1962.

Cowell, Siôn. "Newman and Teilhard: The Challenge of the East." *Ecotheology* 10.1 (2005): 50–65.

Crane, Judith K., and Ronald Sandler. "Identity and Distinction in Spinoza's Ethics." *Pacific Philosophical Quarterly* 86 (2005): 188–200.

Curly, Edwin. "Donogan's Spinoza." *Ethics* 104 (1993):114–34.

Daley, Michael J. "The Sandbox and the Incarnation." *America* 187.13 (2002): 21–24.

Davis, Brian. *An Introduction to the Philosophy of Religion.* Oxford: Oxford University Press, 1982.

D'Agostino, F.B. "Leibniz on Compossibility and Relational Predicates." *Philosophical Quarterly* 26.103 (1976): 125–38.

Deely, John N. *Four Ages of Understanding: the First Post–modern Survey of Philosophy from Ancient Times to the Turn of the Twenty–first Century.* Toronto: University of Toronto Press, 2001.

Desan, Wilfred. *The Marxism of Jean–Paul Sartre.* New York: Anchor Books, 1966.

Descartes, Rene. *Principles of Philosophy.* Translated by John Veitch. Whitefish, MT: Kessinger Publishing, 2005.

Devine, Tony, Joon Ho Seuk, and Andrew Wilson. *Cultivating Heart and Character Educating for Life's Most Essential Goals.* Boone, NC: Character Development Publishing, 2000.

Doncel, Manuel G. "The Kenosis of the Creator and the Created Co-Creator." *Zygon* 39.4 (2004): 791–800.

Downey, James Patrick. "Leibniz Opinion on Descartes's Argument that he is not a Body." *British Journal for the History of Philosophy* 11.3 (2003): 493–98.

Duffy, Simon. "The Logic of Expression in Deleuze's Expressionism in Philosophy: Spinoza: A Strategy of Engagement." *International Journal of Philosophical Studies* 12.1 (2004): 47–60.

Dych, William V. *Karl Rahner.* Collegeville, Minnesota: The Liturgical Press, 1992.

Einstein, Albert. *The World As I See It.* Translated by Allan Harris. New York: Citadel Press, 2006.

Elkington, Trevor G. "Between Order and Chaos: On Peter Greenaway's Postmodern/Poststructuralist Cinema." *Film-Philosophy Journal* 8.1 (January 2004).

Emmet, Dorothy. *Whitehead's Philosophy of Organism.* New York: St. Martin's Press, 1966.

Faricy, Robert. "The Exploitation of Nature and Teilhard's Ecotheology of Love." *Ecotheology* 10.2 (2005): 181–95.

———. *Teilhard de Chardin's Theology of the Christian in the World.* New York: Sheed and Ward, 1967.

Ferraro, Joseph. "Marxism and Thomism: Some Reflections on the Basis for a Dialogue." *International Philosophical Quarterly* 10 (1970): 75–101.

Findlay, J.H. *Hegel: A Re-examination.* New York: Collier Books, 1962.

Flannery, Austin O.P., ed. *Vatican Council II, Conciliar and Post Conciliar Documents.* New York: Costello Publishing Company, 1975.

Fox, Matthew. *Original Blessing.* Santa Fe, NM: Bear & Company Publishing, 1983.

Forsythe, Dennis. *Rastafari: For the Healing of the Nation.* Kingston: Ziaka, 1983.

Fracchia, Josephs. "Dialectical Itineraries." *History & Theory* 38.2 (1999):169–98.

Friedrich, Carl J., ed. *The Philosophy of Hegel.* New York: Modern Library, 1954.

Fuchs, Josef. *Human Values and Christian Morality.* Dublin: Gill and MacMillan, 1970.

———. *Personal Responsibility and Christian Morality.* Washington, DC: Georgetown University Press, 1983.

Futch, Michael. "Leibniz on Plentitude, Infinity, and the Eternity of the World." *British Journal for the History of Philosophy* 10.4 (2002): 541–60.

Galleni, Ludovico. "Is Biosphere Doing Theology?" *Zygon* 36.1 (2001):33–48.

Gilmore, Michael R. "Einstein's God." *Skeptic* 5.2 (1997): 62–65.

Gilson, Etienne. *The Elements of Christian Philosophy.* New York: The New American Library, 1960.

Gorton, David Allyn. *The Monism of Man; Or, The Unity of the Divine and Human.* New York: The Knickerbocker Press, 1893.

Goshen-Gottstein, Alon. "Judaisms and Incarnational Theologies: Mapping out the Parameters of Dialogue." *Journal of Ecumenical Studies* 39.3–4 (2002): 219–47.

Götz, Ignacio L. "Spirituality and the Body." *Religious Education* 96.1 (2001): 2–19.

Graham, Daniel W., "Heraclitus", *The Stanford Encyclopedia of Philosophy* (Winter 2007 edition), http://plato.stanford.edu/entries/heraclitus/.

Gray, Donald P. "The Phenomenon of Teilhard." *Theological Studies* 36.1 (1975): 19–51.

Grey, Mary. "Cosmic Communion: A Contemporary Reflection on the Eucharistic Vision of Teilhard De Chardin." *Ecotheology* 10.2 (2005):165–80.

Grim, John A., and Mary Evelyn Tucker. "An Overview of Teilhard's Commitment to 'Seeing' as Expressed in his Phenomenology, Metaphysics and Mysticism." *Ecotheology: Journal of Religion, Nature & the Environment* 10.2 (2005):147–64.

Grover, Stephen. "Incommensurability and the Best of All Possible Worlds."*Monist* 81.4 (1998): 648–69.

Gruning, Herb. "God and the New Metaphysics." *Journal of Religion & Psychical Research* 24.2 (2001): 64–70.

Gula, Richard, M. *Reason Informed By Faith: Foundations of Catholic Morality.* New York: Paulist Press, 1989.

Haeckel, Ernst. *The Riddle of the Universe.* Translated by Joseph McCabe. New York: Prometheus Books, 1992.

Haight, Roger. *Jesus: Symbol of God.* New York: Orbis Books, 1999.

Hamlyn, D. W. *The Theory of Knowledge.* New York: Anchor Books, 1970.

Hankey, Wayne J. "Why Philosophy Abides for Aquinas." *Heythrop Journal* XLII (2001): 329–48.

Harrison, Paul. "Scientific Pantheism: Reverence of Nature and Cosmos." http://www.pantheism.net/paul/.

Harrison-Barbet, Anthony. *Philosophical Connections: Merleau–Ponty.* http://philosophos.org/philosophical_connections/.

Hartshorne, Charles. *The Logic of Perfection.* La Salle, Illinois: Open Court, 1962.

———. *Anselm's Discovery: A Re-Examination of the Ontological Proof for God's Existence.* La Salle, Illinois: Open Court, 1991.

Hartshorne, Charles, and William Reese. *Philosophers Speak of God.* Chicago: University of Chicago Press, 1953.

Hartz, Glenn A. "Why Corporeal Substances Keep Popping up in Leibniz's Later Philosophy." *British Journal for the History of Philosophy* 6.2 (1998): 198–207.

Haught, John F. "In Search of a God for Evolution: Paul Tillich and Pierre Teilhard De Chardin." *Zygon* 37.3 (2002): 539–53.

Hegel, G.W. *Encyclopaedia of the Philosophical Sciences, The Logic.* Translated by William Wallace. Oxford: Clarendon Press, 1984.

———. *Encyclopaedia of the Philosophical Sciences, Part One.* Black Mask Online: http://www.worldlibrary.org/Collection/9/Blackmask%20Online%20Collection/Blackmask–Online–Collection.

———. *Hegel's Phenomenology of Spirit.* Translated by A.V. Miller. Oxford: Oxford University Press, 1977.

———. *Hegel's Logic.* Translated by William Wallace. Oxford: Oxford University Press, 1975.

———. *Hegel: The Essential Writings.* Edited by Frederick G. Weiss. New York: Harper Torchbooks, 1974.

———. *The Philosophy of Mind.* Translated by A.V. Miller. Oxford: Oxford University Press, 1971.

———. *Hegel's Philosophy of Nature.* Edited and translated by M.J. Petry. London: Humanities Press, Inc., 1970.

———. *Science of Logic.* Translated by A.V Miller. London: Allen & Unwin, 1969.

———. "Philosophy of Religion." In *Hegel: A Re-examination.* Translated by J.H. Findlay. New York: Collier Books, 1962.

———. "Logic of Hegel." In *Hegel: A Re-examination.* New York: Collier Books, 1962.

———. *The Philosophy of History.* Translated by J. Sibree and Karl Hegel. New York: Dover Publication, 1956.

———. *The Philosophy of Hegel.* Edited by Carl J. Friedrich. New York: Modern Library, 1954.

———. "Lectures on Aesthetics." University lectures given in Heidelberg and Berlin in 1820/21, 1823, 1826 and 1828/29. Compiled by Heinrich Gustav Hotho in 1835. (http://plato.stanford.edu/entries/hegel–aesthetics/).

Henriot, Peter, J., Edward P. DeBerri, and Michael J. Schultheis. *Catholic Social Teaching: Our Best Kept Secret.* New York: Orbis Books, 1995.

Heraclitus. *The Fragments: of the Work of Heraclitus of Ephesus On Nature.* Translated by George T.W. Patrick. Whitefish, MT: Kessinger Publishing, 2007.

Herbert, G., Bruce May, and M. Metzger, eds. *New Oxford Annotated Bible with the Apocrypha.* New York: Oxford University Press, 1977.

Hick, John. *Disputed Questions in Theology and the Philosophy of Religion.* New Haven: Yale University Press, 1993.

Hooker, Richard. *Yin and Yang, Chinese Philosophy.* http://richard-hooker.com/sites/worldcultures/GLOSSARY/YINYANG.HTM. Accessed October 10, 2010.

Hopkins, Jasper. *Nicholas of Cusa On Learned Ignorance: A translation and an appraisal of De Docta Ignorantia.* 2nd ed. Minneapolis: The Arthur J. Banning Press, 1985.

———. *Nicholas of Cusa on God as Not-other: A translation and an appraisal of De Li Non Aliud.* Minnesota: The Author Banning Press, 1983.

———. *Nicholas of Cusa's Dialectical Mysticism: Text, translation and interpretive study of De Visione Dei.* Minnesota: The Author Banning Press, 1985.

Hoskins, Richard. "Social and Transcendent: The Trinitarian Theology of John Richardson Illingworth Re-examined." *International Journal of Systematic Theology* 1.2 (1999): 185–203.

Hoyle, R.H., M.H. Kernis, M.R. Leary, and M.W. Baldwin. *Selfhood: Identity, Esteem, Regulation.* Boulder, CO: Westview Press, 1999.

Isherwood, Lisa. "The Embodiment of Feminist Liberation Theology: The Spiralling of Incarnation." *The Journal of the Britain & Ireland School of Feminist Theology* 12. 2 (2004):140–56.

Ishiguro, Hide. "Unity without simplicity: Leibniz on organisms." *Monist* 81.4 (1998): 534–53.

Jaarsma, Ada D. "Irigaray's to be Two: The Problem of Evil and the Plasticity of Incarnation." *Hypatia* 18.1 (2003): 44–63.

James, William. *Principles of Psychology.* New York: Holt, 1890.

Jamros, Daniel P. "Hegel on the Incarnation: Unique or universal?" *Theological Studies* 56.2 (1995): 276–301.

Jasper, Allison. "Dangerous Sex." *Theology and Sexuality* 11.2 (January 2005): 7–10.

Johnson, Matthew Raphael. "Nation, State and the Incarnation in the Political Writings of Vladimir Solov'yev: The Transfiguration of Politics." *Religion, State and Society* 30.4 (2002): 347–55.

Johnson-Hill, Jack A. *I-Sight: The World of Rastafari.* Metuchen, NJ: The Scarecrow Press, 1995.

Jolley, Nicholas. "Causality and creation in Leibniz." *Monist* 81.4 (1998): 591–612.

Kant, Immanuel. *Critique of Practical Reason.* Translated by L.W. Beck. New York: Bobbs-Merill, 1956.

———. *Religion Within the Limits of Reason Alone.* 2nd ed. Translated by T. M. Greene and H.H. Hudson. La Salle, IL: Open Court, 1960.

———. *Critique of Pure Reason.* Translated by N. K. Smith. London: Macmillan, 1968.

———. *Critique of Pure Reason.* Translated by Paul Guyer and Allen W. Wood. Cambridge: Cambridge University Press, 1998.

———. *Prolegomena to Any Future Metaphysics.* New York: Macmillan, 1987.

Keenan, James, F. *Virtues for Ordinary Christians.* Kansas City: Sheed & Ward, 1996.

———. "Proposing Cardinal Virtues." *Theological Studies* 56 (1995): 709–29.

Kenig Curd, Patricia. "Parmenidean Monism." *Phronesis* 36.3 (1991): 241–64.

Kim, Chin–Tai. "Transcendence and Immanence." *Journal of the American Academy of Religion* 55.3 (Autumn 1987): 537–49.

King, Thomas M. "Globalization and the Soul – According to Teilhard, Friedman and Others." *Zygon* 37.1 (2002): 25–33.

King, Ursula. "Consumed by Fire from Within: Teilhard De Chardin's Panchristic Mysticism in Relation to the Catholic Tradition." *Heythrop Journal* XL (1999): 456–77.

———. "One Planet, One Spirit: Searching for an Ecologically Balanced Spirituality." *Ecotheology* 10.1 (2005): 66–87.

———. Theories of Love: Sorokin, Teilhard and Tillich." *Zygon* 39.1 (March 2004): 77–102.

Kirk, G.S., J.E. Raven, and M. Schofield. *The Presocratic Philosophers.* Cambridge: Cambridge University Press, 1990.

Klauder, Francis J. *Aspects of the Thought of Teilhard de Chardin.* Boston, MA: The Christopher Publishing House, 1971.

——. "Teilhard and the Environment." *Ecotheology* 10.1 (2005): 88–98.

Knitter, Paul F. "Toward a Liberative Interreligious Dialogue." *Cross Currents* 45.4 (1995): 451–69.

Kotva, Joseph J. *The Christian Case for Virtue Ethics.* Washington, DC: Georgetown University Press, 1996.

Kress, Robert. *A Rahner Handbook.* Atlanta: John Knox Publishing, 1982.

Lafitte, Paul. *The Person in Psychology.* London: Routledge, 1999.

LeBuffe, Michael. "Spinoza's *Summum Bonum.*" *Pacific Philosophical Quarterly* 86 (2005): 243–66.

Leibniz, G.W. *The Monadology and Other Philosophical Writings.* Translated by Robert Latta. London: Oxford University Press, 1898.

——. *G.W. Leibniz: Political Writings.* 2nd ed. Translated by Riley Patrick. Cambridge: Cambridge University Press, 1988.

——. *New Essays on Human Understanding.* Translated by Peter Remnant and Jonathan Bennett. Cambridge: Cambridge University Press, 1985.

——. *Theodicy: Essays on the Goodness of God, the Freedom of Man, and the Origin of Evil.* Translated by E.M. Huggard. Chicago: Open Court, 1951.

——. "Principles of Nature and Grace, Founded on Reason." In *The Monadology and Other Philosophical Writings.* London: Oxford University Press, 1948.

——. *G.W. Leibniz: Philosophical Essays.* Translated by Roger Ariew and Daniel Garber. Indianapolis: Hackett Publishing Company, 1989.

Lodge, Paul. "Leibniz Notion of an Aggregate?" *British Journal for the History of Philosophy* 9.3 (2001): 467–86.

——. "The Debate Over Extended Substance in Leibniz's Correspondence with De Volder?" *International Studies in the Philosophy of Science* 15.2 (2001):155–65.

Lodge, Paul, and Marc Bobro. "Stepping back inside Leibniz's mill." *Monist* 81.4 (1998): 553–73.

Look, Brandon C. "Hylozoism and Dogmatism in Kant, Leibniz, and Newton." *Internationalen Kant Kongresses* IV (2001): 490–97.

——. "On Monadic Domination in Leibniz's Metaphysics." *British Journal for the History of Philosophy* 10.3 (2002): 379–99.

Lucero–Montano, Alfredo. "Spinoza's Ethics, Determinism and Freedom." www.PhiloSophos.com. Accessed June 25, 2009.

Luoma, Tapio. *Incarnation and Physics: Natural Science in the Theology of Thomas F. Torrance.* Oxford: Oxford University Press, 2002.

MacIntyre, Alasdair. *After Virtue: A Study in Moral Theory.* 2nd ed. Notre Dame: University of Notre Dame Press, 1984.

Mac Cormac, Earl R. "Metaphor and Pluralism." *Monist* 73.3 (July 1990): 411–21.

Macquarrie, John. *Principles of Christian Theology.* 2nd ed. New York: Charles Scribner's Sons, 1977.

Madigan, Kevin. "The Metaphysics of the Incarnation: Thomas Aquinas to Duns Scotus." *Journal of Religion* 84.4 (2004): 641–42.

Mansueto, Anthony. "Organization, Teleology and Value: The Ontological Foundations of the Theory of Value." *Journal of Religion* 77.1 (1997): 68–87.

Mansingh, Ajai and Laxmi Mansingh. "Hindu Influences on Rastafarianism." *Caribbean Quarterly* Monograph (1986): 96–115.

——. "The Impact of East Indians on Jamaican Religious Thoughts and Expressions." *Caribbean Journal of Religious Studies* 10.2 (1989): 36–52.

Maritain, Jacques. *The Person and the Common Good.* Notre Dame: University of Notre Dame Press, 1966.

Marley, Robert. "One Love/People Get Ready." New York: Universal Music Publishing Group, 1965.

Marx, Karl. *Karl Marx: Selected Writings.* 2nd ed. Edited by David McLellan. Oxford: Oxford University Press, 1987.

Marx, Karl, and Frederick Engels. *Karl Marx, Frederick Engels, Collected Works.* New York: International Publishers, 1975.

Maser, Jack D., and Gordon G. Gallup Jr. "Theism as a By–Product of Natural Selection." *Journal of Religion* 70.4 (1990): 515–33.

Mason, Richard. "Spinoza on Modality." *The Philosophical Quarterly* 36.144 (1986): 313–42.

Matthews, Lionel, Elvin Gabriel, Warren Joseph, and Ken Crane. "The Social Morality of Reconsidered: A Christian Interactionist Perspective." *Journal of Research on Christian Education* 13.1 (2004): 5–21.

McLellan, D., ed. *Karl Marx: Selected Writings.* Oxford: Oxford University Press, 1987.

Merleau-Ponty, Maurice. *Phenomenology of Perception.* London: Routledge Classics, 2002.

Merton, Thomas. *Seeds of Contemplation.* New York: Dell, 1949.

Milbank, John. "History of the One God." *Heythrop Journal* XXXVIII (1997): 371–400.

Miller, John F. "A Modern Symposium: In Praise of Love." *Journal of Religion & Physical Research* 21.1 (1998): 40–46.

Milosz, Czeslaw. *The Captive Mind.* New York: Vintage Books, 1990.

Min, Anselm K. "The Dialectic of Divine Love: Pannenberg's Hegelian Trinitarianism." *International Journal of Systematic Theology.* 6.3 (2004): 252–69.

Molnar, Paul D. "Incarnation, Resurrection and the Doctrine of the Trinity: A Comparison of Thomas F. Torrance and Roger Haight." *International Journal of Systematic Theology* 5.2 (2003): 147–67.

———. "Love of God and Love of Neighbour in the Theology of Karl Rahner and Karl Barth." *Modern Theology* 20.4 (2004): 567–99.

Mooney, Christopher, F. *Teilhard de Chardin and the Mystery of Christ.* New York: Harper & Row, 1966.

Moore, Norah. "The Archetype of the Way: Part 1 Tao and Individuation." *Journal Analytical Psychology* 28 (1983): 119–40.

Morris, Thomas, ed. *God and the Philosophers.* New York: Oxford University Press, 1994.

Morrish, Ivor. *Obeah, Christ and Rastaman: Jamaica and its Religion.* Cambridge: James Clark, 1982.

Musser, Donald W., and Joseph L. Price, eds. *A New Handbook of Christian Theologians.* Nashville: Abingdon Press, 1996.

Nash, Carroll B. "Double-Aspect Monism." *The Journal of Religion and Psychical Research* 19.2 (96): 68–71.

Nelson, James S. "Ralph Burhoe & Teilhard de Chardin: An Affinity in Mysticism." *Zygon* 35.3 (2000): 687–98.

Nettleford, Rex. *Caribbean Cultural Identity: The Case of Jamaica.* Kingston: Institute of Jamaica, 1978.

Nicholas of Cusa. *On Learned Ignorance: A translation and an appraisal of De Docta Ignorantia.* 2nd ed. Translated by Jasper Hopkins. Minneapolis: The Arthur J. Banning Press, 1985.

———. *On Learned Ignorance.* Translated by D.J.B. Hawkins. London: Routledge & Kegan Paul Ltd, 1954.

———. *God as not–other.* Edited by Jasper Hopkins. Minnesota: The Author Banning Press, 1983.

Nicholson, Graeme. *Illustrations of Being: Drawing Upon Heidegger and Upon Metaphysics.* Atlantic Highlands, NJ: Humanity Books, 1992.

Nussbaum, Martha C. *The Fragility of Goodness: Luck and Ethics in Greek Tragedy and Philosophy.* Cambridge: Cambridge University Press, 2001.

Nutu, Liliana M. "The Seduction of Words and Flesh and The Desire Of God: A Poststructuralist Reading Of John 1:1, 14 and The Pillow Book." *Biblical Interpretation* 11.1 (2003): 79–97.

O'Connell, Timothy E. *Principle for a Catholic Morality.* Minneapolis: The Seabury Press, 1978.

O'Donovan, Leo J., ed. *A World of Grace: An Introduction to the Themes and Foundations of Karl Rahner's Theology.* Washington, DC: Georgetown University Press, 1995.

Ogden, Schubert, M. *On Theology.* San Francisco: Harper & Row, 1986.

———. *The Point of Christology.* San Francisco: Harper & Row, 1982.

———. *The Reality of God.* New York: Harper & Row, 1966.

Okolo, Chukwudum, B. "Self as a problem in African philosophy." In *The African Philosophy Reader,* edited by P.H. Coetzee and P.J. Roux, 209–15. 2nd ed. New York: Routledge, 2003.

O'Murchù, Diarmuid. "Teilhard: A Mystical Survivor!" *Ecotheology* 10.1 (2005): 99–108.

Ontario Consultants on Religious Tolerance. "Taoism." http://www.religioustolerance.org/taoism.htm.

Owens, Joseph. *Dread – The Rastafarians of Jamaica.* Introduction by Rex Nettleford. Kingston: Sangster's Book Stores, 1976.

Page, Ruth. *The Incarnation of Freedom and Love.* Cleveland: The Pilgrim Press, 1991.

Parkinson, G.H.R. "Moral luck, freedom, and Leibniz." *Monist* 81.4 (1998): 633–78.

Pearl, Thomas. "Dialectical Panentheism: On the Hegelian Character of Rahner's Key Christological Writings." *Irish Theological Quarterly* 42 (1975): 119–37.

Petry, M.J., ed. *Hegel's Philosophy of Nature.* Translated by M.J. Petry. London: Humanities Press, 1970.

Phemister, Pauline. "Exploring Leibniz's Kingdoms: A Philosophical Analysis of Nature and Grace." *Ecotheology* 7.2 (2003) 126–45.

———. "Leibniz and the Elements of Compound Bodies." *British Journal for the History of Philosophy* 7.1 (1999): 57–78.

Plotinus. *Enneads.* Translated by Stephen MacKenna. London: Penguin Books, 1991.

Popper, Karl. *Conjectures and Refutations: The Growth of Scientific Knowledge.* New York: Basic Books, 1962.

Priddy, Robert C. *The Human Whole: An Outline of the 'Higher' Psychology.* Accessed June 27, 2009. http://robertpriddy.com/P/.

Priest, Stephen, ed. *Jean Paul Sartre: Basic Writings.* London and New York: Routledge, 2001.

Privette, Jeffrey S. "Must Theology Re-Kant?" *Heythrop Journal* XL (1999):166–83.

Rahner, Karl. *Foundations of Christian Faith: An Introduction to the Idea of Christianity.* Translated by William Dych. New York: Crossroad, 1992.

———. *Hearer of the Word: Laying the Foundation for a Philosophy of Religion.* Translated by Joseph Donceel. New York: Continuum, 1994.

———. *Hominisation: The Evolution Origin of Man as a Theological Problem.* New York: Herder and Herder, 1965.

———. "Trinity, Divine." In *Encyclopedia of Theology.* New York: The Seabury Press, 1975.

———. *Theological Investigations.* 23 vols. Translated by Kevin Smyth. Baltimore: Helicon Press, 1966.

———. *The Christian Commitment.* New York: Sheed and Ward, 1963.

———. *Trinity.* New York: Herder and Herder, 1970.

Rahner, Karl, and Herbert Vorgrimler. *Dictionary of Theology.* New revised ed. New York: Crossroad, 1985.

Rathus, Spencer A. *Essentials of Psychology.* 6th ed. Fort Worth: Harcourt College Publishers, 2001.

Ramati, Ayval. "Harmony at a Distance." *Journal of the History of Science in Society* 87.3 (1996):430–53.

Rea, Michael C. "How to be an Eleatic Monist." *Philosophical Perspectives* 15 (2001): 129–51.

Reese, William L. *Dictionary of Philosophy and Religion.* Amherst: Humanity Books, 1996.

Rescher, Nicholas. *Process Metaphysics: An Introduction to Process Philosophy.* New York: State University of New York Press, 1996.

———. *Process Philosophy: A Survey of Basic Issues.* Pittsburgh: University of Pittsburgh Press, 2000.

Rifkin, Jeremy. *Entropy Into the Greenhouse World.* New York: Bantam Books, 1989.

Ribas, Albert. "Leibniz' Discourse on the Natural Theology of the Chinese and the Leibniz–Clarke Controversy." *Philosophy East & West* 53.1 (2003): 64–86.

Roberts, Elizabeth, and Elias Amidon, eds. *Life Prayers from around the World.* San Francisco: Harper, 1996.

Rutherford, Donald. "Salvation as a State of Mind: The Place of Acquiescentia in Spinoza's Ethics." *British Journal for the History of Philosophy* 7.3 (1999): 447–73.

Salmon, James F., and Nicole Schmitz–Moormann. "Evolution as Revelation of a Triune God." *Zygon* 37.4 (2002): 853–71.

Sartre, Jean Paul. Being and Nothingness . Translated by Hazel E. Barnes. New York: Philosophical Library, 1948.

Sia, Santiago. *God in Process Thought.* Dordrecht, Boston, Lancaster: Martinus Nijhoff Publishers, 1985.

Schade, Martin J. *'God is Love and the totality of reality': Karl Rahner: A Proposal of Dialectical Incarnationalism.* STL diss. Weston Jesuit School of Theology, 1997.

———. "Riddim of Creation: An Incarnational Expression of Caribbean Theology." *Caribbean Journal of Religious Studies* 19.1 (1998): 28–38.

———. "Christ the *Alpha* and the Rasta: A Reflection on Christology within the Emergence of Rastafari." *Caribbean Journal of Religious Studies*, 17.1 (1996): 38–64.

Scott, Alex. "Merleau-Ponty's *Phenomenology of Perception.*" http://www.angelfire.com/md2/timewarp/merleauponty.html.

Scott, Peter Manley. "Trinitarian Theology and the Politics of Nature." *Ecotheology* 9.1 (2004): 29–48.

Segal, Gideon. "Beyond Subjectivity: Spinoza's Cognitivism of the Emotions." *British Journal for the History of Philosophy* 8.1 (2000): 1–19.

Seigworth, Gregory J., and Michael E. Gardiner. "Rethinking Everyday Life and Then Nothing Turns Itself Inside Out." *Cultural Studies* 18.2–3 (2004): 139–59.

Sesonske, Alexander. "Pre-established harmony and other comic strategies." *Journal of Aesthetic and Art Criticism* 55.3 (1997): 253–62.

Sessions, George. "Ecocentrism and The Anthropocentric Detour." *Revision* 13.3 (1991):109–16.

Shafer, Ingrid H. "From Noosphere to Theosphere: Cyclotrons, Cyberspace and Teilhard's vision of Cosmic Love." *Zygon* 37.4 (2002): 825–52.

Shim, Michael K. "What Kind of Idealist was Leibniz?" *British Journal for the History of Philosophy* 13.1 (2005): 91–110.

Siegel, Harvey. "Dangerous Dualism or Murky Monism? A Reply to Jim Garrison." *Journal of Philosophy of Education* 35.4 (2001): 577–95.

Sivadge, Steven Paul. "A Critical Evaluation of John Hick's Interpretation of the Divine Carnation as Metaphor." Diss., Trinity International University, 2000. http://place.asburyseminary.edu/trendissertations/4915/.

Skehan, James W. "Exploring Teilhard's 'New Mysticism': 'Building the Cosmos'." *Ecotheology* 10.1 (2005):11–34.

Skrbina, David. "Participation, Organization, and Mind: Toward a Participatory Worldview." Doctoral thesis, University of Bath, 2008. With permission from the author.

Slowik, Edward. "Descartes and Individual Corporeal Substance." *British Journal of the History of Philosophy* 9.1 (2001): 1–15.

Smith, Huston. "The Ambiguity of Matter." *Cross Currents* 48.1 (1998): 49–61.

Smith, James K.A. "A Principle of Incarnation in Derridas's (Theologische?) Jugendschriften: Towards a Confessional Theology." *Modern Theology*18.2 (2002): 217–30.

Solomon, Hester. "The Transcendent Function and Hegel's Dialectical Vision." *Journal of Analytic Philosophy* 39 (1999): 77–100.

Spinoza, Baruch. *The Collected Works of Spinoza.* Translated by Edwin Curly. Princeton, NJ: Princeton University Press, 1985.

Sprinsted, Eric O. "Conditions of Dialogue: John Hick and Simon Weil." *Journal of Religion* 72.1 (1992): 19–37.

Stanton, Glenn T. "The Conservative Humanist." *Christianity Today* 50.4 (2006):42–45.

Stapp, Henry. *Mind, Matter and Quantum Mechanics.* Berlin, Heidelberg: Springer, 2009.

———. "S-Matrix Interpretation of Quantum Theory." *Physical Review* 3.6 (1971): 1303.

Steiner-Aeschliman, Sherrie. "Immanent Dualism as an Alternative to Dualism and Monism: The World View of Max Weber." *Worldviews: Environment Culture Religion* 4.3 (2000): 235–63.

Stevenson, Leslie, and David L Haberman. *Ten Theories of Human Nature.* New York: Oxford University Press, 2004.

Stone, Jerome A. "Religious Naturalism and the Religion–Science Dialogue: A Minimalist View." *Zygon* 37.2 (2002): 381–94.

Strawson, P.F. *Individuals: An Essay in Descriptive Metaphysics.* London: Methuen & Co. Ltd., 1964.

Stumpf, Samuel Enoch. *Socrates to Sartre: A History of Philosophy.* New York: McGraw-Hill Book Company, 1966.

Suzuki, D.T. *On Indian Mahayana Buddhism.* New York: Harper & Row, 1968.

Taliaferro, Charles. "The Ethics of the Incarnation." *Anglican Theological Review* 81. 4 (1999): 597–607.

Tarnas, Richard. *Cosmos and Psyche.* New York: Viking, 2006.

Taylor, Barbara Brown. "Practicing Incarnation." *Christian Century* 122.7 (2005): 39.

Taylor, Mark Lloyd. *GOD IS LOVE: A Study in the Theology of Karl Rahner.* Atlanta: Scholars Press, 1986.

Teilhard de Chardin, Pierre. *Hymn of the Universe.* New York, Harper & Row, 1961.

——— . *The Future of Man.* New York: Harper & Row, 1964.

——— . *The Divine Milieu.* New York: Harper & Row, 1968.

——— . *The Phenomenon of Man.* New York: Harper & Row, 1975.

Thessaloniki Museum of Technology. "Ancient Greek Scientists." http://www.noesis.edu.gr/.

Tillich, Paul. *Love, Power, and Justice.* New York: Oxford University Press, 1954.

——— . *Theology of Culture.* Edited by Robert C. Kimball. New York: Oxford University Press, 1959.

——— . *The Courage to Be.* New York: Yale University Press, 1980.

Trigg, Roger. *Ideas of Human Nature: An Historical Introduction.* Malden: Blackwell Publishing, 1999.

Vacek, Edward Collins. *Love, Human and Divine.* Washington, DC: Georgetown University Press, 1994.

Vale, Carol Jean. "Teilhard de Chardin: Ontogenesis vs. Ontology." *Theological Studies* 53.2 (1992): 313–38.

Vailati, Ezio. "Leibniz on Divine Concurrence With Secondary Causes." *British Journal for the History of Philosophy* 10.2 (2002): 200–230.

Vandrunen, David. "Iconoclasm, Incarnation and Eschatology: Toward Catholic Understanding of the Reformed Doctrine of the 'Second' Commandment." *International Journal of Systematic Theology* 6.2 (2004):130–47.

Vanin, Cristina. "The Significance of the Incarnation for Ecological Theology: A Challenging Approach." *Ecotheology* 6.1 (2001): 108–22.

Velasquez, Manuel, and Cynthia Rostankowski. *Ethics: Theory and Practice.* Englewood Cliffs, NJ: Prentice Hall, 1985.

Volf, Miroslav. "The Trinity is our Social Program: The Doctrine of the Trinity and the Shape of Social Engagement." *Modern Theology* 14.3 (1998): 403–23.

Weger, Karl Heinz. *Karl Rahner: An Introduction to His Theology.* New York: The Seabury Press, 1980.

Weiss, Frederick G., ed. *Hegel: The Essential Writings.* New York: Harper and Row, 1974.

Welshon, Rex. "Anomalous Monism and Epiphenomenalism." *Pacific Philosophical Quarterly* 80 (1999): 103–20.

West, David. "Spinoza on Positive Freedom." *Political Studies* XLI (1993): 284–96.

Whitehead, Alfred North. *Process and Reality: An Essay in Cosmology.* Edited by David Ray Griffin and Donald Sherburne. New York: The Free Press, 1978.

Reese, William L. "Socratic Method." Dictionary of Philosophy and Religion. Amherst: Humanity Books, 1996.

Wikiquote. "Immanuel Kant." https://en.wikiquote.org/wiki/Immanuel_Kant.

Wildiers, N.W. *An Introduction to Teilhard de Chardin.* New York: Harper & Row, 1967.

Wittgenstein, Ludwig. *Tractatus Logico–Philosophicus*. London: Routledge Classics, 2001.

Witvliet, Theo. *A Place in the sun: An Introduction to Liberation Theology in the Third World*. New York: Orbis Books, 1985.

Wojtyla, Karol. *The Acting Person*. Translated by Andrzej Potocki. Dordrecht, Netherlands: Springer, 1979.

Wolter, Allan B. "John Duns Scotus on the Primacy and Personality of Christ." In *Franciscan Christology*, edited by Damian McElrath, 139–82. St. Bonaventure, NY: Franciscan Institute of St. Bonaventure, 1980.

Wood, Allen W. *Karl Marx*. 2nd ed. New York and London: Routledge, Taylor & Francis Group, 2004.

Yerkes, James. *The Christology of Hegel*. Albany, NY: State University of New York Press, 1983.

Youpa, Andrew, "Leibniz's Ethics", *The Stanford Encyclopedia of Philosophy* (Summer 2011 edition): http://plato.stanford.edu/entries/leibniz-ethics/.

Zaehner, R.C. *The Convergent Spirit: Toward a Dialectics of Religion*. London: Routledge and Kegan Paul, 1963.

———. *Dialectical Christianity and Christian Materialism*. New York: Oxford University Press, 1971.

Ziporyn, Brook. "Setup, Punch Line, and The Mind-Body Problem: A Neo-Tiantai Approach." *Philosophy East & West* 50.4 (2000): 584–614.

Zukav, Gary. *The Dancing Wu Li Masters: An Overview of the New Physics*. New York: Harper Collins Publishers, 1979.